GOD

and

DONALD
TRUMP

★ ★ ★ ★ ★

GOD
— and —
DONALD TRUMP

★ ★ ★ ★ ★

STEPHEN E. STRANG

FRONT
LINE

EARLY PRAISE FOR
GOD AND DONALD TRUMP

★★★★★

If you woke up the day after the 2016 election wondering "What just happened?" then this is the book for you. Stephen Strang gives you the inside facts of how an unlikely candidate appealed to an unlikely group of voters to win the presidency. More importantly this book will energize your prayers for America because you will know that prayer changes the course of nations.

—GORDON ROBERTSON
CEO, THE CHRISTIAN BROADCASTING NETWORK
VIRGINIA BEACH, VIRGINIA

God and Donald Trump may very well be one of the most important books about the Trump presidency. Steve Strang has delivered a terrific book that cuts through the mainstream media narrative to explore the spiritual life of the forty-fifth president, and in doing so, we get to see the true heart of Donald Trump.

—TODD STARNES
FOX NEWS CHANNEL
BROOKLYN, NEW YORK

Everyone is curious about the topic of God and Donald Trump. That's why I'm so thankful that a trusted Christian writer like Steve Strang took on this timely challenge. I know President Trump personally. I like him as a man, and I enjoy serving on his Faith Advisory Board. President Trump sincerely cares about protecting every American's religious liberty rights under our brilliant First Amendment.

In *God and Donald Trump* you'll find a comprehensive, realistic, and fair assessment of President Trump's faith. In fact, I'm confident you'll be pleased by what you read. I've come to trust and rely upon Steve's words since I began reading his columns in *Charisma* magazine in the 1980s. Enjoy this important book!

—HON. MICHELE BACHMANN
2012 PRESIDENTIAL CANDIDATE
FORMER MEMBER, US HOUSE OF REPRESENTATIVES
MINNEAPOLIS, MINNESOTA

After Donald Trump stunned the nation by becoming the Republican nominee in the 2016 presidential election, his victory over Hillary Clinton took the world by storm. Steve Strang, an acclaimed journalist and Christian publishing veteran, takes a closer look at how and why this happened. In more than fifty years of ministry I have observed how people of faith can change elections. Our votes matter. But more importantly now our prayers matter. Mr. Trump heard the voice of Christians during the campaign. Now President Trump must hear the voice of wisdom during these turbulent times. Church leaders and all believers must speak the truth in love while fervently praying for those in authority.

—JAMES ROBISON
FOUNDER AND PRESIDENT, LIFE OUTREACH INTERNATIONAL
FOUNDER AND PUBLISHER, THE STREAM (STREAM.ORG)
FORT WORTH, TEXAS

God and Donald Trump is not a book about President Trump's religious or political views. It's a well-written, much-needed look at the undeniable hand of God working in our nation's most recent presidential election. It will restore your hope that America can be a great and godly nation once again by placing our hope in the God who hears the prayers of His people and responds.

—DR. ROBERT JEFFRESS
SENIOR PASTOR, FIRST BAPTIST CHURCH
DALLAS, TEXAS

Did you know George Soros was a Nazi collaborator? I found that out reading Stephen Strang's new book, *God and Donald Trump*. I am excited about this new president, and I am excited about Stephen's book. Read it. It's good!

—KENNETH COPELAND
FOUNDER, KENNETH COPELAND MINISTRIES
NEWARK, TEXAS

This book is one of the most fascinating and informative works I have read in a long time. It is a must-read because every US president reflects and/or mirrors the moral and spiritual identity of our democracy. In other words, when we understand who our president is and who he is becoming, it gives us insight into our own national spiritual makeup.

It is a miracle that Donald J. Trump has become president, but what was the purpose of this miracle? What was in the heart of God when He chose this man? These questions are answered in this amazing book. When you start reading it, you won't put it down.

—BISHOP HARRY JACKSON
SENIOR PASTOR, HOPE CHRISTIAN CHURCH
BELTSVILLE, MARYLAND

Visit the author's website at godanddonaldtrumpbook.com.

Library of Congress Cataloging-in-Publication Data:
An application to register this book for cataloging has been
submitted to the Library of Congress.
International Standard Book Number: 978-1-62999-486-4
E-book ISBN: 978-1-62999-487-1

While the author has made every effort to provide accurate
Internet addresses at the time of publication, neither the publisher
nor the author assumes any responsibility for errors or for changes
that occur after publication.

17 18 19 20 21 — 987654321
Printed in the United States of America

CONTENTS

★★★★★

FOREWORD

★★★★★

DONALD TRUMP WAS not my first choice for president—I was my first choice. But as we know, Trump not only received far more votes than any Republican in the history of the primaries—more than Ronald Reagan, the Bushes, John McCain, and Mitt Romney—on November 8, 2016, he went on to win one of the most unprecedented presidential elections our country has ever experienced.

Every prediction about the 2016 race was wrong. Those of us who brought years of experience and effective governing to the race found that voters were not interested. They blamed everyone from Washington for the mess and even blamed those of us who had never worked in DC.

Knowing who to vote for doesn't always come easy for the Christian, and this past election was no different. Many struggled with the fact that Donald Trump's stance on pro-life issues, same-sex marriage, and Israel didn't necessarily come from a deep conviction either politically or biblically. You can think whatever you like about Donald Trump, but there's no denying that he broke the code, owned the media, and inspired the masses. And when he became the nominee at the Republican National Convention in Cleveland, Ohio, I predicted then and there that he would defeat Hillary Clinton and become the forty-fifth president of the United States.

Some wondered how I could get behind a candidate like Trump, but you see, I went into the 2016 race knowing Hillary Clinton better than the other sixteen Republican candidates. I served ten and a half years as governor of Arkansas, where the Clintons lived and served. It was the Clintons who left behind the government I inherited. I left the 2016 race still knowing her better, but also knowing the other GOP candidates, including Donald Trump. I was—and still am—convinced that Donald Trump is our best hope of turning the tide of the insider political nonsense that has left people seething and that would have continued if Hillary Clinton had won the election.

The growing support Trump gathered from many leaders in the evangelical community along the way shows that they too saw the value of coalescing behind him to defeat Clinton and change the course of our nation. And the results of the election show that Americans did not want to continue in the direction in which eight years of the Obama White House had taken us.

Since his election I'm encouraged by the way President Trump has surrounded himself with a number of evangelical Christians, starting with Vice President Mike Pence, and genuinely desires their counsel. I believe his continued openness to input from Christian leaders shows that he wasn't only pandering for votes but that he truly understands and welcomes godly advice and he sees the value of prayer. Trump once said, "Imagine what our country could accomplish if we started working together as one people, under one God, saluting one flag."[1] I believe that is still his dream, and he intends to see it through as he leads our country from the Oval Office.

In this book, *God and Donald Trump*, Stephen Strang gives us an insightful look back at the events that unfolded during Donald Trump's election. Over the years I've gotten to know Steve and the passion he has in his heart to impact our culture through his faith and to see biblical values restored in our society. From Steve's unique vantage point at the forefront of Christian media for the past four decades, he is able to pull back the curtain and show us inside the minds and hearts of Christian leaders and share with us their journey to support the most unlikely GOP candidate in American history.

I believe you'll enjoy reading every word of this book, and as you do, remember to pray for our president. As he undertakes the pressures and responsibilities of governing our nation, he needs the wisdom and strength that can only come from heaven through the power of a praying people. Remember also to pray for our country. I believe Trump's historic battle for the White House in 2016 metaphorically reminds us that America too is in a historic battle not only for its political future but also for its very soul.

—MIKE HUCKABEE
GOVERNOR OF ARKANSAS FROM 1996 TO 2007
REPUBLICAN PRESIDENTIAL CANDIDATE IN 2008 AND 2016

INTRODUCTION

★★★★★

NㅤEWS REPORTS IN the wake of the 2016 election revealed that evangelical Christians backed Donald J. Trump more than any Republican presidential candidate in history. What makes this remarkable is that few Evangelicals supported him in the beginning. For Bible-believing Christians, Trump would be the most unlikely candidate anyone could imagine. He fathered children by three wives, made some of his wealth in the gambling industry, and was well known for using some of the most vulgar and degrading language imaginable.

Even though he made it known during the campaign that he'd never smoked cigarettes and didn't drink alcohol, he was no one's image of a choirboy. But at some point, to everyone's surprise, Donald Trump managed to win the confidence of enough voters to overcome seemingly insurmountable odds. And in the process he persuaded the largest number of Evangelicals in history to vote for him on Election Day, which was nothing short of a miracle.

While all of that is compelling, I should make it clear that this will not be merely another book about how Donald Trump became the forty-fifth president of the United States. The campaign tactics and political drama are really a small part of the story. Instead, my purpose has been to explore the spiritual dimensions of the 2016 presidential election and to determine what role faith and the religious impulse may have played in Trump's unlikely win.

In the interest of full disclosure I have spent most of my career as a journalist, author, and publisher in the Christian community. I have met and written about most of America's well-known religious leaders, and I believe the spiritual aspect of life is vitally important. But like most people who followed the political gymnastics of the 2016 campaign, I wanted to know why Donald Trump was elected. I wanted to look closely at the religious and spiritual dynamics of the race and to find out what impact they may have had.

The "faith factor" was brought up repeatedly throughout the campaign, often to the amusement of Trump's critics in the media. Not only did the candidate make his faith an issue, but he went to the trouble of creating a faith advisory board of pastors, evangelists, and ministry leaders years before he entered the race. Trump obviously believed that religion was an issue, and he understood that the evangelical community of more than sixty-five million to eighty million potential voters[1] was an audience he needed to know more about.

As he gathered advisers and strategists to his side, he discovered that the people in the so-called flyover zone (how people on the East and West Coasts refer to middle America) were profoundly angry with Washington. They were tired of the government's lurch toward globalism in the Obama administration. They were concerned about the impact undocumented immigrants were having on their communities, and they were rightfully afraid of the threat of radical Islamic terrorism. I believe Donald Trump shared those emotions, but how much of what he promised on the campaign stump was merely tactical, and how much was inspired by a genuine concern for the future of the nation?

Since the election I have been intrigued by the public reaction to Trump's victory, and I've been surprised by the comments of people who say they have a sense that God had something to do with it. Some posted comments on the Internet saying they had never thought about the possibility before, but maybe there was a God, and maybe He was doing something nobody understands. I thought of Benjamin Franklin's surprising declaration during the Constitutional Convention of 1787, when he said famously, "God governs in the affairs of men." And it struck me that a lot of Facebookers and chat room prowlers were starting to come to the same conclusion.

So that's the real reason for this book. I want to tell the untold story of why Donald J. Trump, the flamboyant outsider who broke all the rules and shattered political protocol, became the forty-fifth president of the United States. This book is neither biography nor commentary but delves into issues and trends in society, looking at where the country is going and the degree to which the actions of the evangelical community may have influenced Trump's election. In short, where was God in all this? And what difference does it make?

THE REST OF THE STORY

There are a number of little-known stories that proved to be critical in helping to turn the tide of this historic election, and those stories need to be brought to light. So I have written about not only the enormous evangelical support for Trump's campaign but also the early support of some charismatic leaders, an angle few have written about thus far. I examine how Trump has attempted to reach across the racial divide and how a California pastor wrote an amazing article giving a rationale for voting for Trump, especially for those who didn't like him, and wound up with more than 4.1 million shares on the Internet. I have also spoken with several religious leaders identified as modern-day prophets. Many of these individuals prophesied well before the election that God was raising up Donald Trump like the ancient Persian king Cyrus the Great, a pagan chosen by God for a purpose only he could accomplish. The prophets told me they had certain knowledge that Trump would win. And, lo and behold, he did.

I confess that, like most Evangelicals, I supported Trump only after Ted Cruz dropped out of the race in May 2016. But once I was on board, I did whatever I could to help elect this most unlikely candidate. I became involved behind the scenes, meeting for strategy sessions with Christian leaders, posting more than one hundred articles on our CharismaNews.com website, and writing columns about the stakes in this election. We devoted the entire October issue of *Charisma* magazine to what I considered to be the most important election of my lifetime. That issue included my exclusive interview with Donald Trump, from August 11, 2016, and I've included that conversation in this book.

I know, of course, that Trump made some unwise public statements and attacked others when he should have held his tongue—he could have been more diplomatic in his replies to critics. But I'm reminded of the words of my friend Archbishop Russell McClanahan of Tallahassee, Florida, who said recently, "Trump's strength is he's not a politician. Trump's weakness is he's not a politician." For all his abrasive words and deeds, a near majority of the American people, and an overwhelming plurality in the electoral college, were willing to overlook the negatives and accentuate the positives to give the political outsider from Manhattan the victory. Since the election I think even those who had their doubts are coming to believe they did the right thing.

I can't begin to imagine what life would have been like with four years of Hillary Clinton in the White House. Pundits of both the Left and the Right have suggested it would simply have been Obama's third term, and that would have been inconceivable. During the campaign I got to know some of the people you will meet in these pages—people whose credibility I readily vouch for—and they provided insights on what was happening behind the scenes that few people could have known. I soon realized those stories of what was happening on a spiritual level needed to be included in this book, so that's part of what you will find in these pages.

In 2003 I had the privilege of publishing *The Faith of George W. Bush,* which was Charisma House's first *New York Times* best seller. *Time* magazine wrote about the impact of the book on the evangelical community. Yet as appealing as the story of President Bush's spiritual journey may have been, I believe the story of Donald Trump's journey to the White House is infinitely more interesting. Donald Trump is certainly no theologian, and he has been described by some observers as a "baby Christian" at best. But Christian leaders I respect have told me he is a chosen vessel being used by God despite his flaws. Like General Patton, they said, he is a man with a heaven-sent mission, and the rough edges, crusty language, and arrogance are essential aspects of his character and force of will.

By the time I flew to New York to attend the election evening party at the New York Hilton on the evening of November 8, 2016, I had already come to believe Trump was going to win. If I didn't believe that, I would have stayed home. But I believed God had spoken, and I wanted to see this amazing part of history as it unfolded. There are other books about Donald Trump, and reams have been written about the election. But most of them ignore the God story, and I'm convinced that is not merely *part* of the story—it is the *biggest* part of the story.

Maybe you're a skeptic. Maybe you don't like President Trump. You don't have to like him to realize this has been an exceptional election, and there are apparently forces at work we barely understand. As you read this book, I hope it may cause you to think that perhaps God really does get involved in the affairs of men, and better yet that the turn taking place in this nation under Donald Trump's presidency will prove to be a turn in the right direction.

—STEPHEN E. STRANG
ST. AUGUSTINE, FLORIDA
JULY 4, 2017

PART I

THE
ELECTION

★★★★★

CHAPTER 1

TRUMP'S MIRACULOUS WIN

★★★★★

O N JANUARY 20, 2017, Donald J. Trump stepped forward to take the oath of office on the steps of the US Capitol, in Washington, DC, to become the forty-fifth president of the United States. It was a moment no one in the mainstream media or the political establishment had seriously considered. That auspicious occasion marked the culmination of one of the most contentious election campaigns in US history and the beginning of one of the most heated ideological struggles ever seen in this country.

Outlasting a field of sixteen other GOP contenders while attracting the largest number of evangelical voters in history, the New York billionaire had delivered a stunning blow to his Democratic rival and sent shock waves of amazement and disbelief across the nation and around the world. By some miracle "The Donald" had actually won.

Washington elites from both political parties had spent months pounding on candidate Trump, questioning his intelligence, his sanity, his motives, his fitness for public office, and even his religion. Thrice married, a casino owner, and someone known for his outrageous and often salty language, Trump did not have the persona of a model Christian, and his detractors were certain the conservative Republican base would never vote for such a man. And if they did, the pundits suggested, it would certainly be a betrayal of everything they once claimed to believe.

The *New York Times* pointed out that evangelical leaders had spent decades developing and fielding a cadre of strong conservative candidates capable of winning high public office. Gov. Mike Huckabee, Sen. Ted Cruz, Sen. Marco Rubio, Sen. Rick Santorum, Gov. Rick Perry, and Rep. Michele Bachmann were among the beneficiaries of that effort, yet none of them attracted the kind of support in the 2016 campaign accorded to the egotistical and unrestrained reality-TV star from Queens.

Trump, they wrote, "is unabashedly ignorant of the biblical

imperatives that form the foundation of evangelical culture and politics. That Mr. Trump is a Presbyterian and not Evangelical is not the issue. It's that he doesn't pretend to understand evangelicalism, or even his own mainline Protestantism."[1] The *New York Times* pontificating on the biblical imperatives of evangelical Christians ought to elicit at least a few chuckles for the irony.

Nevertheless, Donald Trump never claimed to be a paragon of virtue; in fact, he has admitted repeatedly in interviews with reporters and biographers that he had been rude and undisciplined for much of his life. But evangelical leaders who have met with him, as I have, believe he understands the importance of sincere faith, and—especially over the last few years—he has made a sincere effort to expand his knowledge of and his fluency with essential Christian beliefs.

During the 1950s Trump attended Sunday school and church with his parents, Fred and Mary Trump, at First Presbyterian Church in Jamaica, Queens, which has been described as the oldest Presbyterian congregation in America. He was even awarded a Bible at his confirmation in 1959. After the family transferred membership to Marble Collegiate Church in Manhattan, Trump was strongly attracted to the preaching of Dr. Norman Vincent Peale, who served that congregation as pastor for more than fifty years, from 1932 to 1984.

Peale's message that faith in God and a positive attitude are the keys to success in every area of life had an obvious appeal to the young Trump. Looking at Peale's book *The Power of Positive Thinking*, which has sold more than twenty million copies, it's easy to see how his message would have resonated in Trump's life and business practices. Shortly before his retirement Peale wrote to Trump, congratulating him on completion of his landmark structure, the lavish Trump Tower. Peale reminded Trump that he had once predicted he would become "America's greatest builder" and added, "You have already arrived at that status, and believe me, as your friend, I am very proud of you."[2] Four years later Trump hosted Peale's ninetieth birthday party at the Waldorf-Astoria hotel in Manhattan.

But Trump's education in biblical imperatives didn't end there. It's fair to say that he values the Christian faith because it defines a key part of the America he loves, not necessarily because he is a born-again Evangelical. He has been taught, counseled, witnessed to, and preached at for years, and he professes belief but keeps a healthy arm's length from overtly doctrinaire and fundamental Christianity. From a purely pragmatic point of view, perhaps that's for the best. His understanding, despite all he has said, may appear somewhat superficial to the faithful, but a majority of the American people have decided that's OK. They were seeking a true American leader, not a theologian. And in comparison with the Democratic alternative, there was never a serious debate.

THE REAL STORY OF WHY TRUMP WON

This perspective was articulated beautifully by my longtime friend and fellow publisher Don Nori Sr. in a blog post for the readers of CharismaNews.com in October 2015, a year before the election. Don wrote, "'We the people' have found our voice, and we intend to use it to shape the conversation, not to conform to another's view of our country or our faith."[3] The mainstream media are so blinded by their own parochialism that they've missed the real story.

Don wrote, "The media stand in amazement that a non-politician such as Trump can garner such widespread support among so many American sub-cultures....'He doesn't act like much of a politician,' they say in stunned amazement. But that is the point. We don't want a politician. Therefore, we are not surprised when he does not act like one. They are surprised and horrified. Really? I want to hear the truth as a candidate sees it and not how someone spins it. Trump is not too 'spinnable.'"[4]

Don went on to list what he saw as evidence of Trump's belief in Jesus Christ, not because of the litmus tests many denominations employ but because of his simple faith. "He believes Jesus is His Savior, reads his Bible, and prays every day. He is pro-life, wants to defund Planned Parenthood, and will stop the persecution of believers here in America."[5] Don wrote that his favorite quote of Trump's was "Christianity is under attack. It's time for Christians to stand up for themselves. I'll stand up for Christianity."[6]

What ought to be readily apparent is that Donald Trump believes in the American Dream. He has achieved it himself, in a big way. Growing up in a middle-class neighborhood in the New York borough of Queens during the 1950s, Trump watched his father, with only a high school education, achieve his dream of becoming the most successful builder and real estate entrepreneur in Brooklyn and Queens. At an early age Trump decided to follow in his father's footsteps. He worked for him, learning the ropes from the bottom up, and would eventually exceed his father's accomplishments many times over. But he understood that the American Dream was within the reach of anyone willing to work hard and play fair, and that too requires a certain biblical ethic. That attitude apparently struck a chord with men and women in the heartland during the bruising 2016 campaign.

Michele Bachmann, who had made an impressive run for the White House with major Tea Party support in 2012, didn't hesitate to assure her supporters that Donald Trump was the best man for the Republican nomination in 2016. In a taped interview with CBN News commentator David Brody she referred to the Old Testament Book of Daniel, saying, "The bottom line of the Book of Daniel is this: it teaches us that the most high God lifts up who He will and takes down who He will."[7]

Bachmann had not been a Trump supporter from the first but eventually decided he was the only electable candidate. "I actually supported Ted Cruz," she said. "I thought he was fabulous, but I also see that at the end of the day God raised up, I believe, Donald Trump, who was going to be the nominee in this election. I don't think God sits things out. He's a sovereign God.... I think it's very likely that in the day that we live in that Donald Trump is the only individual who could win in a general election of the seventeen who ran."[8]

This is a perspective I have encountered more than once as I've observed and participated in the vetting and exploratory process of the election. There are ministry leaders and prophetic voices who are convinced God brought Donald Trump, who had said for many years that he was not at all interested in running for public office, to this place for this time. It may well be, as Bachmann and certain prophetic voices have suggested, that Trump was sent by God as a bull in a china shop to break up the globalist agenda and interrupt the Left's campaign to remake America in their own image. A man with a milder, gentler, less aggressive personality could never hope to take on the forces within the political establishment and prosper, which explains why Donald J. Trump was the perfect choice for this hour.

If you consider the level of shock in all quarters once it became clear that Trump had actually won, you would have to believe that some kind of backlash was to be expected. Democrats were stunned, and many Republicans were in disbelief as well. Even Trump's most ardent supporters could hardly believe what had happened. Panic and anger ensued on one side, and euphoria on the other, but the impossible had actually happened. The Never-Trumpers and self-righteous conservatives and libertarians were utterly confounded, but the reaction from hard-left groups funded by George Soros and other counterculture organizations escalated the anger and violent protests to unprecedented levels.

The Left reacted furiously because their long-term agenda was being derailed. The Obama administration had been organized and commissioned as a catalytic operation—set into motion, no doubt, decades earlier. Saul Alinsky, a mentor of both Barack Obama and Hillary Clinton, taught that the historic framework of democracy in America must be destroyed. This was also the goal of the "new world order." The powers that elevated Obama to prominence and supported his rise to the presidency in 2008 had given him a mandate. His administration was to be the key to unlock the gates of the antiquated American Democracy, to bring America at long last into the "community of nations,"[9] and to clear the way for the global government President George H. W. Bush had promised seventeen years earlier in his 1991 State of the Union address before Congress.

Bush had called it "a new world order, where diverse nations are drawn together in common cause to achieve the universal aspirations of mankind."[10] Once Obama opened the door, the Clinton campaign would be poised to take it from there, to capitalize on that promise and complete the transformation. But something unexpected happened on the way to global government: a grassroots rebellion and an act of God of magnificent proportions. A comparison of the platforms of the two political parties reveals the depth of division between them. But what those documents do not show is the depth of resentment of the men and women in the flyover zones who felt their country was being ripped from their fingers and their moral heritage was being squandered.

Neither party and few mainstream pundits had recognized the tension building up in Middle America. Consequently Trump's victory led to a wave of outrage from the Left followed by a massive campaign of resistance and retaliation. Even before the inauguration the liberal media were in full Terminator mode. There were vitriolic attacks on the president-elect like nothing we had ever seen. I will take a closer look at this development in a later chapter, but it would be foolish indeed to ignore the unprecedented hostility that began rising all around us.

THE UNPATRIOTIC RESISTANCE

Democrats had hoped to win back the House and the Senate as part of Clinton's inevitable White House win, but, in fact, they managed to lose all three. So no one is really surprised the Democrats would react to Donald Trump's victory with alarm. Their agenda and their cushy appointed jobs in the government were being threatened for the first time in a decade, or maybe two, and that was enough to make them a bit crazy. Even more extraordinary was the level of hatred spewing from Clinton's supporters in every corner of the country, not only in Washington, but also in New York, Hollywood, and many other places across the fruited plain.

Faced with an overwhelmingly negative press, vulgar broadsides by the sitting president and members of Congress, insults by celebrities, and stereotyping by the media as a racist and bigot, Donald Trump knew he faced a difficult race. He would need a way to fight back, and he found it with Twitter, the news and social-networking service that allows users to post short comments of up to 140 characters to their online followers—in Trump's case, that would be thirty-five million followers on @realDonaldTrump. Later he would add another twenty million followers on @POTUS, and Twitter would become Donald Trump's direct link to the American people.

Hollywood actress Meryl Streep carried the banner for the celebrity Trump haters in her acceptance speech at the Golden Globe Awards in January 2017, calling for organized resistance to the Trump presidency. Without calling him by name, she painted the president as a heartless racist and bigot. Never one to dodge a fight, however, Trump tweeted in response to Streep's Golden Globes tirade, "Meryl Streep, one of the most over-rated actresses in Hollywood, doesn't know me but attacked last night at the Golden Globes. She is a . . ."[11] and stopped short, leaving it for his followers to fill in the blank. Meghan McCain, daughter of the 2008 Republican nominee, went on defense for the president and tweeted that Streep's speech provided a perfect example of why Trump won. "And if people in Hollywood don't start recognizing why and how," she said, "you will help him get re-elected."[12]

Name-calling by celebrities is one thing, but name-calling by a former president constitutes another matter, and Barack Obama—whose tasteless jibes at Trump during the 2011 White House Correspondents' Dinner may have helped persuade Trump to make his bid for the presidency[13]—has not been greatly concerned about precedent or decorum. By long-standing tradition, former presidents do not criticize their successors. Bush never did, but Obama has referred to his successor as a liar, using a vulgar slur I can't repeat.[14] But even that appears insignificant compared with the diatribes routinely leveled at Trump by the likes of representatives Nancy Pelosi, Elijah Cummings, Maxine Waters, and Sen. Chuck Schumer and their like-minded cohorts in the House and Senate.

The bitterness on display in the halls of Congress and in hundreds of cities and towns feels disheartening. I think this kind of behavior displays a warning sign of what's to come if the Christian consensus in this country continues its decades-old decline. While we expect our political adversaries to disagree with us on certain issues, our leaders shouldn't have to face unrestrained hatred and violence every day.

But what has been most surprising over the past eighteen months is the hostility and vocal resistance to the Trump presidency posed by the substantial group of Republican and Libertarian journalists known as "Never-Trumpers." Columnist George Will, an outspoken Never-Trumper, said in one televised diatribe that he would resign his membership in the Republican Party if Donald Trump became the nominee, which Will did.[15]

Former presidential candidates John McCain and Mitt Romney constantly criticized Trump from the time he entered the race, even accusing him of collusion with the Russians and interfering with Justice Department investigations. At least three of the Republican candidates Trump defeated in the primary—John Kasich, Ted Cruz, and Jeb Bush—along with Jeb's father and brother (Bush forty-one and Bush forty-three), have spoken out against Trump.

Many in his own Republican Party, not just the Democrats, were working to destroy him. He didn't have the ground game that Clinton had. He was far behind on fundraising and had minimal staff to work on solving these problems. A Trump campaign insider told me during a private conversation that major Republican National Committee donors met several times with party hierarchy to figure out how they could derail the Trump campaign. Clearly Trump needed a miracle to overcome all the resistance, and the fact that the media caught its collective hair on fire every time he tweeted something outlandish only made the challenge that much greater. In all fairness Trump's tweets about his opponents during the campaign were often offensive, and some viewed him as a bully. But many others were delighted by Trump's attacks, exposing his political enemies.

Weekly Standard editor at large Bill Kristol said in a tweet that if he were forced to choose between loyalty to Trump and joining with the gang of government bureaucrats working undercover to embarrass and cripple the president, he would side with the "deep state."[16] In other words, he would choose treason over party loyalty. Until recently few in the general public knew the term *deep state*. Basically these are the government bureaucrats who run the government out of public view—the government that doesn't change no matter which party holds power. The bureaucracy, the lobbyists, the insiders, the establishment, and even the intelligence agencies are involved.

Even if most Americans are unaware of these men and women, they know intuitively that something is wrong with the way the government operates. When Trump ad-libbed on the campaign trail that he was going to "drain the swamp," he was talking about the permanent bureaucracy and the deep state, and the crowds erupted in cheers. Finally someone was going to deal with the unaccountable cadre that looks out after its own interests rather than the interests of the American people.

For many years only right-wing political conspiracy theorists talked about the deep state. The Washington establishment and the left-leaning media ignored it because, as they said repeatedly, that was just right-wing conspiracy talk. Now, however, everyone knows that US intelligence agencies were eavesdropping on Trump's campaign and giving information to the press and the Clinton campaign. Leaks from intelligence sources in the NSA, CIA, FBI, and Department of State were given to the press to help destroy the Trump campaign.

If these weren't obstacles enough, Trump's campaign was threatened by wide-scale election fraud. Illegal voting has become a standard campaign strategy in major cities where Democrats control the voting process. This issue is only getting worse and making it more difficult for Republican candidates to win in the swing states, particularly in the Midwest. I've heard some experts suggest that if there had been no illegal voting in the 2016 election, Trump would have also won the popular vote and possibly added more states to his electoral college total. When you add all this up, it makes Trump's victory even more miraculous. The whole entrenched political system—including both political parties, the media, academia, covert corporate interests, and the deep state—was against him and created a roadblock to the White House, yet he won.

Meanwhile notorious antidemocratic groups such as MoveOn.org, funded by Hungarian billionaire and former Nazi collaborator George Soros, were on the warpath.[17] A laundry list of self-styled anarchist cells and racially motivated groups such as Black Lives Matter and UnidosUS (formerly called La Raza), along with rent-a-mob

organizations and union thugs, were on the march, intimidating conservative gatherings, congressional town hall meetings, and even
Christian churches. By stalking conservatives, screaming vulgar epi-
thets, and threatening physical violence, these groups have been able
to subvert the natural course of government and violate the rights
of citizens to participate in the political process. All together such
activity represents a dangerous—and I would add demonic—attempt
to undermine free speech and our most basic freedoms.

THE MEDIA'S LOSS OF CREDIBILITY

We would like to think that public disapproval of such tactics would
be a hot topic in the media. We would like to think the newsrooms of
America would be ablaze with impassioned defenders of free speech
unmasking the villains and crying out for justice. But that hasn't happened. We can no longer trust the mainstream media to give us a "fair
and balanced" account of political events. Instead it has become only
too clear that the mainstream media stands on the other side. If any
good news can be found in this scenario, it is that the public is not
blind to what has been happening. They've been watching, and they're
not buying everything they're told.

Shortly after the election in November 2016 a Media Research
Center (MRC) poll of more than two thousand adults found that, even
as they fanned the flames of controversy, the mainstream media managed to alienate virtually every politically active American. The survey
found that 78 percent of respondents thought that media coverage of
the 2016 presidential campaign was biased, 69 percent believed the
news media were not "honest and truthful," and 59 percent said the
media were biased in favor of Hillary Clinton, while just 21 percent
said the media were biased in favor of Trump. But perhaps most telling
was the fact that fully 97 percent of registered US voters in the survey
said they did not let the media bias influence their vote.[18] In other
words, for them the media had already lost all credibility.

It's hardly surprising the voters lost confidence. Across the board, in
broadcast, print, and electronic coverage of the campaign, the media
had already chosen their candidate, and it was not Donald Trump.
Meanwhile, in October, just twenty-nine days before the election,
then Fox News commentator Bill O'Reilly reported that at least three
media organizations had "ordered their employees to destroy Donald

Trump," and he was "100 percent convinced" the order was not merely rhetorical.[19]

An Investor's Business Daily/TIPP Poll conducted in September 2016 found very similar results to the MRC study, showing that more than two-thirds of registered voters (67 percent) believed the media's reports on the candidates were inaccurate, while only a quarter of respondents trusted the accuracy of news stories. Slightly less than half of voters felt the media were being too easy on the Democratic candidate, and only 16 percent said the media had been too tough on her. And most telling, more than two-thirds of Americans (69 percent) said the news media wields too much influence on the election process.[20]

In reality Trump's defeat of Clinton's weak campaign should not have come as a surprise to anyone. Her negative numbers were enormous, and her history of scandals was all too familiar to the voters. In short, the Democrats could not have given themselves a worse candidate. When she started her presidential campaign, Clinton believed she had already won the race. She wrapped up the East Coast, from Maine to Virginia, with the exception of little New Hampshire. She had promises of 97 electoral votes from her Democratic base. On the West Coast, from California to Washington state, she was guaranteed another 74 electoral votes. With 171 votes out of the required 270, Clinton was convinced she had the election locked up when she launched her campaign.[21]

In contrast, there were a lot fewer solid Republican states that Trump could count on. Chances are he would win the South, from Kentucky to Texas, and probably Kansas. The big question was the swing states, mostly in the Midwest, which in times past had been a Democratic stronghold. In recent elections if the Democratic candidate won either Ohio or Florida, he went on to win the presidency. By all rights Clinton should have won. The numbers were all on her side. Who would have imagined that Trump could win not only Florida and Ohio but also Wisconsin, Michigan, and Pennsylvania. It was politically unthinkable.

Of course the media went along with all this, showing Clinton's road to victory but never Trump's road to victory. Even when it became obvious Trump had won, the networks were reporting that Clinton still had some sort of path to reach 270 electoral votes. It's difficult to imagine the insularity that exists in America's newsrooms, but that's a dilemma conservatives and Evangelicals have wrestled with ever since I worked in newsrooms back in the 1970s. In a post-election column in the *New*

York Times journalist Jim Rutenberg admitted that the media missed the boat. They failed to capture "the boiling anger of a large portion of the American electorate that feels left behind by a selective recovery." He said he was amazed at how often "the news media has missed the populist movements that have been rocking national politics since at least 2008."[22]

The media have been challenged repeatedly, and countless polls show the levels of public dissatisfaction. Furthermore, the success of Fox News, Breitbart, the Drudge Report, Infowars, and other conservative news outlets, including my own Charisma News, ought to have given them a clue they were betting on the wrong horse. But clearly there exists a blind spot in the media's worldview. The reporters, editors, and bureau chiefs who fashion the headlines are opinionated and unwilling to change their bad habits. Apparently nothing short of a miracle will ever change that.

A poll conducted by the liberal Shorenstein Center on Media, Politics and Public Policy at Harvard reported that coverage of Donald Trump during the election run-up was overwhelmingly negative. While the authors of the study suggested that coverage of the Clinton campaign seemed equally negative, their own study doesn't support that conclusion.[23] The numbers speak for themselves.

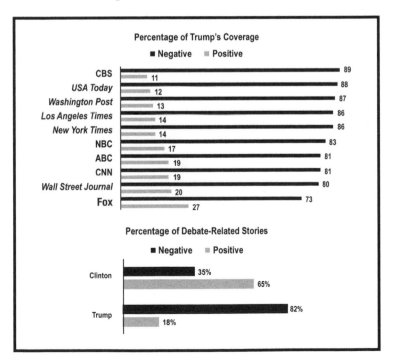

Percentage of Trump's Coverage

■ Negative ▪ Positive

	Negative	Positive
CBS	89	11
USA Today	88	12
Washington Post	87	13
Los Angeles Times	86	14
New York Times	86	14
NBC	83	17
ABC	81	19
CNN	81	19
Wall Street Journal	80	20
Fox	73	27

Percentage of Debate-Related Stories

■ Negative ▪ Positive

	Negative	Positive
Clinton	35%	65%
Trump	82%	18%

The Shorenstein Center's analysis of reporting on the presidential debates reveals how one-sided the mainstream media's coverage had been. So-called objective reporting on Trump by all ten of the major national news organizations was overwhelmingly negative, even at Fox News, which is commonly thought to be the only "conservative network." More than 70 percent of Fox's coverage was negative while less than 30 percent was somewhat positive. And much of the positive reporting came from the network's three outspoken commentators, Bill O'Reilly, Sean Hannity, and Tucker Carlson. The Shorenstein Center's charts illustrate what an uphill struggle the Trump campaign was in for.

With so much negative press and attacks from members of both parties, how did Trump win? A comment from a longtime friend of Trump's at the election night party at the New York Hilton may provide the answer. As we waited the long hours and watched the election returns on the TV screens set up around the ballroom, a wealthy businessman standing close to me said (a couple of hours before the election was called for Trump), "If the results show that Trump wins, that proves there is a God." Reason: "If Donald Trump wins, it will be a miracle!" And that's what Christians had been praying for.

CHAPTER 2

AN ANSWER TO PRAYER

★★★★★

W HILE SOME PEOPLE interpreted Donald Trump's win as a political revolution, many conservative Christians saw it as a cultural counter-revolution and an answer to prayer. Respected journalist David Aikman articulated this very well in an op-ed published by *Charisma* magazine. I've known Aikman, who is now retired, since the 1970s when he worked as a senior foreign correspondent for *Time* magazine, a post he held for twenty-three years. An outspoken Charismatic, Aikman served as *Time*'s bureau chief in Berlin, Jerusalem, and Beijing and covered Middle East affairs from Jerusalem. He had reported from five continents and more than fifty-five countries and wrote three "Man of the Year" cover stories for *Time*. He has an excellent grasp of social and cultural issues.

During his distinguished career Aikman interviewed many world figures, from Alexander Solzhenitsyn to Mother Teresa of Calcutta to Billy Graham. As a journalist Aikman understood the animosity of the members of the media toward Trump, who publicly denounced reporters at almost every opportunity. When his audiences erupted in raucous approval, the media who covered those events were seething with disgust. But Trump didn't oppose the press just because most of them backed Clinton, Aikman says. He opposed them because they seemed clueless to "the economic and cultural resentment" of the voters all over America.[1]

The fact that so many journalists were oblivious about the extent of Trump's support showed that very few of them had spent any time in the so-called flyover zones where Trump had millions of followers. The beltway pundits were blinded by their own wishful thinking about the upcoming election, Aikman says. An op-ed that ran in the *New York Times* showed how out of touch they were. Robert Leonard, the news director for a couple of Iowa radio stations, wrote that he'd had a flash of insight—an epiphany, he said—about the media's disconnect when he spoke with Oklahoma Baptist pastor J. C. Watts, who had served in the US House of Representatives from 1995–2003. Listening to Watts, Leonard said, suddenly the lights went on.

"The difference between Republicans and Democrats," Watts told Leonard, "is that Republicans believe people are fundamentally bad, while Democrats see people as fundamentally good." Watts told Leonard that Democrats believe we are born good, that we create God in our own image. God didn't create us; we created Him. But Watts pointed out that young children don't have to be taught how to behave badly: "They are born knowing how to do that," Watts said. "We are born bad. We teach [our children] how to be good. We become good by being reborn—born again."[2]

Aikman wrote that "if reporters who covered Trump had realized what a huge subterranean Christian prayer movement was under-girding the Trump campaign, even if the reporters themselves did not believe in God or the power of prayer, they might have been less dumbfounded by the actual election result."[3] This tells us, he said, that many Americans who heard Trump saying he wanted to "make America great again" hoped he was also saying that he wanted to make America "morally great again."[4] For conservative Christians this moral greatness only comes from spiritual revival, something many believers had been praying for. They weren't praying to elect Donald Trump so much as they were praying for a change of direction and a new moral and spiritual awakening.

For most voters in the heartland, their concerns had little to do with Obamacare, gun control, or defense spending, although most would have an opinion on such matters. Rather the moral issues and downward spiritual spiral of the nation had them fired up. Supreme Court rulings taking prayer out of school in 1962[5] and Bible reading out of school in 1963[6] were just the beginning. Legalizing abortion on demand under the Supreme Court's faulty 1973 ruling in *Roe v. Wade*[7] signified a tragedy of even greater magnitude. Removing restrictions on Internet pornography and legalizing same-sex marriage after the *Obergefell v. Hodges* Supreme Court ruling in 2015[8] were among the reasons conservatives believed they were under attack. And that's why the cultural revolution was becoming a major issue in the election.

Mike Bickle, founder of the International House of Prayer in Kansas

City, Missouri, explained his perspective on the election to me, saying, "We prayed God would raise up a righteous voice. We didn't have anyone in mind."[9] That's because his organization focuses on causing America to wake up. And if the person who could wake them up turned out to be Donald Trump, Bickle said, that would be fine with him.

Chuck Pierce, who heads an apostolic and prophetic ministry in Texas called Glory of Zion International, said much the same thing. Donald Trump, he told me in a recent conversation, is not just a candidate; he is the path to a spiritual remedy for America. "I think you have to look past his unrighteous modes in the past to see how God has righteously chosen him to affect the way that this nation goes forward." Pierce told me he had predicted in 2008 that "America must learn to play the Trump card" and explained that's because once you play the trump card, your opponent can't play over it. "It was as if the Lord was saying that He has a plan the opponent cannot stop."[10]

A New Cultural Agenda

Americans who grew up in the 1950s, or whose lives were formed at an early age by people from that era, tend to look back on that time not only as a wonderful era of American prosperity but also as a time of moral righteousness on a national level. Many Americans look back fondly to this period of history as a time when there were no disputes about right and wrong, good and evil. Everybody seemed to agree about such things. Small groups and individuals who had a more liberal perspective worked behind the scenes, we now know. But no one preached rebellion against the conventional moral code. Of course it was also a time of segregation in part of the country, and minorities who lived under the injustice of Jim Crow laws that weren't changed until a decade later don't look back fondly on those days. The fifties weren't perfect in other ways: for example, many adults who deal with sexual abuse as children were molested in the fifties, but it wasn't talked about. And the "stable" fifties were the incubator for the social fomenting of the 1960s.

Nonetheless, David Aikman writes that America had a civic religion in those days, a basic Christian morality reinforced by the preaching of evangelists such as Billy Graham, who was greatly admired by all regardless of their political leanings. Trump himself was a product of that era, and although there's not a lot of evidence he had a religious side, it was only much later in life that he became morally libertarian.[11]

"The American civic religion was largely eroded," Aikman said, "after the campus upheavals and the antiwar movement of the 1960s. The entire culture began to experience a shift that introduced new gate-keepers and new worldviews in Hollywood, academia, and the media."[12] Some of those worldviews, such as Marxism, he said, reemerged after years of unpopularity. But constant pressure from the Left, and the explosion of hedonism and self-gratification in the 1970s and 1980s, escalated the pace of change.

"Most of the new cultural paradigm rejected the view of a created world and of a deity who was still interested in human behavior," Aikman writes. "As of 2017, America has undergone seven decades during which the existence of God and even the very notion that there might be design behind the formation of the universe has been repeat-edly mocked or utterly dismissed on college campuses and in public schools. It has been repeatedly ridiculed by Hollywood."[13]

While Donald Trump never said anything about wanting to change the American culture, his attacks on "political correctness" and his insistence on restoring the freedom to say "Merry Christmas" endeared him to the audiences on his tours. After the election many Christians and other supporters of traditional American values began to think that President Trump might be favorable to any grassroots movement that sought to make America "morally" great once again.[14]

Part of Trump's appeal for many voters was that he wasn't Hillary Clinton. "We would have voted for any conservative who could beat Hillary," Mike Bickle told me after the election. "When it came down to Trump or Hillary, there was no question." Unfortunately the candi-date kept shooting himself in the foot with one outlandish tweet after another. But he was the comeback kid, Bickle said. The more outra-geous he was, the more the people loved him. And things that would have destroyed any other candidate didn't seem to slow him down.[15]

As Election Day drew near, Aikman said, it often looked as if Clinton might actually win. The polls certainly suggested she would win. But if she did, not only would it be a continuation of America's unfortu-nate lurch to the left; it also would be the doorway to a new era of corruption like nothing we had ever seen. It would unleash an all-out effort to transform the culture, to dismantle "Christian America," and to make the hope of renewal and restoration many Christians were praying for much, much harder to achieve.[16]

Evangelist and media personality James Robison told me in a recent telephone interview that "a lot of Christians were praying that we wouldn't lose freedom, that we would not lose the opportunities this nation offers with the protections and safeguards, and government functioning as a protector, and not potentially replacing God and our love for one another."[17] Robison, who serves on the president's Faith Advisory Board and remains a friend and confidant of Trump's, believes now that Donald Trump represents a supernatural answer to prayer, but he didn't come in the package people wanted. Of the seventeen Republican nominees, he ranked as the last choice of most Evangelicals. "He would have been my last choice," Robison told me. "Many conservatives said that we don't know where Donald Trump is going to end up taking us, but we know exactly where Hillary Clinton would take us, and that would be a continuation of everything that's wrong, destructive, and that would ruin America by taking away our freedoms."[18]

During the week of Trump's inauguration, thousands of Evangelicals converged on Washington, DC, to celebrate the big win and to thank God for answering their prayers. There were inaugural galas and plenty of prayer meetings all over the District of Columbia and neighboring towns. Over and over Christian leaders who did not initially back Trump thanked God for a reprieve. Even establishment conservatives in the respected Council for National Policy (CNP) were elated by Trump's win when they met right after the election. Ray Moore from South Carolina, whom I introduce later, is a member of CNP. After one session he walked alongside Tony Perkins, who besides being president of the Family Research Council is also president of CNP. "I put my arm around Tony's shoulder," Ray remembers, "and thanked him for his part in getting Trump elected and saving America."[19] When I attended the first post-election CNP meeting as a guest in February 2017, the general mood was "we dodged a bullet."

The secular pundits, on the other hand, saw Trump's victory only as a battle between Democrat and Republican, or between the Left and the Right. But Robison saw it as a supernatural spiritual battle. "What happened," he told me, "is that God overpowered the foolishness of political correctness and the liberal (not just deceived but possessed) Left, which is far too often dead-set against a biblical worldview and against America's traditional Judeo-Christian ethics. But they were being totally pushed back."[20]

The secular Left in this country, Robison said, are being manipulated by the powers that Jesus was talking about when He said of those who crucified Him, "They don't know what they're doing." They knew exactly what they were doing, but Jesus said no, they didn't. "They were under the control of another force, another power in the invisible supernatural realm of the Spirit. They were deceived by the deceiver." Millions of Christians were praying for that deception to be overthrown, to prevent the government from being raised up as another form of Pharaoh or some kind of an overseeing Caesar. The people were praying, "God, we've got to let You be God. We've got to stop this nonsense." And Robison added, "Christians were praying for this to be stopped, but they never dreamed that it would be some person totally disconnected with politics, totally unable to even express himself like a politician, and someone who was best known as a shrewd maneuverer."[21]

Trump spoke with conviction about what's wrong in this country, Robison told me. "He was totally open about everything that was wrong. Most of us would agree that he didn't address those problems in the most statesmanlike or diplomatic terms, but everything he was saying was right on track. He was saying that many things in this country are bad and they needed to be dealt with. And he was 100 percent correct."[22]

REDEEMING THE NATION

Christians who were concerned about "government masquerading as God," to use Robison's expression, knew the government needed to be brought under control, so Trump's win served as evidence that their prayers were being answered. "Trump was coming in as a builder. He was first going to tear down things that needed to be torn down before replacing them with something better, which is exactly what you do when you tear down the old and build something new.

"He understood what it means to lay a foundation," Robison said. "He is a builder. What he didn't realize was that he was actually returning to the foundation of our freedom, and we know that the solid rock upon which we are to build is the transforming truth Jesus referred to when He said, 'You shall know the truth, and the truth shall make you free'" (John 8:32, NKJV).[23]

As many evangelical leaders did, Robison had initially backed Ted Cruz. He told me he had known Ted's father, Rafael, ever since Ted was nine years old. But he also knew several other presidential contenders, including his lifelong friend Rick Perry. He was an adviser to George W. Bush and a friend to all the Bush family. He knows Rand Paul and Carly Fiorina and has prayed with all of them. "They all looked like they had such great qualifications," he said, "and frankly I was astounded that Donald Trump was even being considered and gaining momentum."[24]

Mike Huckabee was the first to tell Robison to get behind Trump after Huckabee dropped out of the race. Robison had been recruiting Huckabee to counsel Cruz, but the governor told him, "James, the man who listens to counsel the best of anybody I've been around is Donald Trump." Robison was surprised to hear that and said, "Mike, have you lost your mind?" Mike said, "No, I haven't. I've known him, James. I've watched him, and I know it sounds crazy, but I believe he's the right man at this time."[25] Robison remembers hearing Jerry Falwell Jr. saying much the same thing.

After Ben Carson dropped out of the race, Robison prayed with him nearly every day on the phone. "The week that Dr. Carson decided to endorse Trump, we probably talked on average about two hours a day. Then all of a sudden he told me, 'I'm endorsing Donald Trump.' And I said, 'Ben, you've lost your mind! What are you doing?' He said, 'James, listen to me. I've spent two hours with him this week and two hours another day. It's just not the way it looks.' So I asked him, 'What do you mean?' And Ben Carson told me, 'James, I'm telling you, he'll listen to wisdom. And my endorsement comes with the assurance that he will be willing to listen to those who have deep convictions and the ability to communicate their importance, and he agreed to do that.'"[26]

Apparently Trump did listen, and before long Robison was flying with him to campaign events, giving him advice, and offering spiritual counsel whenever possible. Robison said he has met with several presidents. "None of them were as open as Donald Trump," he told me. "Mr. Trump called frequently on his cell phone, and he took my calls. We were able to have very open, honest exchanges where I could share the real concerns of pro-family, pro-faith leaders. He was always very appreciative and responsive. I was also able to travel with him on the plane and ride with him in the car in very important moments when I shared serious, deep concerns we had, which many thought Donald Trump would not listen to or even consider. But not only did he hear me with graciousness; he was very expressive in his appreciation for me and love for my family."[27]

In an interview for his organization's website, Robison asked Jack Graham, pastor of the forty-two-thousand-member Prestonwood Baptist Church in Plano, Texas, how he assesses the president's attitude toward people of faith. Robison said, "You've seen him in settings where someone is sharing their concern....Do you find it amazing the way this president responds to people no matter who they are?"[28]

Graham answered, "Beyond just personal skills, I am convinced he has a genuine spiritual interest and a desire to hear the viewpoint of others. In particular, it's apparent he wants to know what conservative, Bible-believing Christians think. It's been very gratifying and satisfying. And not only him but the people he has put into place. Vice President Pence is a great Christian. Eight or nine of his cabinet members, the people closest to him, are Christians, and they are having Bible study and prayer together."[29]

Graham also said, "I am grateful this president has given us the opportunity to speak into his life. When we prayed for him in the Oval Office earlier this week, though he was under a great deal of pressure, he was buoyant and joyful. We stayed in there for a good while conversing and praying. It was a God moment and a powerful experience." Robison and Graham agreed that Trump's words and actions indicate that this president values the opinions of the Christian leaders. And Graham added that "Vice President Pence was with us and he is a great man of prayer, a legitimate Bible-believing Christian. This president and his team have been nothing but responsive. I am very hopeful about the future of America right now because of this."[30]

The sudden groundswell of support for Trump that David Aikman referenced in his op-ed didn't only occur at Trump's political rallies. You could see it in churches, prayer groups, and rallies of all sorts. The respected charismatic teacher Dutch Sheets traveled to seventy-seven cities holding rallies, not for Trump but for righteousness to prevail. His main teaching was, "God, show us mercy."[31]

Cindy Jacobs, cofounder of Generals International and the Reformation Prayer Network, is not well known in evangelical circles but is widely respected by Charismatics as a prophet and teacher. She mobilized ten thousand intercessors to "prayer walk" the seven critical states that helped Trump win in November. These men and women would walk around courthouses or through the centers of towns praying for righteousness to prevail. In addition, a coalition of prayer leaders called As One also mobilized its networks two different times to prayer walk for forty days. "It was an urgent, Pentecostal type of prayer," she told me.[32] They knew this was not just another election. There were "battles in the heavenlies" for the soul of America, and Cindy's prayer warriors were engaged in those battles, praying that God's will would reign in America once again.

Cindy has ministered about such things all over the world, and as the campaign grew more intense in the fall of 2016, she began receiving calls from friends in Europe, China, and Latin America saying intercessors were praying fervently that Trump would be elected. Many took the election so seriously, they told her they were fasting and praying for hours each day. Cindy's close friend Lou Engle, a revivalist and cofounder of TheCall, a group that hosts twelve-hour prayer rallies, sent out a call to friends and supporters to begin a three-day Esther fast—meaning no food and no water—as a petition for God's mercy. He rallied thousands to join him because things looked so bleak. Conservative Christians believed that if Hillary Clinton won this election, it would be "game over" for religious freedom.

The night before the election Jerry Johnson, president of National Religious Broadcasters, attended a prayer meeting in Washington, DC, and came away telling friends he believed Trump would win. I had been praying too, and I felt optimistic that Trump was going to win. That's why I accepted the invitation from Darrell Scott, pastor of the New Spirit Revival Center in Cleveland Heights, Ohio, to fly to New York to watch the election returns at the New York Hilton on election night. Scott was joined by several other African American pastors. That event, with the whole world watching, turned out to be a huge victory celebration. For part of the evening I stood near pastor Robert Jeffress of First Baptist Church in Dallas, Texas, who told me what a miracle he thought it would be if Trump actually won.

CANCEL THE FIREWORKS

For most of the evening the television commentators kept predicting that Clinton would be victorious. Even Fox News, which was broadcast live on TV screens in the Hilton ballroom, was reporting that Clinton had the edge and Trump had too much ground to make up. Yet by 10:00 p.m. Eastern time it seemed to me that Trump's lead in electoral votes would be enough so that even a surge of West Coast victories couldn't make up the difference.

The networks were showing all of the jubilation from the Hilton ballroom. It was packed with people who had worked diligently for the campaign. The level of tension increased throughout the evening as the numbers for Trump kept getting better and better. Victory seemed possible, and then when Trump's numbers hit the 270 mark, the networks went silent. The liberal commentators were stunned silent by the realization that Trump had actually won. But at the Hilton ballroom the celebration became one of sheer joy.

Anyone watching what was happening at the Jacob K. Javits Convention Center, where Clinton's supporters were gathered to watch the election returns, witnessed a very different scene. The Clinton campaign had erected a two-million-dollar stage, and the balloons and confetti that were being held up by huge nets were ready to descend when Clinton's win was finally announced. But the announcement never came.

As I made my way to New York earlier that day, I heard the news that the Democrats had canceled their big fireworks display over the Hudson River in New York. I wondered then if Clinton's people had a suspicion that maybe they weren't going to win. The Democrats' "victory celebration" continued for a while with champagne and all the commotion of a political rally. But by midnight the scene was more like a funeral wake than a coronation.

Where I was standing, in the Hilton ballroom, my Christian friends were shouting, and a few shed tears of joy. It was as if God had answered our prayers and the impossible had happened. We had a new president, one we believed God had raised up for such a time as this. And perhaps best of all, we each thanked God in our own way that Hillary Clinton was not going to be the next commander in chief.

CHAPTER 3

AFTER THE ELECTION

★★★★★

I T WAS AS if all the air had suddenly been sucked out of the room. Hillary Clinton's election night rally at the Javits Center in New York City was supposed to be a colossal event, a spectacle, a coronation ceremony for the first woman president of the United States. Supporters, many of whom arrived early and celebrated throughout the day, were expecting to dance the night away, to celebrate with champagne as balloons and streamers cascaded down from high in the rafters. But the victory celebration never came that night. Something happened, something completely unexpected by the restless crowd, and as the evening wore on, it was becoming apparent that Hillary Clinton would not be moving to the White House.

For the men and women on Clinton's advisory team, the election had not gone as planned. The pollsters, once again, had missed it. States once thought to be secure Democratic territory were going for the Republican candidate, and the brightly colored maps displayed on the TV screens around the convention hall were now mostly red. One state after another was being called for Trump, and while the East and West Coasts performed as expected, remaining solidly blue throughout the night, the rest of America was going the other way. The heartland was voting for the political outsider who promised to "make America great again."

The crowds inside and outside the hall had been nervous and impatient all evening, but they wanted to hear from the candidate. They needed reassurance. Surely they hadn't lost, had they? But the candidate was nowhere to be seen, and by 11:00 p.m. the music had stopped, the house lights had gone out with a thump, and campaign officials could be seen scurrying away unceremoniously, taking refuge behind the enormous floor-to-ceiling curtains.

When Clinton's campaign chairman, John Podesta, addressed the bewildered stragglers, he tried to reassure them it wasn't over.[1] But it was over, and it was becoming crystal clear that the media, the networks, the pundits, and all the talking heads had gotten it wrong. The *New York Times* insisted that all its polling data confirmed that Clinton had the election in hand and her chances of winning were between 70 and 99 percent.[2] None of the models compiled by analytics experts showed the Democrats with less than 60 percent of the vote. But now everyone understood that the prognosticators had guessed wrong and Clinton had lost.

Clinton did not come out that night. She wouldn't officially concede the race until the next morning, but at 2:00 a.m. John Podesta said she would have a public statement the following day. "It's been a long night," he said, "and it's been a long campaign, but…we can wait a little longer, can't we? They're still counting votes, and every vote should count.…So we're not going to have anything more to say tonight."[3]

Shortly before 3:00 a.m. New York time on November 9, and shortly after the television networks announced that the battleground states of Pennsylvania and Wisconsin had gone for the Republican candidate, Donald Trump took the stage at the Hilton hotel. I stood there and took video of him walking out at 2:47 a.m. with his family, Gov. Mike Pence, and several close associates, including Reince Priebus. My cell phone battery died right before he made a short speech, so I wasn't able to alert my team what was happening. But Trump took the stage and gave a speech, which lasted only about fifteen minutes, in which he called for a time of healing and a new spirit of unity.

He said Hillary Clinton had called him moments earlier. "She congratulated us," he said. "It's about us…on our victory. And I congratulated her and her family on a very, very hard-fought campaign. She fought very hard. Hillary has worked very long and very hard over a long period of time, and we owe her a major debt of gratitude for her service to our country. I mean that very sincerely.

"Now it's time for America to bind the wounds of division," Trump said. "To all Republicans and Democrats and Independents across this nation, I say it is time for us to come together as one united people. It's time. I pledge to every citizen of our land that I will be president for all Americans."[4] To say the crowd in the Hilton ballroom was jubilant would be an understatement. The mood was like Chicago Cubs fans after their first World Series victory in more than one hundred years!

Judge Jeanine Pirro of Fox News was behind me, standing on one of the few chairs in the ballroom, whooping like a cowgirl.

The Trump campaign team was ecstatic. Their diligence paid off, and their man had won. Cheers and chants broke out around the hall, at which point the president-elect raised his hand and made a strong conciliatory appeal, saying, "For those who have chosen not to support me in the past—of which there were a few people—I'm reaching out to you for your guidance and your help." Then he added that he would be announcing a series of new projects of "national growth and renewal," and he said, "we will get along with all other nations willing to get along with us." Regarding the ongoing immigration crisis, Trump said he would work for closer relationships with bordering nations. "We will seek common ground, not hostility," he said. "Partnership, not conflict." He also said, "America will no longer settle for anything less than the best. We must reclaim our country's destiny."[5]

Two Very Different Strategies

Shortly after delivering his victory speech, the president-elect, along with his family and close supporters, moved backstage where Paula White Cain, pastor of New Destiny Christian Center in Apopka, Florida, had been waiting. Then, with vice–president–elect Mike Pence and his family looking on, Paula began praying for the two men, asking for divine guidance, wisdom, and safety as they began their momentous journey. There was no question, she said, that God had prepared the way. Christians all over the country had been in constant prayer for months, seeking divine intervention in the election.

In the days leading up to the election, Paula and a group of Christian leaders were fasting and praying continuously for a favorable outcome. The founder of Focus on the Family and host of the radio program *Family Talk*, Dr. James Dobson, told supporters that he believes Donald Trump actively seeks God's guidance in his life. Many others had come to the same conclusion.

Unlike the Clinton camp, which had been consumed by shock and dismay during the final hours of the election, thousands of Christian believers were confident and enthusiastic about what they expected to happen. A small percentage of Never-Trump believers could never reconcile their beliefs with the candidate's language and behavior, but the vast majority of evangelical and charismatic Christians supported

Trump's candidacy and turned out in record numbers to help him secure the win.

The candidate and his campaign manager, Kellyanne Conway, had been watching the vote count from Trump Tower when the final tabulations were being announced. Several of Trump's key evangelical advisers were already at the hotel by that time, waiting with other team members for the victory celebration and the forthcoming victory speech. Liberty University president Jerry Falwell Jr., who had given the candidate a bully pulpit on at least two occasions, was on the phone with Trump when the candidate realized he was about to win. Trump said, "Jerry, I think they are going to call Pennsylvania." Pennsylvania and Wisconsin were two of the states that could swing the balance and ensure that Republicans would win the White House. "The next thing I know," Falwell said, "I'm getting texts from his son-in-law they were on their way over [to the hotel]."[6]

Pastor Robert Jeffress, who serves on Trump's Faith Advisory Board, was in the Hilton ballroom watching as all this was taking place. We talked during the long hours as the election results trickled in from around the country, and he told me he had assured the candidate that the evangelical community would stand with him on Election Day. In a short time we would all find out how true his reassurance actually proved to be.

During the third and final presidential debate Trump had reaffirmed his commitment to appointing strong conservative jurists to the Supreme Court. That statement struck home with a lot of Christian voters, and the promise that he would work to overturn Roe v. Wade influenced thousands who had been skeptical to give Trump a chance. Jeffress told Trump that support from the evangelical community was growing daily. "He asked me how I thought the evangelical turnout would be," Jeffress said. "I told him I thought it would be very strong."[7]

As it turned out, the evangelical vote accounted for nearly a third of all the votes cast for Trump. His campaign gained the support of more than 80 percent of the white born-again Christians while Clinton received just 16 percent—the lowest number ever recorded for a Democratic presidential candidate.[8] From the beginning Donald Trump understood the importance of the Christian vote. He courted evangelical support, spoke openly about his faith, accepted invitations to speak to the Christian media, and promised to stand strong for the issues that would bring Christians to the polls. It proved to be a winning strategy.

But this strategy differed greatly from the one adopted by the Clinton campaign, which had essentially ignored the Christian electorate. The fact that so many evangelical Christians showed up and voted for Trump should not have come as a surprise to anyone, according to pastor Darrell Scott. Evangelicals, he said, were overlooked by the other side. They were "derided, denigrated by the liberal Left."[9] As it turned out, Trump's support from the evangelical community and the prayers of the faithful put his campaign over the top.

In the final hours of the campaign, while Hillary Clinton remained secluded in her suite at the Peninsula Hotel, her fans and supporters at the Javits Center were left to find their way out in the dark. For several hours a pall hung over the crowds, but as news spread that Clinton had lost and Trump had won, disappointment turned to anger, and before long there were gangs of professional agitators pushing their way through the crowds outside the Javits Center, coaxing the most disappointed and vulnerable into a state of rage.

The following day the world would see graphic images of a large effigy of Donald Trump's head being set ablaze outside the Los Angeles City Hall.[10] In New York thousands of protesters filled the streets of Manhattan carrying signs and waving flags and banners of all kinds. The televised images showed thousands of mostly young people marching down Fifth Avenue in front of Trump Tower yelling, "New York hates you!" "Not my president!" and a variety of unprintable profanities. As the delirium began to spread, the throngs that included large numbers of millennials, immigrants, and paid provocateurs continued to grow, eventually stretching more than five city blocks. And the pictures were much the same in other urban centers.

For days afterward there were dozens of anti-Trump demonstrations around the country. In Boston, Chicago, Philadelphia, Portland, San Francisco, and other blue cities much the same occurred.[11] Violence and vandalism and shocking physical and verbal assaults came from the same people who were protesting against free speech on college campuses all over the country. As reported by the *Los Angeles Times*, the crowd in New York was dominated by young people, many of whom had just voted in their first presidential election.[12]

A Time for Change

On the day after the election former House speaker Newt Gingrich appeared on the national Sean Hannity radio program in a celebratory mood. "You and I, along with millions of other Americans," he said, "are just beginning one of the great adventures of our lifetime. The eight years of Donald Trump are going to be among the most extraordinary, creative, inventive, and exciting periods in all of American political history, and will, I think, both move America back to being great again, dramatically drain the swamp in Washington, and move our systems into the twenty-first century to provide much, much better experiences for every American. My only point is, compared to all that, the little whiny, sniffling, negative cowards who were Never-Trumpers are beneath our paying attention to them. Let them drift off into the ashbin of history while we go ahead and work with Donald Trump and with the House and Senate Republicans to create a dramatically new future."[13]

Meanwhile, Bernie Sanders, who had lost the Democratic primary to Clinton, was calling for change as well. Speaking to a crowd of some four thousand liberal activists at the annual People's Summit in Chicago, Sanders blasted the Democratic Party for its manifest failures. The Vermont socialist was calling for a new progressive revolution. "Let us be very, very clear," he said. "The current model and the current strategy of the Democratic Party is an absolute failure.... This is not my opinion, this is the facts.... Over the last nine years, Democrats have lost almost one thousand legislative seats in states all across this country."[14]

Sanders pointed out that "in almost half of the states in America, the Democratic Party has almost no political presence at all. Now if that's not a failure, if that's not a failed model, I don't know what a failed model is."[15] Ironically, the revolutionary agenda Sanders was proposing is precisely the sort of agenda that drove millions of American voters to the polls to support Donald Trump. The anger and deceit the voters had witnessed over the past eight years repulsed a large segment of the middle class and drove even stalwart supporters of the previous administration into the waiting arms of the Republicans. The Democratic Party may need fundamental change, but most American voters apparently believe the Bernie Sanders model would prove to be a recipe for disaster.

A hallmark of our American system of government has always been the peaceful transition of power. That's how it's supposed to work. The voters have an opportunity every four years to select their leaders at the highest level. They have the same opportunity to choose local, regional, and state officials, and it is expected that they will do so in a principled and honorable manner, as it has been done throughout the nation's history. Unfortunately the leftward lurch of the government in many parts of the country and the invasion of the culture by leftist culture warriors the past fifty to sixty years has changed that for many Americans who are apparently convinced they have the right to undo "the will of the people" by public protest and violence.

When their candidate lost the election, the mainstream media did not blame their flawed candidate, but they were quick to blame Trump's victory on anything else—the electoral college, former FBI Director James Comey, or on Russian interference in the election process. Although the FBI has found no evidence of collusion and no inappropriate contact between the Trump campaign and Russian officials, the media and the leftist activists are determined to resist, obstruct, and destroy the new president. The words *resist and obstruct* have become the battle cry of anti-Trump activist networks in this country and abroad, and there may be no amount of reason that will shake their diabolical resolve. But the president is not without support, for a faithful army of prayer warriors surrounds him.

A FAITHFUL DEFENSE

In opposition to the rabble of protesters trying to deter or destroy the president stands a stout wall of defenders who meet together weekly in the nation's capital to study the Bible, pray, and seek God's counsel for President Trump and his allies in the government. The meetings are known as the Trump Cabinet Bible Study, and most of the attendees are elected officials and cabinet officers who serve in the Trump administration, which has been called the most evangelical cabinet in history. All attendees have been handpicked by President Trump and Vice President Pence. According to a report by CBN News, Pence and eight cabinet secretaries serve as sponsors of these meetings, which are often led by evangelical minister Ralph Drollinger, the founder of Capitol Ministries.

In addition to the vice president, the list of sponsors includes some of the most influential people in the federal government, such as secretaries Betsy DeVos, Ben Carson, Sonny Perdue, Rick Perry, and Tom Price, and Attorney General Jeff Sessions, along with Environmental Protection Agency Administrator Scott Pruitt and

CIA Director Mike Pompeo. Although his schedule normally keeps him occupied at these times, the president is always welcome to join the meetings and receives a copy of Drollinger's teaching each week. In addition to the cabinet-level Bible study, both the House of Representatives and the Senate hold Bible studies on a weekly basis, and participants are expected to actively take part in the sessions and seek for ways to apply biblical principles to their work and every area of their lives.[16]

Former congresswoman Michele Bachmann has expressed support for the efforts of the Drollinger teams. "This is a strategic moment in our nation's history," she says. "Prior to [Capitol Ministries'] arrival, there was little in the way of ministry that was intent on expositing God's Word and making disciples amongst the members of both Houses."[17]

In his endorsement on the group's website Rep. Trent Franks of Arizona says, "The Member's Bible Study Ralph Drollinger teaches on Capitol Hill gives members of Congress a core, theological foundation derived from an in-depth, exegetical analysis of Scripture itself by which to weigh and measure the critical policy issues and decisions they face in Congress. It is next to impossible to build or rebuild any nation without this necessary component."[18] In addition to the Bible study groups meeting in the capitol, there are other ministry and government leaders meeting regularly and praying for the welfare of the nation under the new administration. Among them: Jerry Falwell Jr., Robert Jeffress, Jack Graham, Ben Carson, James Robison, Michele Bachmann, James Dobson, and many others.

In an interview on the Fox Business Network, Rev. Franklin Graham told host Lou Dobbs that he believes Donald Trump's victory over his Democratic rival showed clear evidence of "the hand of God" on the election.[19] Franklin Graham's father, the evangelist Billy Graham, was asked to meet with and pray for every US president since World War II, from Truman to Obama.[20] Now Franklin Graham carries the torch and continues to seek God's blessings for the nation and our new president.

The power of faithful prayer in times of crisis and change cannot be overestimated, and without question the Trump administration has inherited a nation in crisis. Being surrounded by faithful prayer warriors, and repeatedly expressing his own gratitude for the men and women who joined together to offer a faithful defense through intercessory prayer, President Trump must know there can be no doubt that God put His imprint on the election and showed His favor on the nation. "I think God intervened and put His hand on Donald Trump for some reason," Graham told Dobbs. "It's obvious that there was something behind this, and it was more than people understand. I just think it was God."[21]

PART II

THE RELIGIOUS RESPONSE

★★★★★

CHAPTER 4

TRUMP AND EVANGELICALS

★★★★★

ALTHOUGH DONALD TRUMP professes faith in God, he failed the litmus test for many Evangelicals early in the campaign. There were prominent elements among the wider evangelical leadership who said they despised Trump and, until the very end, worked diligently to derail his election. They couldn't see beyond his past lifestyle, and they were so blinded by their dislike for him they couldn't recognize the benefits a Trump presidency would bring for the country and the church compared with the immensely greater dangers of the Clinton alternative.

In their contempt for Trump some of the Never-Trump Evangelicals would apparently do anything to destroy him, even if it meant sending the Clintons and their far-left agenda back to the White House for four more years. As in every political persuasion there were different levels of animosity, but the heated debate taking place among the faithful not only divided loyalties and ended many long-standing friendships; it also gave the media plenty of fodder to show that the Evangelicals were a deeply divided lot.

This was especially true after the *Access Hollywood* tapes were released October 7, 2016, with video of a ten-year-old conversation in which Trump discussed women sexually and even described groping for their private parts. By then most Evangelicals had already decided to vote for Trump, but the evangelical Never-Trumpers still came out swinging, determined to halt Trump's momentum barely a month before the election.

WORLD magazine, which purports to be the weekly Christian equivalent to *Time* magazine, immediately called for Trump to drop out of the race.[1] A former *WORLD* staffer told me the editors had called for President Bill Clinton to resign over the Monica Lewinsky scandal almost twenty years earlier, and it just seemed fair to do the same for Trump when he was found to be immoral—as if there were any equivalence between the two events.

The frustrations of Middle America that would ultimately catapult Donald Trump to the White House were shared by Evangelicals, who make up perhaps the largest segment of Middle America. They were frustrated by the Republican establishment repeatedly taking their support for granted. They were wooed during the election and promptly forgotten when it came time to govern. Many had concluded there wasn't much difference between moderate Democrats and establishment Republicans on most issues, and that attitude had kept large numbers of evangelical voters away from the polls for years.

Trump appears to be anything but evangelical. Raised as a mainline Presbyterian, he rarely identified with Evangelicals. His marital failures and some of the business interests he has pursued weren't the sort of things Christians were supposed to do. But what was the alternative? Hillary Clinton had been raised a Methodist but became radicalized during her college years at Wellesley and was an acolyte of the radical socialist Saul Alinsky. Over the decades she drifted even further to the left, not only politically but also socially. She became the number one supporter of Planned Parenthood, an advocate for late-term abortions,[2] and a proponent of same-sex marriage. She has never had a meaningful outreach to evangelical Christians and referred to conservatives as a "basket of deplorables."[3]

Not only were her platform policies anathema to all but a few Evangelicals, but her history of corruption, the e-mail scandal that erupted over her private server, and the "pay for play" favoritism she had manipulated through the Clinton Foundation while she served as secretary of state were enough to turn the stomach of anyone who believed in honesty and transparency in government. It seemed inconceivable that any evangelical Christian could overlook such a record, but many apparently did.

CHRISTIAN NEVER-TRUMPERS

The president of the Ethics and Religious Liberty Commission (ERLC) of the Southern Baptist Convention, Russell Moore, found himself in a costly spat when he called Donald Trump "an awful candidate" and said the Christians who support him are guilty of serious error. "The religious Right," he said, "turns out to be the people the religious Right warned us about."[4] In an October 9, 2016, Twitter post, Moore said, "The damage done to the gospel this year, by so-called Evangelicals, will take longer to recover from than the '80s TV evangelist scandals."[5] Many in his denomination, however, took exception to Moore's attacks. Rev. Bill Harrell, who helped organize the ERLC, said Moore had gone too far and was out of step with other Baptists. "Since Dr. Moore has taken over," he said, "there are a lot of things that are being said on various issues that the Southern Baptist people at large don't agree with." He added, "It's developed into a very touchy situation, and it needs to be addressed in some way."[6]

Mike Huckabee, former governor of Arkansas and Baptist minister, expressed a similar view: "I am utterly stunned that Russell Moore is being paid by Southern Baptists to insult them." Likewise, Christian talk-show host Janet Mefferd said Moore's criticism of Trump supporters was unfair and ill-advised. "Most Evangelicals that I've talked to," she said, "became Trump voters late in the process....I think Russell Moore has made the error of saying Evangelicals who supported Trump are selling out their principles." Later, in response to his critics, Moore said he didn't mean to criticize everyone who voted for Trump. "If that's what you heard me say, that was not at all my intention, and I apologize."[7]

Dr. Al Mohler Jr., president of the Southern Baptist Theological Seminary in Louisville, Kentucky, took his dissent to another level with an op-ed critical of Trump and his supporters in the *Washington Post.* Mohler called the Republican candidate an "immediate and excruciating crisis" and added, "I am among those who see evangelical support for Trump as a horrifying embarrassment—a price for possible political gain that is simply unthinkable and too high to pay." Mohler was quick to avoid Russell Moore's mistake of questioning the ethics of fellow Baptists, however, and noted that many friends were Trump supporters. "The leaders I have in mind are principled men and women of Christian character and conviction," he said. Nevertheless, he insisted, "They are wrong, I believe, to serve as apologists for Donald Trump."[8]

In a similar vein Andy Crouch, former executive editor of *Christianity Today,* joined the opposition with a strong critique of Trump supporters, saying, "Enthusiasm for a candidate like Trump gives our neighbors ample reason to doubt that we believe Jesus is Lord. They see that some of us are so self-interested, and so self-protective, that we will ally ourselves with someone who violates all that is sacred to us—in hope, almost certainly a vain hope given his mendacity and record of betrayal, that his rule will save us."[9]

Popular author and columnist Beth Moore surprised a lot of Christians when she went on the attack shortly after the *Access Hollywood* tapes were revealed with a series of angry Twitter posts: "Wake up, Sleepers, to what women have dealt with all along in environments of gross entitlement & power. Are we sickened? Yes. Surprised? NO."[10] A short time later she tweeted: "I'm one among many women sexually abused, misused, stared down, heckled, talked naughty to. Like we liked it. We didn't. We're tired of it." [11] As a victim of sexual abuse herself, she said she could not get past Trump's vulgar language in the ten-year-old cell-phone video.

Several writers and Trump supporters criticized Russell Moore and his fellow Never-Trumpers for driving voters into Hillary Clinton's waiting arms, noting that Trump had come out strongly in defense of Juanita Broaddrick, Paula Jones, Gennifer Flowers, Kathleen Willey, and other women who had been abused by Bill Clinton while he served in public office. Trump invited them to sit on the front row of his campaign appearances, while Hillary Clinton waged a bitter war against them and publicly defended her husband's inexcusable behavior.

In a well-reasoned response to all the rancor and bombast, former *Wall Street Journal* columnist Stephen Moore pointed out the risks the Never-Trumpers were taking. In an article for the *American Spectator* he said, "One's vote is a matter of personal conscience. But to actively support Hillary is to put the other team's jersey on and then run a lap around the stadium."[12] What made the Never-Trump position so dangerous, as any thinking person should know, was that a Hillary Clinton presidency would be four more years of everything we hated about the Obama presidency. If that happened, the columnist said, "there won't be a conservative movement left to rebuild. The Republicans will move to the left. Worse, for Obama to win effectively a third term will be a voter validation of all of the destructive policies of the last eight years."[13]

Those who were saying Trump's chances of winning were hopeless, he said, "are the same political geniuses who a year ago assured us that Trump could never win a primary (he won most of them), then that he couldn't win 50 percent of the vote (he did), then that he couldn't win 50 percent outside of New York (he did), then they said he couldn't win a majority of the delegates (he did).... On every occasion the Trump haters were wrong."[14]

Fortunately the vast majority of Evangelicals obviously ignored the warnings of the Never-Trump leaders—especially when respected evangelical leaders said they would stand by Trump even though they said they objected to what he said on the tapes. The voters understood the difference between the candidates and decided to give their votes and their support to Donald Trump. Even those who said they would have to close their eyes and hold their noses turned out when it counted. I call them ABC voters: Anybody But Clinton.

Setting Aside Differences

Looking back, it was the willingness of Evangelicals, Charismatics, and pro-life Roman Catholics to make the commonsense choice that was the real difference in this election. According to the Pew Research Center, eight out of ten self-identified white born-again evangelical Christians said they voted for Trump, while just 16 percent voted for Clinton. This gave Trump a 65-percentage-point margin of victory among white born-again evangelical Christian voters. White Catholics supported Trump by a 23-percentage-point margin (60 percent to 37 percent).[15]

The critical element was that each of these communities decided to set aside their differences and disappointments to put Trump over the top. They weren't going to elect a pastor. As Franklin Graham had suggested, they voted for the only candidate who wanted to make America great again, knowing that a win by Clinton would change America forever and would threaten religious liberty as we know it.

During the primaries some evangelical leaders eager for a standard bearer they could believe in were more likely to vote for "anybody but Trump." But after Trump won the nomination, they took a closer look, listened to some of their colleagues and fellow believers who had a broader view, and eventually came around to his message and joined the movement. Ironically it was a secret campaign to unite the movement behind one standard bearer that may have made it possible for Trump to prevail.

According to the *National Review*, in early 2014 a group of about fifty evangelical leaders with significant numbers of followers and robust e-mail lists began meeting in various cities around the country to develop a united strategy. They planned to review the options and then take a vote of the members before the Iowa caucuses. If they reached a 75 percent supermajority about whom to support, everyone would pledge to give his or her full support to the person the group had picked.[16]

As it turned out, they selected Sen. Ted Cruz of Texas, and the idea was that each member of the group would roll out his or her endorsement individually rather than issuing a collective statement. This, the group members felt, would help create the perception that the evangelical Right stood solidly behind one candidate. With so many evangelical candidates in the race, they were concerned that splitting their votes could shatter the spirit of unity and allow a candidate they did not support, such as Jeb Bush, to run away with the nomination.[17]

But there were other concerns. To avoid the appearance of backroom dealing, all members of the group were sworn to secrecy. They didn't want to give the group a name, as if they were members of a secret society, so they called themselves "The Group."[18]

But nothing in politics remains secret for long, and someone who was present leaked the deliberations of the group's final meeting on December 7, 2015, in the boardroom of the Sheraton Hotel in Tysons Corner, Virginia. Barely a week later Tim Alberta penned a detailed article for the *National Review* about The Group, describing the meeting and the fact that it took five ballots to get to the 75 percent supermajority required to bind the membership to support Senator Cruz.[19]

Alberta wrote that the group's effort was "aimed at one thing: coalescing the conservative movement's leaders behind a single presidential candidate in a show of strength and solidarity that would position them to defeat the establishment-backed candidate in the head-to-head stage of the 2016 Republican primary." Cruz was the heavy favorite coming into the December gathering, Alberta wrote. "He had won each of the previous three straw polls and for two years had tirelessly courted the evangelical leaders who formed the group's backbone."[20]

Whoever leaked the information to Alberta even included vote counts for various candidates in the straw polls. At each meeting participants were asked to list their first, second, and third choices in the straw polls. A first-place vote was weighted with three points, second was two points, and third was one point. In only one ballot, taken in September 2015 at the Family Research Council's Washington, DC, headquarters, did Trump receive even a single vote. The final tally, the article reported, was Cruz, 48; Rubio, 39; Huckabee, 27; Jindal, 13; Carson, 12; Fiorina, 7; and Rand Paul, 2. Jeb Bush and Donald Trump each received 5 votes. Other than that, Trump was not mentioned in the article. It was all about how Rubio was giving Cruz a run for his money in the evangelical endorsement sweepstakes.[21]

A WINNING STRATEGY

An unintended twist of providence was the outcome for Rubio supporters within the evangelical leadership. The *National Review* reported the leader of the Rubio faction was John Stemberger, a prominent Florida attorney who heads up the respected Florida Family Policy Council. Stemberger had been very close to Rubio since his days in the Florida state house and was a dedicated supporter.[22] He did not endorse any candidate, but when Trump defeated Rubio in the Florida primary, Rubio withdrew from the race, and Stemberger said during an interview that he would be voting for Trump.[23]

By the time the race for the White House was under way and the alternatives were clear, many Evangelicals had come around to support the party's nominee. Trump eventually won them over by convincing the Evangelicals he had their best interests at heart. And in his first hundred days in office he made good on many of his campaign promises, including confirming the most conservative Supreme Court justice in decades, signing an executive order to ease restrictions on political speech in churches under the Johnson Amendment, and authorizing the military to launch a series of devastating attacks on ISIS compounds in Syria and Iraq. And in a stunning operation he authorized dropping what was known as "the mother of all bombs" (called MOAB) on a large ISIS compound in Afghanistan.

Even before he decided to make his run for the White House, Trump understood that the evangelical Right was a powerful and growing voting bloc. His credentials may have been slim by their standards, but he professed his faith openly and often, and he started on an accelerated learning curve by listening to the Christians he met through his business interests and others he knew only from their television ministries. He made several trips to Virginia Beach, for example, to speak with Pat Robertson, whose presidential campaign in 1988 has been credited with awakening the evangelical political movement. Over a two-year period Trump made nine separate appearances on Robertson's daily television broadcast, *The 700 Club*, and in the process managed to earn Robertson's endorsement.

Early in his campaign Trump organized a group of Christian leaders who met with the candidate. This group was initially assembled by

Paula White Cain and was made up mostly of Charismatics, including pastor Darrell Scott, Kenneth and Gloria Copeland, and a few Evangelicals such as pastor Robert Jeffress, Jerry Falwell Jr., Ralph Reed, Tim Clinton, and Mark Burns. Then in June 2016 the Faith Advisory Board was officially launched and names were added such as Dr. James Dobson, Richard Land, James Robison, Baptist minister Ronnie Floyd, and megachurch pastors Jim Garlow, David Jeremiah, and Jack Graham, along with several others, including Michele Bachmann and Bishop Harry Jackson, representing a wide range of social and ethnic communities.

To assure the members of the board that he was actually listening to them, Trump met with them regularly and sought their advice on important issues. He had endeared himself to many Evangelicals when he said in his acceptance speech at the Republican National Convention, "At this moment I would like to thank the evangelical and religious community because, I'll tell you what, the support they have given me—and I'm not sure I totally deserve it—has been so amazing and has had such a big reason for me being here tonight....They have much to contribute to our politics, yet our laws prevent you from speaking your minds from your own pulpits."[24] Of course he needed their support, but showing a bit of humility and addressing evangelical concerns in this way was a wise move. On another occasion while meeting with a group of pastors, he said, "While you all were pursuing a higher calling I was running around building buildings and making money," implying that he respected their chosen profession as much as his own.[25]

For all the fuss made over the "evangelical community," it's only fair to point out that the evangelical movement was never just one monolithic group; it has always had a wide variety of expressions. The term dates back to the time of Martin Luther and before, but it was not widely used in America until after World War II. After the founding of the World Council of Churches in 1948, a group of 348 mostly mainline churches made up of conservative Protestants wanted to differentiate themselves from their more liberal counterparts. So they adopted the term *evangelical* to let everyone know they were born-again believers who teach the Bible as the inerrant Word of God. The National Association of Evangelicals (NAE) traces its origin to an April 1942 gathering of a group of 147 people in St. Louis who met in hopes of reshaping the direction of evangelical Christianity in

America. Today the organization is less conservative than most of the groups that refer to themselves as Evangelicals.

Evangelicals have been considered an important political force for many years, but before the 1970s evangelical involvement in politics seemed almost invisible. *Newsweek* published a cover story that called 1976 "The Year of the Evangelical," and in the fall of that year Jimmy Carter, a Baptist Sunday school teacher, was elected president. Suddenly the media were writing about these Bible-believing Christians, many of whom supported Carter as "one of them." But as Carter's liberal policies turned out to be a big disappointment, the evangelical community shifted its focus and rallied around a movie actor from California named Ronald Reagan.

As Carter's star was descending and Reagan's was reaching its full ascent, evangelical broadcaster Pat Robertson delivered a stirring talk at the Washington for Jesus rally in April 1980. That event put born-again Evangelicals on the political map in a big way and sent the message that simply being a Southern Baptist Sunday school teacher was not all the evangelical community expected from its leaders. During that speech Robertson roared, "You have seen the great silent majority," to a crowd of two hundred thousand on the Capitol Mall, and at that moment a movement was born.[26] Jerry Falwell Sr., who became the unquestioned spokesman for the "moral majority," did not attend the rally that day, but he would soon become the poster boy of the religious Right. And the religious Right ended up voting for Ronald Reagan.

A MUCH-NEEDED AWAKENING

Somewhat like Donald Trump, Ronald Reagan was not immediately recognized as a believer. He had grown up a nominal Christian, but after leaving the Democratic Party, which had been his home for many years in Hollywood, he began his move to the right and began listening to Christian friends and advisers who schooled him on essential evangelical beliefs. Perhaps his most successful remark to a Christian audience came during a national affairs rally in Dallas attended by several well-known pastors. He began his remarks by saying, "Now I know this is a nonpartisan gathering, and so I know that you can't endorse me, but I only brought that up because I want you to know that I endorse you and what you're doing."[27] At that moment Reagan won the hearts of Evangelicals everywhere.

Reagan had been a Hollywood actor, he was divorced, he didn't attend church often, and his wife, Nancy, was apparently into astrology in a big way. Yet Evangelicals did what they would eventually also do with Donald Trump thirty-six years later and adopted Reagan as one of their own. And one reason they did that was because a substantial majority of believers understood the difference between electing a Sunday school teacher and electing a politician who understood the political and spiritual dimensions of his high office. In Donald Trump's case one of America's most respected ministers warned that the nation had fallen too far into sin and only divine intervention could put us back on track.

Addressing a huge crowd gathered outside the North Carolina state capitol, evangelist Franklin Graham said he had been traveling to all fifty states calling for a "Christian revolution," asking believers in every city and town to pray for this nation as never before. Election Day was just two days away, and America's future was hanging in the balance. "I am not telling anyone who to vote for," he had warned earlier in an open letter to friends and followers. "God can do that. But God's people have a responsibility to pray for the nation and to vote. The media want you to think the current presidential election is about personality—but it's not. The biggest impact this election will have on our nation will involve whom the next president appoints to fill vacancies on the Supreme Court. This will affect the course of America for decades to come."[28]

On the night before the election Graham prayed for the country during a Facebook Live event that was shared by an estimated 1.3 million people. Once again he called for a Christian revolution and urged every participant to vote. In the 2012 election he said twenty million to thirty million Christians stayed home, and that made the critical difference. "We can't let this happen again," he said. "The future of our nation is riding on this election: religious freedom, the Supreme Court, protecting the unborn and our families, and so much more. The Christian voice needs to be heard on November 8."[29]

Other Evangelicals, such as Tim Wildmon of the American Family Association, without endorsing Trump let Evangelicals know that it absolutely mattered who our president would be. If men and women with no fear of God are allowed to rule over us, our very way of life will be at stake. The Constitution, the Bill of Rights, freedom of speech, and freedom of religion will be at stake. "It is silly to underestimate the power of the executive branch of government," Wildmon said. "Secular progressives are on the warpath against Christianity, and they will continue to come after us in many ways, should they win the White House.

Yes, God cares about these things. America has been a beacon of light for the world in so many ways based on her Christian heritage."[30]

Focus on the Family founder Dr. James Dobson, who now hosts the daily *Family Talk* radio broadcasts, has urged Evangelicals to follow the path spelled out in 2 Chronicles 7:14, which says, "If My people, who are called by My name, will humble themselves and pray, and seek My face and turn from their wicked ways, then I will hear from heaven, and will forgive their sin and will heal their land." That Old Testament promise has been adopted by Christians all over the world because it outlines a clear prescription for national renewal.

In an article published in *Charisma* magazine a month before the election, Dobson told one of our editors, "If we do as instructed, then our gracious Lord will respond with three blessings. He promises to hear from heaven, to forgive our sins, and to heal our land. That is one of the most precious promises in all of Scripture. It's not too late for America. What we need is a revival that will sweep the nation, as it did in the First and Second Great Awakenings. That is the hope of our nation."[31]

On his *Family Talk* radio program Dobson spoke about his trip to Trump Tower in New York on June 21, 2016, when he and a group of a thousand Christian leaders met with the candidate to learn more about his religious beliefs. During the Q&A session Dobson posed a question to the candidate referring to the Christian faith of the founders of our country and the Christian principles contained in America's founding documents. Then he asked Trump how he would defend America's religious liberties if he were elected president. At that point, and also during a smaller, more intimate setting, the candidate assured the leaders of his firm support for religious liberty and his plans not only to appoint conservative Supreme Court justices but also to eliminate the punitive Johnson Amendment and to be a defender of Christian values.

At the end of the evening Dobson was asked for his candid reactions, and he said, "Only the Lord knows the condition of a person's heart. I can only tell you what I've heard. First, Trump appears to be tender to things of the Spirit. I also hear that Paula White has known Trump for years and that she personally led him to Christ. Do I know that for sure? No. Do I know the details of that alleged conversion? I can't say that I do. But there are many Christian leaders who are serving on a faith advisory committee for Trump in the future. I am among them....How will that play out if Trump becomes president? I don't know. It is a good start, I would think."[32]

Then Dobson added, "If anything, this man is a baby Christian who doesn't have a clue about how believers think, talk, and act. All I can tell you is that we have only two choices, Hillary or Donald. Hillary scares me to death. And if Christians stay home because he isn't a better candidate, Hillary will run the world for perhaps eight years. The very thought of that haunts my nights and days. One thing is sure: we need to be in prayer for our nation at this time of crisis."[33]

Later, in his official endorsement, Dobson said, "I am endorsing Donald J. Trump not only because of my apprehensions about Hillary Clinton and the damage she would inflict on this great country. I am also supporting Mr. Trump because I believe he is the most capable candidate to lead the United States of America in this complicated hour."[34]

Evangelical influence in our culture often seems insignificant. The media rarely report on Christian issues except to mock outspoken believers or to accuse opponents of abortion and same-sex marriage of bigotry. But a momentum has started among conservative Evangelicals, and the Trump presidency has given renewed strength and support to a growing Christian resistance movement. The struggle no longer consists of Republican versus Democrat, Left versus Right, or conservative versus socialist, but as I will explore later, an even more critical and widely recognized area of conflict, nationalism versus globalism.

For the past three to four decades the religious Right has been defined by its beliefs concerning "abortion, family, and marriage," and for most of that time the Republican establishment used our limited political position to manipulate Evangelicals, whom they viewed as a useful but troublesome voting bloc. But the momentum that brought record numbers of Evangelicals to the polls in 2016 has introduced a new paradigm that includes a new battle plan with a new narrative. Life and family issues are still very important, and ministries devoted to those causes will continue to wield influence in national affairs, but evangelical resistance to the trendy but toxic globalist agenda has become an even greater area of focus for many believers.

Tom Ertl, a businessman and Presbyterian layman from Tallahassee, Florida, has served as national media coordinator for Christians for Trump and has been an observer of Christian political action groups for decades. His concern, as he told me in a number of conversations, is that Christian leaders have tried to engage in the political arena without a fully developed worldview and epistemology, a fancy word that means "the investigation of what distinguishes justified belief from opinion."[35]

"Their worldview," Ertl says, "has been an odd mixture of a little Bible, general conservative thought, American traditions, Rush Limbaugh, and Fox News sound bites." This limited worldview has resulted in the inability of the Christian Right to advance a Christian position in the political and cultural spheres. For Christians the Bible has always been our source of knowledge. It embodies God's transcendent revealed Word, offering real and practical solutions to all the issues of politics and culture. But when Christian leaders attempt to blend biblical principles with sources outside Scripture, it almost always ends in a compromised and ineffective Christian position.

If the Christian Right ever expects to be effective in helping to shape and transform the culture, Ertl told me, our leaders must be equipped with the proper intellectual tools to do battle against those forces that oppose our beliefs and are working day and night to transform this once Christian country, which was founded on the Word of God, into a secular state and a culture we will no longer recognize. That means Christians will need a comprehensive biblical worldview. It's critical, Ertl says, that Christian activists have the knowledge, tools, and political perspective to do intellectual battle and not simply engage in ideological gymnastics. And that only comes from a thorough understanding and application of the Word of God.

Ultimately, I believe, leaders such as Franklin Graham, James Dobson, and others have been making this argument for years. If Evangelicals are to be a force for good, they must first be a force for God. And that means they must use their God-given reason and understanding to know how to use their rapidly growing influence in the marketplace of ideas. In 2016 Evangelicals managed to come together in sufficient numbers to put a "baby Christian" (to use Dobson's expression) in the White House. If they can continue praying and working in unity, who knows what could happen next?

CHAPTER 5

MOBILIZING THE FAITHFUL

★★★★★

E VEN THOUGH EVANGELICALS almost always vote Republican, they won't vote for just anyone. Because of the vast differences between the platforms and ideology of the Republican and Democratic parties, it is nearly impossible to persuade conscientious Republicans to vote for Democratic candidates. However, it's often just as difficult to get them to vote for candidates in their own party, as we witnessed in the 2008 election, when many Evangelicals stayed home rather than cast their votes for John McCain.

According to Ralph Reed, founder and chairman of the Faith & Freedom Coalition, as many as seventeen million Evangelicals refused to vote for Mitt Romney in 2012,[1] presumably because he is Mormon. The impact of that becomes apparent when you realize that Barack Obama won a second term by a margin of only five million votes.

For a while it looked as if the 2016 election was going to follow the same pattern. Hillary Clinton's nomination for the Democratic ticket was essentially a foregone conclusion. No one in her party had the backing to compete with the Clinton machine, and the Vermont socialist Bernie Sanders was more of a diversion than a bona fide opponent. His only function was apparently to draw the Democratic base further to the left.

For Republicans, however, it was a very different story, and the image fixed in my mind of seventeen smiling candidates standing there on the debate platform, each claiming to be the real conservative and the only true friend of the evangelical base, perfectly illustrates the problem of finding even one candidate the faithful will support. The campaign trail was crowded with sixteen men, one woman, and millions of evangelical voters who couldn't make up their minds. Mike Huckabee, Ted Cruz, Marco Rubio, John Kasich, and Ben Carson were strong early favorites for a variety of reasons, but none of them managed to break out of the pack.

After Ted Cruz finally dropped out on May 3, leaving Donald Trump as the presumptive nominee, many die-hard conservatives said they couldn't bring themselves to vote for Trump and would stay home rather than vote for such an unsavory candidate. That would have almost certainly meant a repeat of the 2008 and 2012 election disasters, and Hillary Clinton would have ascended to her long-awaited destiny as the first female president. But there was change in the air, and by the time Donald Trump passed the threshold of 1,237 delegates on May 26, guaranteeing his nomination, the first inklings of a paradigm shift were beginning to appear on the horizon.

One by one various Christian leaders slowly began speaking out, making a case for voting for Trump, warts and all. One of the most persuasive was Dr. Jim Garlow, pastor of Skyline Wesleyan Church in San Diego. Jim, who has a reputation as one of the most politically astute and doctrinally sound pastors in the evangelical movement, has spoken out on many important issues. He was one of the most visible leaders working to pass California's Proposition 8 in 2008, which amended the state constitution to say that marriage should henceforth be defined as the lawful union of one man and one woman.[2] More recently Jim cofounded The Jefferson Gathering, a worship service for members of Congress in the US Capitol building in Washington, DC.

In July 2015 Jim received a Facebook message from an old friend saying she despised Hillary Clinton, but she just couldn't bring herself to vote for Donald Trump. After thinking it over, he fired off a fifteen-hundred-word reply explaining his own perspectives on the election. That message was picked up and shared an amazing twelve thousand times on Facebook in a matter of days. Realizing he had struck a chord, Jim, whom I've known for more than twenty-five years, contacted me and asked if I might be interested in seeing what he had written. Naturally I was curious to see what had stimulated such widespread interest, so I agreed to take a look, and it didn't take long to realize how insightful Jim's message had been.

His rationale was so good and so succinct, I forwarded a copy to my wife, Joy, who had been debating with her friends about the candidates in this election. Failing to vote for Trump, she said, would be an automatic vote for Clinton, and you can be sure Clinton would immediately nominate a new Supreme Court justice who would trample on our Christian values and drive this country further and further to the left. Joy's logic had changed the minds of several close friends, and now Jim's Facebook post outlined many more good reasons why a vote for Trump was the only logical option. When Joy urged me to spread the word, I decided to publish the document, minus the Facebook references. So I asked him if he'd allow us to publish the article on our organization's website, and he agreed. We posted it on August 11, two weeks after the Democratic National Convention in Philadelphia.

The article began by saying that the Democratic and Republican party platforms are as different as night and day. In his opinion they were as far apart as evil versus good. "I don't care for the 'Right vs. Left' nomenclature," he said. "I am far more concerned with 'right vs. wrong.'" Then he used an analogy only a pastor could bring to a political discussion, saying, "As a pastor, I would rather deal with a church attendee who is blatant and brash in his sinning than one who is devious, lying, cunning, and deceptive. Both are problematic," he said, "but one is easier to deal with than the other. If I were a pastor bringing correction to a parishioner, I would prefer dealing with a 'Trump type' over a 'Hillary type' any day. That's because the chances of making progress with the 'Trump type' are many times greater."

By the next day we could tell the article was attracting a lot of attention. The number of views kept climbing, and by early September it hit one million social interactions, usually called "shares." Someone on Trump's Faith Advisory Board mentioned during a conference call of the board that the article had been shared a million times. As it turned out, Jim was on that conference call as well. Trump said he had already read the article and thanked him for his comments. By Election Day the total had grown to 4.1 million shares.

To Vote or Not to Vote

Dr. Steve Greene, my colleague and the publisher of *Charisma* magazine, said he felt Jim's article had "an anointing"—an Old Testament term used by many Christians when they believe something has been blessed by God. Whether or not there was a supernatural aspect to the message, there's no question it resonated with believers who needed an apologetic for why they should vote for Donald Trump even though there were some things about him they didn't like. When the editors of *Charisma* planned the special election issue for publication in October 2016, Jim's article was displayed prominently with the headline "Deciphering Hillary's Strong Delusion" and subtitled, "Why another Clinton presidency could destroy what's left of America as we know it." Readers who didn't have access to the printed magazine could access it online at CharismaMag.com.

Early in the article Jim wrote, "Not voting is not a viable option, contrary to what the 'purists' claim." A lot of disagreement exists, he acknowledged, but given the fact that refusing to vote for either candidate merely increases Hillary Clinton's chance of winning the presidency, pretending to be more honorable or more righteous is not wise; it is not noble. It is wrong. Jim has a gift of understanding the evangelical mind, and his words obviously struck a nerve. Many Evangelicals said they were afraid of the fact that Donald Trump can be a loose cannon. You never know what he's going to say, or tweet, or who he's going to attack next. And since he had never held political office, no one knew for sure if he would have any idea how to govern a nation of three hundred million people.

To answer this "fear of the unknown," Jim used a very personal analogy. "When my late wife's remarkable and much-loved oncologist said, 'Don't take Carol to that alternative (non-FDA-approved) treatment,' I asked, 'Why not?' He warned me of 'the unknown.'" But Jim told him, "Doctor, your 'known' is much worse than the alternative treatment's 'unknown.'" So Jim took his wife for the alternative treatment, and her improvement was remarkable. A year later that same oncologist went to the alternative treatment facility to find out why Carol had improved so much. Although the treatment did not ultimately save her life, it extended it from two or three years to six.

The application of Jim's analogy was simple: Clinton's *known* is considerably worse than Donald Trump's *unknown*. "Although America has had some scandal-ridden candidates in its history," he said, "we have never seen any one major party candidate more constantly scandalous [than] Hillary and her husband. She seems to exceed all previous boundaries for wrongdoing." And he added, "While I do not excuse Trump's wrongful words or his past personal behavior, I am more deeply concerned with Hillary's devious and illegal actions."

Jim pointed out that America has been blessed with three great freedoms: political, economic, and religious. Few countries in the world have ever had that honor. Donald Trump appears angry and aggressive in his public statements because he perceives that all three of those freedoms are at risk, and he has promised that his administration will defend this great heritage. Even if the privilege of appointing the next two, three, and possibly four Supreme Court justices were the only reason to vote for Trump, Jim said, that ought to have been enough. Trump's marriages, his casinos, and his rants on Twitter didn't come close to justifying the decision to sit out the 2016 election. "Every rational person knows the Supreme Court appointments are paramount," Jim said. "Trump has listed eleven superb potential nominees. Hillary's appointments would snuff out the tiny vestige of the three freedoms that are left."

On the positive side, he said, was the fact that Trump was being surrounded by increasingly good people. As a billionaire builder and businessman, he knows how to pick great managers, and he knows how to delegate. Jim expressed his belief that Trump's choices of leaders for cabinet positions—including the Department of Justice, the State Department, the Central Intelligence Agency, the Pentagon, and the rest of his twenty-four cabinet picks—would be men and women of principle, many of whom would be Christians and all of whom would be fair-minded conservatives. Jim asked, "Can these good people impact him?" He said there's a very good chance they would.

If you stop to consider Trump's beliefs on each of the major issues he addressed throughout his campaign, it would be very hard to find fault with any of them. Jim suggested Trump gets it right on at least 75 percent of the issues. Then he asked people to compare that to Clinton, who he said is wrong on 100 percent of the issues. But there was one more issue that many people failed to consider closely enough, and, according to Jim, it could be the biggest issue of all: the Left's relentless push for globalism. Globalism is more than a geographical issue, he said. It's not simply about eliminating borders. It is a spiritual issue that is demonic at its core. It means the dismantling of American sovereignty, opening our borders to the world, and abandoning our great heritage of freedom and independence based on the Christian worldview of the Founding Fathers. Globalism would transform this country into something we no longer recognize, and Hillary Clinton thrives on it.

Jim suggested that Trump's outspoken resistance to the globalist agenda may be the main reason the Left hates him. Think "principalities and powers," he warned. "This is extremely serious." Meanwhile, Donald Trump has promised to support the Christian pro-life position, while Clinton remains the biggest defender of Planned Parenthood and believes there should be no limits to a woman's right to kill her unborn child. Planned Parenthood traffics body parts from the babies its clinics have killed, which has to be as evil as anything the Nazis ever conceived.

Toward the end of his article, Jim wrote that Donald Trump wants to build a strong military and defend the nation, which is the main purpose of government. Clinton's track record as secretary of state, on the other hand, shows that she is more attuned to the interests of our enemies than our own. Trump has not hesitated to call "Islamic terrorism" what it really is, Jim said. But in the same way that Obama has refused to use those words, and even denies that Islamic extremism has anything to do with the terrorist attacks we've suffered through, Clinton can't bring herself to admit what's really going on. She claims everything is fine in America, which defies every single fact. But facts, Jim said, have never been an interest of hers.

Trump understands, Jim said, that America stands at 11:59 p.m. on the "cultural clock." We are racing toward the end, morally, economically, militarily, and spiritually. America no longer holds our position as the world's leading superpower, and a Clinton presidency would only hasten our final destruction. Trump could either slow that down or possibly, with God's help, reverse it. But we had to give him that chance. Jim concluded his message by saying, "Candidly, I want King Jesus. I want Him to rule here—now. That day is not fully manifested—yet. So we prayerfully navigate this challenging election to honor Jesus."[3]

Jim's op-ed was shared more than twice as much as our previous most-shared viral article on CharismaNews.com. I think the fact that so many people were moved enough to share it with their friends and loved ones showed how important they believed the election to be. And it showed their level of enthusiasm. Many Christians wanted to vote for Trump, but they had to be given permission because, as I said in the previous chapter, they felt he had failed most of our usual litmus tests. My Presbyterian friend Tom Ertl says he thinks Jim's article had a huge influence on the election. "I would say it helped swing the evangelical vote," he told me.[4]

The South Carolina Model

Months before we published Jim Garlow's op-ed, Rev. Ray Moore, a Baptist pastor and former Army chaplain from Columbia, South Carolina, was a pivotal figure in Trump's win in the all-important South Carolina primary, which was held on February 20, 2016. Moore has been involved in public policy issues and Republican politics since the 1980s when he was involved with Pat Robertson's 1988 presidential campaign, which, as I mentioned earlier, gave birth to the Christian Right. With more than forty years in pastoral ministry, Moore understands a lot about how born-again Christians think, as well as how their pastors think, and that can be very important when trying to rally Evangelicals around a political candidate.

Political insiders, pollsters, and policy wonks always follow the South Carolina primary very closely. In every election since 1980, with only one exception, whoever won the South Carolina Republican primary went on to win the GOP nomination. Trump had come in second to Ted Cruz in Iowa. He won the New Hampshire primary, but Cruz, a Southern Baptist, was heavily favored in South Carolina, where Evangelicals make up 58 percent of the state's electorate.[5] Moore said he usually voted for the strongest pro-life candidate and preferred candidates with a strong Christian witness. Cruz met those criteria, and Trump did not, so Moore intended to be a Cruz man.

But one day he had a chat with Ed McMullen, a publicist and political consultant who had worked in South Carolina politics for decades. They debated the virtues of the various candidates, and eventually McMullen convinced Moore that Trump's courageous stands on the issues made him deserve support. McMullen had been a friend of Donald Trump for more than thirty years. They met in George Steinbrenner's box at Yankee Stadium.

McMullen's political work over the years happened mostly behind the scenes, but he remained a close confidant and adviser of Trump. He had been involved in the vetting of vice presidential candidates, and he recommended Mike Pence to Trump as a possible running mate. Moore told me he believes McMullen's recommendation of Pence, who was widely known as a born-again Christian, telegraphed a message to the evangelical Right that "Trump can be trusted."[6]

McMullen is known as a savvy strategist, and during an interview with a reporter from a national newspaper he was asked how Donald Trump could hope to overcome Hillary Clinton's vast ground game that had already been mobilized in the key states. McMullen responded that political strategies had changed, and thanks to the Internet, Trump had been getting his message out in ways no other candidate had been able to duplicate. And perhaps even more importantly, McMullen said, there was a huge volunteer army out there, not readily visible as part of the campaign, working around the clock for Trump.[7]

Hearing that reminded me of a story Tom Ertl told me about a Christian truck driver in South Carolina who always carried a supply of Trump's yard signs with him wherever he went, and he would stop his truck and stick a sign in the ground whenever he got a chance. There were many people with that kind of passion in the palmetto state who never showed up on the party roster. The Trump supporters viewed 2016 as a historic election, and they joined the battle, much as their patriot ancestors had done, fully expecting to win it.

Chances are these people wouldn't have volunteered for a normal establishment candidate, but they saw something different in Donald Trump, and they liked his message. It was a unique situation, a once-in-a-lifetime opportunity to elect an American patriot who would do battle with the established order. Many took time off from their jobs and their normal routines. Some even put their businesses on hold for a season so they could do their part for Trump.

Meanwhile evangelical leaders around the state were still backing Ted Cruz. Virtually every Southern Baptist pastor in the state endorsed Cruz, Moore told me. The few who didn't—such as charismatic pastor Greg Surratt of Seacoast Church in Charleston—gave their support to Sen. Marco Rubio. Both Rubio and Cruz needed a big win to propel them into the Florida primary, but Trump went on to win South Carolina with 32 percent. Rubio and Cruz each received 22 percent of the vote, with Rubio narrowly beating Cruz to take second place to Trump.[8]

Moore speculates that if some of Rubio's supporters had encouraged their man to withdraw earlier and give his support to Cruz, Rubio would have been perfectly situated to become vice president on the Cruz ticket. If that had happened, the Cruz–Rubio ticket could have gone into South Carolina and other southern states with a substantial base of support that would have been too formidable for Trump to overcome. But that didn't happen. Consequently Cruz and Rubio split the evangelical vote, to Trump's advantage.

If Rubio could have been persuaded to wait until 2020 for his presidential run, Tom Ertl believes there is a good chance Cruz would have been the Republican nominee in 2016. And since Cruz was a divisive figure in his own party and not the sort of contender to withstand the barrage the Democrats and their compliant media supporters would put up, he believes Clinton would have become the forty-fifth president of the United States instead of Donald Trump. All this is speculation, but I find it interesting nonetheless.

How did Trump pull off a win in South Carolina? Moore says it was a series of political "miracles," including Trump's first national endorsement from a statewide elected official, Lt. Gov. Henry McMaster, whom Moore has known for more than thirty years. When McMaster came out in favor of Donald Trump, a lot of South Carolinians came along with him. That was a miracle, according to Moore. Conservative Christians ignored what many leaders had been telling them and voted for Trump anyway. He said it may be no coincidence that when South Carolina governor Nikki Haley was nominated and later confirmed as ambassador to the United Nations, Henry McMaster ascended to the governorship.

But the miracle that had been developing for several years was the voters' willingness to ignore what they were being told in order to elect the person with the best chance of becoming our next president. Most Republicans had come to distrust their party's leadership as much as they distrusted the leadership in Washington. And that was true for evangelical voters all over the country. While most Christian leaders were backing Cruz, Trump ended up getting the evangelical vote in state after state.

When There Is No Way

There's more to the evangelical part of Donald Trump's victory than well-reasoned articles like Jim Garlow's or the work of grassroots supporters like Ray Moore appealing to voters by conventional means. There's also a previously untold story of how Evangelicals gave Trump a ground game that many political experts completely ignored. And here again there's a miraculous aspect to it.

Meet David Lane. He is a political adviser, organizer, and planner who generally tries to keep a low profile. He is well-known to the Left, however, because of the Pastors and Pews events he has organized since 1994. Over the years these events have attracted an estimated twenty thousand pastors and ministry leaders from all over the country. Media reports on the meetings often describe them as a subversive operation, mobilizing right-wing conservatives and teaching them to impose their will on the public. Lane, of course, sees it differently: There are sixty-five million to eighty million Evangelicals in this country, he says, and only 50 percent of them (roughly forty million) are registered to vote. Of those registered, only 50 percent (twenty million) actually do vote. And when 75 percent of the evangelical community fails to vote, the nation will inevitably suffer at the hands of the non-Christian Left.

The Pastors and Pews event I went to in Orlando in August 2016 was attended by about five hundred pastors and ministry leaders and their spouses. It was a grand affair with a delicious meal, Disney-quality patriotic music, and some great lead-in speakers, including Gov. Mike Huckabee, who introduced Trump. Lane learned how to put on a great show and connect with people when he worked for several years with Jerry Falwell in the mid-1990s. Earlier he had learned fundraising while working in Washington during the Reagan years. Then he worked as a grassroots organizer in Texas with Dr. Steven F. Hotze, who Lane says is the best precinct-level grassroots organizer in the country. He proved his Pastors and Pews format worked in Texas by helping George W. Bush beat the Democratic governor Ann Richards and by defeating a proposal to make same-sex marriage legal.

A wealthy Republican donor gave Lane the money for his first Pastors and Pews event in Austin in 2005. Lane hoped he could get fifty pastors to meet with the governor. His benefactor said he wanted five hundred to attend the event at the Hilton hotel downtown. In less than four weeks he got five hundred confirmations and had three hundred on a waiting list. "The Lord showed up," he said. "Everything exploded. The hand of God was moving." When that happened, Lane told me, he knew he had found his niche.

His preparation for the work was not what you'd expect, he said. His early life was "wine, women, and song," but he became a Christian at a Bill Gothard seminar he attended at Zig Ziglar's brother's invitation, thinking it was a motivational seminar. "I deserved judgment but was given mercy," he says. Lane was mentored spiritually by retired Texas Court of Appeals judge Paul Pressler of Houston, and his long resume includes a stint as a registered agent for the Nicaraguan resistance in Miami in the 1980s. But his organizational skills clearly come from a higher authority.

I first met Lane when I was involved with Mike Huckabee's campaign in 2008. The former Arkansas governor was a featured speaker, along with other evangelical-friendly Republican candidates, at some of Lane's events. Candidates eager to get ahead of the pack looked forward to speaking at Pastors and Pews events because they were scheduled before the state primaries, and the candidates always wanted the pastors' support.

In January 2015 Lane helped sponsor a prayer rally at Louisiana State University in which Gov. Bobby Jindal played a key part. I was invited to attend the dinner later that evening at the governor's mansion, along with a few other evangelical leaders. Jindal talked about whether or not he would run for president, and he asked for prayer. He did announce his bid for the race on June 24, 2015, but dropped out less than five months later, partly because of all the heat being directed his way by the Trump campaign.

After the Indiana primary, which made Trump the presumptive nominee, someone asked Lane what Trump would do as president. Lane replied, "I don't know, but I know what Hillary will do." Then, making reference to the recent incident in Kentucky when county clerk Kim Davis came under attack for refusing to issue marriage licenses to same-sex couples, Lane said a Clinton presidency would be bad for the country. "If she wins," he said, "what happened to the clerk in Kentucky is just the warm-up act for what's going to happen to you and your kids."

Two things followed the Orlando event I attended that Lane says were miracles. A week later Lane received an e-mail from Paul Manafort, Trump's campaign director at the time, who invited him to come up to New York to discuss mobilizing the evangelical vote. So Lane flew to New York, and as he was getting dressed in his hotel room for the appointment with Manafort, he got a call from a billionaire friend who had supported Lane's previous campaigns. The caller asked him, "How are you doing on that eighteen million dollars?" A year earlier Lane had come up with a plan to mobilize voters and projected it would cost approximately eighteen million dollars. For the moment, Lane told him, that plan was on the shelf, and he admitted he hadn't raised anything so far. "Well," the caller said, "put me down for five million dollars."

Lane thought that was amazing. He hadn't talked to the caller for eight months, and this call came out of the blue. But he thanked the man profusely then went on to his appointment, where he laid out his idea for a way to mobilize evangelical voters. After listening to his idea, Manafort told him there was no money to fund a plan like that. At that moment Lane understood why he had been contacted by his billionaire caller. He said, "I have five million dollars. If you can find four million dollars, I believe we can be competitive in six key states. If the money doesn't come in, then we'll work in three states."

Manafort was clearly surprised by Lane's quick response, but he asked Lane to give him a couple of days to see if he could come up with the money. Lane left the meeting exhilarated but uncertain whether or not Manafort could actually persuade his donors to produce the cash. Manafort never called him back. He resigned the next day as Trump's campaign manager. But this was the Lord's deal, and that same day, Lane's billionaire friend called again and said, "Put me down for another four million dollars." And twenty-four hours later he wired Lane the full nine million dollars.

By this time they were just ten weeks away from the election, and Lane began to worry, how on earth could he mobilize millions of voters in such a short time? That's when the second miracle happened. He got a call from Murphy Nasica, a highly respected campaign firm in Dallas, Texas, that had spent $150,000 training what it called "generals" for the political ground game. It had brought in campaign workers, trained them, and prepared the marching orders when suddenly the funding fell through and Murphy Nasica realized it would have to drop the plan.

Lane couldn't believe his ears. This was exactly what he had been praying for, so he told the folks at Murphy Nasica he would give them five million dollars so that all the people they had trained could get to work. Beginning on August 22, 2016, an army of "generals" orchestrated a million phone calls and door knocks in six key states: Florida, Ohio, Missouri, Virginia, North Carolina, and Iowa. Trump won all but Virginia on Election Day. His victory in the southern states, capped with the unexpected victory in Pennsylvania, gave Trump the win.

On the night of the election Paul Bedard of the *Washington Examiner* tweeted: "Huge: ABC reporting largest turnout of evangelical vote in history. Congrats @GDavidLane."[9] I came across that tweet several weeks later and captured a screenshot as a reminder of the emotions we all felt. I had been standing in the large crowd of Trump supporters gathered at the New York Hilton when we got word that our prayers had been answered. The ground troops had done their job. David Lane and his generals had spread the word. And God had given them the means and the manpower to make it happen. It was amazing, and Bedard's tweet served as a great reminder of what happened that night, when providence, prayer, and persistence made a way where there was no way.

Chapter 6

SURPRISING EARLY SUPPORTERS

★★★★★

W
HILE EVANGELICAL LEADERS were meeting secretly to pick which candidate to back, a group of mostly charismatic leaders had already met together and one by one decided they would support Donald Trump. The same core group had been assembled four years earlier by New Destiny Christian Center pastor Paula White Cain at Trump's request. Paula first got to know Trump in 2003 when she got a call from Trump's office in New York. An assistant told her Trump was on the line, and he was asking to speak to her.

She found out Trump had seen her television program, *Paula Today*, and he was impressed with her ability to apply spiritual understanding to complex social issues and wanted to tap into that. He told her he had a few questions and would be very glad to get her input. So Paula flew to New York and met with him at his office in Trump Tower, and in the course of their conversations she agreed to act as Trump's "spiritual adviser."

Over the next several years they spoke often, comparing notes on current events and the situation in Washington. He decided not to run in 2012, and it would be another three years before he would enter the race for the White House. But Paula was there to counsel and pray, and even as the media taunted Trump over his willingness to take counsel from her, they continued to meet and talk through the issues. And when she came forward to pray at President Trump's swearing-in ceremony, Paula was the first female minister to pray at a presidential inauguration.[1]

I have been covering Charismatics and Pentecostals for four decades. I know how they think and how they act. Pentecostal services are usually louder and livelier than traditional Protestant services, with the kind of spiritual enthusiasm and joy that mainline Protestants refer to as emotionalism. Pentecostal ministers will speak about being "on fire" with the power of the Holy Spirit, and many charismatic churches hold prayer and worship services in which dramatic healings take place. Members of these churches tend to think of traditional Protestant services as cold and lifeless affairs.

The word *charismatic* comes from a Greek word meaning "gifts," as in spiritual gifts. While Charismatics and Pentecostals are subsets of the evangelical movement, many traditional Evangelicals reject Pentecostal/Charismatic doctrine that the gifts did not end with the death of the biblical disciples and apostles in the first century.

Charismatics (and many Evangelicals) believe that God is central to everything they do, not just on Sunday but every day, and that He has a purpose for every person. He cares whom they marry, how they live their lives, what jobs they hold, and even whom they vote for. Charismatics also believe that God actually speaks to people today, either individually through the "still, quiet voice" of the Holy Spirit or through modern-day prophets. And many Charismatics believed that certain men and women with prophetic gifts would hold the key to the 2016 presidential election.

As a rule, Charismatics are not politically active, partly because they prefer to focus their energies on spiritual pursuits such as evangelism, missions, or providing assistance for the poor and disadvantaged. And since Charismatics are often ignored or marginalized by their evangelical counterparts, they tend to keep a low profile. As one charismatic leader said to me, "They're only interested in us at election time, and no other."[2]

But the 2016 election was going to be different. As the race began heating up in the fall of 2015, a group of charismatic and Pentecostal leaders began talking about the various candidates and what each one had to offer. Very early on charismatic leaders began rallying around Donald Trump, partly because of his outspoken defense of America and traditional American values but also because they felt the Lord had told them Trump had His favor.

Few officially endorsed him at that time, but those who attended the meetings in which Trump was invited to speak began to see in him what the majority of Evangelicals would come to see before the election, when more than 80 percent of evangelical Christians supported him. Though he seemed in many ways just a beginner, he was a person of faith, and he had their interests at heart.

Paula was instrumental in putting together that first group of charismatic leaders, and later she would be chairman of Trump's Faith Advisory Board, which had weekly phone calls with the candidate before the election. Those meetings have continued with periodic calls after the election, although mainly now with White House staffers. Paula began by inviting people she knew to participate. She rarely attended the "evangelical" meetings with political leaders, but she wasn't taking part in any of the events for political reasons. Donald Trump had become a friend, she said, and she wanted her Christian friends to know him and support him as she did.

Having known Paula for more than twenty years, I remember her talking about the meetings with Trump in 2003. At that time most people only knew Trump as the billionaire businessman and television celebrity. He was a popular but controversial figure, and his widely publicized feuds with celebrities always made headlines. No one would have suspected in those days that he would ever be the president of the United States. Yet Paula and the others who were getting to know him had come to believe that God was laying a foundation for what was going to happen.

RECEIVING THE BLESSING

In September 2015, someone put an iPhone video on YouTube showing Donald Trump being prayed for at Trump Tower. At that time Trump was ahead in the polls with a 39 percent advantage, up from 26 percent the month before.[3] But it was still four months before the Iowa caucuses, and anything could happen.

There's nothing unusual about a presidential candidate meeting with ministers. Over the years I've attended several events with political leaders who were courting the evangelical vote. The first was George H. W. Bush, who invited a group of Christian leaders to the vice presidential residence in Washington, DC, in 1986. I also attended in 2008 when candidate Barack Obama reached out to the evangelical community—something his opponent John McCain rarely did. That time Franklin Graham, Max Lucado, Sam Rodriguez, T. D. Jakes, and several leaders of mainline Protestant denominations were present. But there were no prayers in any of those meetings, and there was certainly no "laying on of hands," as there was in this meeting with Trump.[4]

At the end of Trump's meeting with the charismatic pastors that Paula and her fellow ministers had brought together, there were prayers and several pastors gathered around the candidate to lay hands of blessing on him. Others reached out their hands, and they prayed fervently, one by one, for God's hand of blessing to be upon him throughout the campaign. Trump seemed to be in unfamiliar territory, but he stood respectfully while holding a Bible. And even though he looked uncomfortable, at one point he reached over and patted the hand of the man who was praying for him.

Kenneth Copeland, the Word of Faith teacher whose daily broadcasts are seen by millions around the world, prayed: "No man can be successful as president of the United States without Your wisdom, Lord. And so we ask You today to give this man Your wisdom, boldly. Make sure and certain that he hears. Manifest Yourself to him. And we thank You and praise You for a bold man, a strong man, and an obedient man."[5]

Paula prayed last and said, "Even as we lay hands on him right now, let Your hand be laid upon him." She prayed that "any veil would be removed and his eyes would be open to see the glory and the goodness of God all the days of his life." [6]

That a political figure would submit himself to such prayers truly surprised me. I could not envision Mitt Romney or John McCain or even the reserved Bushes standing quietly while a group of pastors prayed in this way. Later as videos emerged of Trump and his running mate, Mike Pence, visiting charismatic services and submitting to their prayers, it seemed apparent that both men may have believed that such prayers not only helped their chances of being elected but also were helping them to understand the hearts of God's people.

It was just a beginning, but in time these meetings with pastors and Christian leaders would grow to include thousands of Evangelicals of all stripes. Why did this happen? I believe it was because Trump and Pence understood the importance of these events. Yes, they wanted the support of the large evangelical community, but they also wanted to know that they would have God's blessings in the bare-knuckles political battle they had entered. On the other side the Christian pastors and teachers wanted to know firsthand what kind of man Donald Trump was.

It was not just during the election. Trump continued to invite evangelical leaders to the White House on various occasions. One example that went viral was when pastor Rodney Howard-Browne, of The River at Tampa Bay Church in Florida, was among a group of religious leaders who met with President Trump in the Oval Office shortly after his trip in July 2017 to meet with French president Emmanuel Macron in Paris. Howard-Browne took a cell-phone video of the moment as several pastors prayed with Trump, laying hands on him. As reported by both *Fox & Friends* and CBN News, the pastor said he was surprised by Trump's openness and felt that was important for people of faith. "I see this as a last-minute reprieve for America, and the Church," he said. "This is the time for the body of Christ to arise like never before. We have to get vocal. It is crucial." He added, "I see President Trump as an answer to prayer to give America one last opportunity. We have to pray."[7] The screenshot of the video Howard-Browne took of that meeting on July 12, 2017, appeared the next day on the Drudge Report online and immediately went viral.

While most early Trump supporters were Charismatics, three major non-charismatic evangelical leaders came out for Trump, which was not only a foreshadowing of evangelical support later, but it also sent a signal to others it was OK to vote for the unconventional business mogul.

The first was Robert Jeffress, pastor of First Baptist Church, who has been quoted many times in this book. In January he told James Robison on a television program that as a pastor he would never "endorse" a candidate. But he met with Trump several times and is pictured standing awkwardly among a group of mostly Charismatics who were praying passionately over Trump in September 2015.

In January, right before the Iowa caucus, Liberty University president Jerry Falwell Jr. also came out for Trump, and the candidate tweeted: "Great honor- Jerry Falwell Jr. of Liberty University, one of the most respected religious leaders in our nation, has just endorsed me!"[8] Both Jeffress and Falwell took a lot of heat for their stand. Jeffress was called a hypocrite by the Baptist Standard,[9] and Falwell had a near insurrection among some of the faculty and students at Liberty.[10]

Then on March 11, 2016, right before the Missouri primary, Phyllis Schlafly, the conservative icon, gave Trump perhaps the greatest endorsement of all. Trump was a former Democrat and had never been involved in conservative political action. That Schlafly, who would die six months later, would give him her conservative stamp of approval sent a signal to the furthest right of the evangelical world that Trump could be trusted to uphold conservative values. "He does look like he's the last hope," Schlafly said. "We don't hear anybody saying what he's saying. In fact, most of the people who ought to be lining up with him are attacking him."[11] The month before, in an interview with Breitbart News, Schlafly said that Trump seemed to be best positioned to defeat the "kingmakers" of the Republican establishment but that Cruz should be his first Supreme Court nominee.[12]

When she died on September 5, Trump tweeted: "The truly great Phyllis Schlafly, who honored me with her strong endorsement for president, has passed away at 92. She was very special!"[13] When he spoke at her funeral, Trump said: "Her legacy will live on every time some underdog, outmatched and outgunned, defies the odds and delivers a win for the people."[14] The day she died, Trump posted on Facebook: "Phyllis Schlafly is a conservative icon who led millions to action, reshaped the conservative movement, and fearlessly battled globalism and the 'kingmakers' on behalf of America's workers and families. I was honored to spend time with her during this campaign as she waged one more great battle for national sovereignty."[15]

In her last book, *The Conservative Case for Trump*, released the day after her death, Schlafly argued that conservative Christians should follow high-profile evangelical leaders, including Liberty University president Jerry Falwell Jr. and Family Research Council president Tony Perkins, and support Trump's candidacy.

OPENNESS TO CHANGE

Lance Wallnau, a Bible teacher, consultant, and businessman, attended several of those meetings between evangelical leaders and Trump, and he described one such event for the readers of *Charisma* magazine.[16] The article was widely shared on the Internet, and Wallnau revealed how much his own view of Trump had changed. His first meeting with Trump, he wrote, was December 30, 2015, in the boardroom on the twenty-sixth floor of Trump Tower. He recognized several of those present, but most of the people in the room didn't know one another personally prior to the meeting. "It was a rather eclectic sampling of Evangelicals," he said, "a group within the larger self-described 'Christian' community that makes up nearly 30 percent of the American population—some 30 million potential voters."

Wallnau said he was immediately struck by what most people see when they meet Donald Trump for the first time. He is a big man, broad chested, and an imposing figure at six feet three inches tall. "Add heels and hair," says Lance, "and he grows another inch." But equally surprising to Wallnau was Trump's manner. He was much more restrained than what we generally see on television. Wallnau writes, "He was gracious, nonconfrontational, and surprisingly open to 'give and take.' I got the impression that Trump takes in information quickly but filters it equally fast to distinguish one idea from another. It's an executive skill I've noticed in CEOs in whatever field I meet them."

As each person spoke, he said, Trump was reading them and

weighing their relative authority and grasp of the issues. A Messianic rabbi named Kirt Schneider spoke up at one point, saying, "Your comments don't always represent you in the best light. People want to know you have a presidential temperament. They want to know that you are a person they can trust with a finger on a nuclear button." At that point Trump paused for a moment, pursed his lips as we've seen him do a hundred times on television, and said, "I hear you."

As the conversation turned to some of the well-publicized verbal battles that had transpired during the campaign, Trump said, "You know, people aren't aware of what is coming at me...what I am responding to, like the storm that broke out when I took a stand on immigration. It can get pretty vicious." Most of those in the room understood his point: they had experienced their own share of controversy. Then, looking toward his questioner, he said, "You don't always know the backstory. I can say this, I never punch indiscriminately. I'm a counter puncher...but I fully hear what you are saying. I know where you're coming from."

Several of the men and women in the room smiled and exchanged knowing glances. There was no need to drill down much deeper on that subject. It was apparent that Trump understood how his critics in the media perceive him. But, Wallnau said, "there was no flippant or disingenuous commitment to change. He would do as occasion required—till he clinched the nomination." Some of the pastors in the room that day were taking a risk by even coming to New York to meet with Trump, including a number of African American ministers who were present on the occasion. "Almost to a man," Wallnau writes, "they described to me the backlash they had encountered for even being willing to meet with a Republican. It was interesting to watch the interaction."

According to Wallnau, Cleveland, Ohio, pastor Darrell Scott spoke up and said, "I wouldn't change a thing. Be you and keep being consistent. That's what people like about you. You're not playing politics."

Trump seemed to be pleasantly surprised by Scott's words. He looked around the boardroom table and laughed. "So you're saying, 'Don't change'?" he asked. "Well, that's interesting!"

Scott answered, "Right! People would see you change, they would know it isn't you. You would start to look political, and that would make you look like everyone else. Just be you!" The majority of African American Evangelicals would be voting for the Democratic candidate in November. That was no secret. But Scott told the candidate he had come to New York with an open mind. "There are three branches of government," he said, "legislative, executive and judicial. You are clearly gifted for the executive branch. That's what you do."

The conversation continued for several more minutes before Wallnau realized that Trump apparently knew several of the preachers and teachers in the room. He had never met them, but he had watched their broadcasts on television. As he reflected on that fact, he thought, of course! "Media is one of his domains. He is very much dialed in on all sorts of TV programing, including Christian programing." At one point Trump said he had been flipping around the dial the previous evening and came across the late-night program *Politically Incorrect*, a popular left-wing talk show hosted by Bill Maher on HBO. "It's amazing how antagonistic they are about people of faith," Trump said. "It was painful to watch."

As several people nodded in agreement, Trump said it hadn't always been that way in America. Then, turning toward Jan Crouch, the cofounder of the TBN television network, he asked, "This seems to have been going on for a while, hasn't it?" Everyone agreed. Crouch, who died of a stroke before she would have the chance to vote for Trump, could have given a litany of all the attacks she and her husband, Paul, had endured over the years. As Trump scanned the room, he said, "I think we had such a long period of Christian consensus in our culture, and we kind of got…spoiled. Is that the right word?"

The ministers either nodded or smiled, but then Trump said something that surprised everyone. "Every other ideological group in the country has a voice," he said. "If you don't mind me saying so, you guys have gotten soft." Wallnau said that's the line he won't forget. After a brief moment of reflection, Trump looked around the room and corrected himself. "I mean, we, myself included, we've had it easy as Christians for a long time in America. That's been changing." Trump wanted these pastors and teachers to understand that, in a sense, he was one of them. He might not have their knowledge of Scripture or their level of experience as a believer, but he considers himself a person of faith, and he wants to be in tune with the beliefs and concerns of Evangelicals.

Not long after that meeting, Trump announced that he would propose ending the Johnson Amendment. The ban that then senator Lyndon Johnson had devised to silence his Christian opponents in 1954 had become an IRS sword hanging over the heads of churches in America. Wallnau prayed that would happen, but the truth of the matter, he said, was that even if the Johnson Amendment were lifted, most pastors would be living in fear of offending their flocks.

"What [Trump] said next may have been lost on others," Wallnau said, "but it hit me in a particularly striking way...'People who identify themselves as "Christian" make up probably the single largest constituency in the country, but there is absolutely no unity, no punch...not in political consensus or any other area I can see.'" The point was well taken, but there was at least a hope now that all these things were beginning to change.

PLAYING THE TRUMP CARD

In meetings like this Trump was gradually winning over more and more Christian leaders. In addition, charismatic "apostles and prophets," most of whom never actually met the man, were convinced the Holy Spirit had revealed that the political battle between the first female and first billionaire nominees for president would turn out to be the most important election in American history. This election had all the markings of a prophetic showdown.

As far back as 2007 the late Kim Clement had prophesied, "Trump shall become a trumpet....I will raise up the Trump to become a trumpet, and Bill Gates to open up the gate of a financial realm for the church."[17] The first has come true, but we'll have to wait and see about the second part. "This is the year the tide turns," Prophet Cindy Jacobs, cofounder of Generals International, told *Charisma* before the election. "God gave us a word earlier this year that there would be a flood of violence," she said, "and we've certainly seen that happen. He also gave us a word to look to Isaiah 59:19, which states, 'When the enemy shall come in like a flood, the Spirit of the LORD shall lift up a standard against him.'"[18]

Cindy says the Lord gave her a word long before the campaigns began about a coming conservative revolt. God is "preparing a patriot" to lead our nation, she said. But, she added, we must pray and agree with the Lord if this prophecy is to be realized. Besides Clement and Jacobs, other prophets began saying Trump would be elected. Before the election, *Charisma* published an article quoting Bill Hamon, founder of Christian International, who prophesied in November 2015 that God had chosen Trump to be the next president, and his election would be part of a global awakening that would lead to a restoration of biblical Israel, a return of the Jewish nation, and rebuilding of the temple.[19]

For those who don't understand or believe this, it's important to know that Charismatics believe that God speaks today and that one of the gifts of the Spirit described by the apostle Paul (1 Cor. 12:4–11) is the gift of prophecy. Over the years, I've received many prophecies that have come to pass. Most were encouraging words at the right time. However, another type of prophecy speaks to the nations and informs us of God's will. I suspect many people, including many Christians, don't believe in gifts such as prophecy because there have been so many flaky prophecies, such as the Y2K disaster, which never happened. In 2008 one respected pastor prophesied that Rudy Giuliani would be the next president. Obviously that never happened.

However, on May 31, 2008, Chuck Pierce, a prophet I respect, predicted Trump would win the White House eight years later. He told me he received this word during a four-hour "visitation" from the Lord in Liberty Park, New Jersey. He said the Lord showed him many things during the next few years, and he felt the Lord was saying that "America must learn to play the trump card." Then, three months later, as he was driving to speak at the International Church of Las Vegas and driving past Trump hotel, Pierce said he received another message. "When I drove by the Trump hotel, I knew exactly what God was saying—that it would take someone like Donald Trump, who would not have the political background of either party, and he would be willing to address the structure that was presently taking America in the wrong direction." Pierce also told my wife, Joy, and me over lunch early in 2008 when it seemed Hillary Clinton would get the Democratic nomination that Barack Obama would be elected twice, and he was right.

OTHER PROPHETIC "WORDS"

Three years after Chuck Pierce's prophecy, another prophetic word came from an unlikely source. In April 2011 Mark Taylor, a retired fireman from Central Florida, said he received a prophecy that God had chosen Donald Trump to be the leader of the United States, to "bring honor, respect, and restoration" back to the nation. Five years later he shared that word in an interview with pastor Rick Wiles of TruNews.com, and the prophecy went viral.[20]

The word came to him, Taylor said, on April 28, 2011, in the middle of a debilitating illness. He told the story online, including a news article on CharismaNews.com. Taylor said that Donald Trump would be elected, but that wasn't all. There would be a series of dramatic changes around the world, blessings and cursings, widespread revival and desperate reprisals unleashed by the enemy of mankind.[21] Many people who read Taylor's story said they were convinced that God had actually spoken to him, and his early warning ought to be a wake-up call to the church.

Cindy Jacobs said in the October issue of *Charisma* that she didn't want to predict who would win the 2016 election. But, like Pierce, she had prophesied that God had a "trump card" in his hand, and He was going to play it. In hindsight she believes that was a foreshadowing that Donald Trump would win.[22] Pastor Darrell Scott, the African American pastor quoted earlier, told me in a podcast one week before the election that he had predicted Trump would win and would be the greatest president in our history. It wasn't as much a prophecy, he said, as it was a political prediction,[23] but he was right on the first part, and we will have to wait and see about the other part.

Darrell was a guest on *The Jim Bakker Show*, along with my friend Frank Amedia, a few days before the election. Four months before, I went on Jim Bakker's show to talk about Trump, ironically the same day I'd been invited to join a thousand other evangelical leaders to meet with Trump in New York. I decided keeping my appointment with Jim Bakker was more important than flying to that meeting. Besides I was hoping for a private interview with Trump, which I got on August 11.

When I was on Jim's program, I talked about how I was endorsing Trump and how we were working on our October issue, where we wrote about the election. I assumed Jim's invitation was his way of discussing politics by interviewing me due to the restrictions on nonprofits to be involved politically. But as time passed, Jim invited more guests on the show to talk about the election and supporting Trump. Two strong supporters I suggested he invite were Jim Garlow and Frank Amedia, which he did. To me, no one was more pro-Trump than Jim Bakker.

In an interview a week before the election, Frank Amedia told Jim what he had told me privately, that as soon as Donald Trump announced he would run in June 2015, he felt the Lord saying, "My hand is on this man." He also believed the Lord had given Trump a "breaker anointing" to make a major shift in the nation, the world, and the church. I've known Frank for nearly ten years, ever since we met in Israel at the Western Wall. He was the first person I ever heard talking about how Trump would win. He went all out for Trump, and his efforts got him a private meeting with the candidate in March 2015, along with prominent charismatic ministers

Sid Roth, Rick Joyner, and several others. That meeting took place at Trump Tower, and immediately afterward Frank began sending out messages and advice on campaign issues, including the importance of moving the American embassy in Israel to Jerusalem—something that made its way into the Republican platform and that Trump has promised to do. Frank says God showed him that Trump would win the primary election—putting him in a position to take on the political establishments of both parties.

Frank is one of the boldest prophetic leaders I know. During the campaign he told me in private conversations that he was committed to being a prophetic voice to the church and secular spheres and that Trump's journey to the White House was an extraordinary one, destined by God. He didn't say it just in church settings. He was a guest in June 2016 of liberal radio host Alan Colmes, who was intrigued with Frank's claim that Trump had a breaker anointing and said on the air that Trump would win by a landslide of the electoral college. Colmes, who said he didn't know if God existed, conceded that if it did indeed happen, he would believe in miracles. We'll never know what Colmes thought. He died of lymphoma at age sixty-six on February 23, 2017, a month after Trump was inaugurated.

Frank first came to the attention of the Trump campaign when he led excited crowds in "declarations" calling for transformation dealing with all the issues Evangelicals care about and stating that God had raised Trump for this purpose while Trump listened. How did the candidate respond? "Trump was OK with it," Frank told me. "In fact, he embraced it."

At the conclusion of a rally at pastor Darrell Scott's church in Ohio, Frank gave a rousing benediction in Pentecostal form, urging those assembled to give a "Jericho shout to the Lord" (a reference to how the children of Israel shouted before they won the battle at Jericho). This time it was in celebration of the anticipated victory of Trump and Pence, who were standing right behind Frank in the pulpit.[24]

The event happened on September 21, 2016. In the video we posted at CharismaNews.com, Trump had a big smile and embraced Frank after the prayer.[25] Frank was so bold. What if he were wrong? Well, he wasn't wrong, and I did what I could to put the prophecies of Frank Amedia and many others online and on the record through our magazine and podcasts. Earlier I had recorded a podcast with Lance Wallnau, who said God was raising up Donald Trump as He did the

Persian king Cyrus the Great.[26] If God could use a pagan king to rescue His people and restore the nation of Israel, why couldn't He do it again here in America?

Wallnau was not the only one to use the Cyrus analogy. Presbyterian pastor Dr. Derek W. H. Thomas made the comparison in a sermon at First Presbyterian Church of Columbia, South Carolina, a church where the governor and other establishment Evangelicals worship. Without naming Trump or Clinton, he said God can raise up a leader in the most unlikely ways. Thomas asked, "Would you have voted for Cyrus the Great?" According to Jerome Corsi in an article for WorldNetDaily.com, "Thomas' point is that Cyrus the Great, a brutal dictator, was raised up by God to serve God's purpose in returning the Jews, God's chosen people, to the land of Israel."[27] Without naming the candidates, he made it clear that God can use even the most unlikely people to accomplish His purposes.

Of course not everyone agrees. James Robison said he respects those with this view, but God ultimately destroyed Cyrus, who was a wicked pagan king. He doesn't believe Trump is that type of leader. When the article I posted on Lance Wallnau's message went viral, becoming our most listened to podcast ever,[28] I believed it was a foreshadowing that the evangelical and charismatic communities would come together as never before to bring about Donald Trump's victory on Election Day. Today we know that's exactly what happened.

As 1 Corinthians 13 says, "Now we see as through a glass, dimly" (v. 12). So it's never clear how to interpret prophetic words. This is illustrated by a contrarian voice of Tom Horn, a prolific writer of books on the end times and frequent guest on *The Jim Bakker Show*. In an op-ed on CharismaNews.com that was an excerpt from his new book, *Saboteurs*, Horn wrote: "Curiously, Cyrus isn't the only example of a pagan leader used by God to providentially influence the ancient Jewish nation. Nebuchadnezzar was also called 'the Servant of the Most High God,' and I understand why many modern believers prefer not to think about that example."[29]

Unlike Cyrus the deliverer, Horn points out, Nebuchadnezzar was the instrument of God's judgment against Judah, which meant most of the people being brought into captivity and their land being destroyed. The contrast between these two characters raises a very serious question, according to Horn. If Trump is God's choice for America's president, is he Cyrus (our deliverer) or Nebuchadnezzar (our agent of judgment)? "I want to believe Trump was God's way of putting His foot down on the socialist-globalist runaway agenda to allow a respite and opportunity for spiritual awakening in this country. But what if I'm wrong?" Horn writes.[30]

First Corinthians 13 also says, "We know in part, and we prophesy in part" (v. 9), so I believe there are many things we cannot understand. We must wait and see. However, it's clear America needs to repent. And God seems to be speaking to us. Will we listen and obey?

CHAPTER 7

ETHNIC ISSUES

★★★★★

IN THE WAKE of the riots and violent protests in Ferguson, Missouri, in August 2014, the *New York Times* published a heavily sourced article on the state of race relations in America. "America's racial divide," the writers stated, "is older than the republic itself, a central fault line that has shaped the nation's history." Pointing to the "racial fissures between blacks and whites" that erupted suddenly in that summer of rage, the article said, "Five decades past the era of legal segregation, a chasm remains between black and white Americans—and in some important respects it's as wide as ever."[1]

The writers admitted there are "bright spots" in the image of over-arching gloom they were painting, including the "rising number of blacks in executive and managerial jobs...and converging levels of life expectancy" between blacks and whites. Yet while acknowledging that the gaps between men and women and between Hispanics and non-Hispanics have actually shrunk in recent years, they nevertheless leaped to the inevitable conclusion that little hope exists of crossing the racial divide between whites and the racial minorities in this country anytime soon.[2]

No one denies that there are significant differences and important areas of disagreement between the various ethnic communities in this country—as in any country where there are large and diverse populations. But most Americans, regardless of race or socioeconomic status, still want essentially the same things. We all want to live in clean and safe neighborhoods; we want to be safe in our homes, to be able to make a decent living, to feed our families, to educate our children, to be able to work and play without undue restraint, and to be free to worship according to our beliefs and traditions. What tends to divide us—and what has led many minorities into the waiting arms of the Democratic

Party—is the rhetoric that persuades people to distrust their neighbors and believe that only government can fulfill their needs.

The politics of race has been a huge factor for so long that many people have come to accept the idea, as the *New York Times* apparently believes, that things will never change. But if there was one factor in the 2016 presidential election that may prove them wrong, it was the emergence of a wave of spiritual unity, touching men and women in all ethnic groups and all segments of society and drawing them together in the hope that the outspoken political outsider from New York, Donald Trump, may actually be the political leader they've been hoping for—not because he is better or wiser than anyone else but because he had the courage to make faith in God, belief in American ideals, and the importance of moral renewal major themes of his campaign.

Since the election many sources have reported that the evangelical vote gave Trump the edge he needed to win. I have cited these sources in several places already, and the evidence is compelling. But it's important to notice that Evangelicals are a diverse group, made up of all ethnic and socioeconomic groups. There are undoubtedly many reasons why they came over to support Trump in November, but I find it most remarkable that so many African Americans, Hispanics, Asians, and other minorities—many of whom have supported the Democratic party for generations—decided that this time around they would vote for the Republican.

There's no doubt that Trump moved the needle in making inroads into those communities. He won 29 percent of the Hispanic vote—2 percent more than Romney.[3] While he won only 8 percent of the black vote,[4] anecdotal evidence suggests that a large number of African Americans stayed home rather than voted for Clinton. They couldn't vote for Trump, but by staying home they robbed Clinton of votes she was counting on in places such as Michigan, Wisconsin, Pennsylvania, and Florida.[5] Churchgoing blacks and Hispanics generally reject abortion and favor traditional marriage. They are more apt to have a strong work ethic and traditional values. Democrats have used identity politics so successfully that many blacks and Hispanics vote Democratic simply because that's what you do. But the Trump campaign may have changed that.

Newt Gingrich, former Speaker of the House and former presidential candidate, writes in his book *Understanding Trump* that Republicans now have a chance to win those voters. "The truth is," he writes, "if the Republican Party could shrug off the Left's brand and engage Latinos, African Americans, Asian Americans, and others, we would build a huge coalition of Americans who favor traditional values. These are Americans who want to work hard, provide for their families, and pursue their own happiness without government intrusion. Frankly, that needs to be one of President Trump's main goals. If he's successful, it would be the most important accomplishment he could achieve for the Republican Party as president."[6]

When trying to estimate the Hispanic vote, pollsters were expecting single-digit backing for Trump because of his position on immigration and his tweets about building "the wall." I attended a board meeting of the National Hispanic Christian Leadership Conference (NHCLC) in May 2016—the same month Trump wrapped up the Republican nomination. I knew many of the board members, mostly pastors, and I knew they were conservative when it comes to traditional marriage and pro-life issues. Yet I heard them worrying out loud that if Trump deported all the illegals, they could lose 25 percent to 35 percent of their Pentecostal congregations. As a result, the board decided to remain middle of the road. At their big conference event they played video greetings from both Trump and Clinton[7] and endorsed neither candidate.

THE TIPPING POINT

On Election Day exit polls showed that of the 30 percent of Hispanics who voted for Trump, the biggest group was Evangelicals, who backed him by 66 percent. In Florida and Pennsylvania the evangelical Hispanic vote made up the margin of victory. Without those two states, analysts reported, Trump would have lost the election.[8] So what actually happened? My longtime friend Sam Rodriguez, president of NHCLC, told me it came down to Trump's support for the issue the Hispanic community cares most about: the Supreme Court and what kind of judges would be appointed by either Clinton or Trump. "When it came down to it," he said, "the Supreme Court trumped Trump's wall and Trump's tweets."[9]

The tipping point came in the third debate, Rodriguez told me, when moderator Chris Wallace said to Hillary Clinton that she had been quoted as saying the unborn have no rights, and she did not deny the comment. During the debate he got texts from friends saying, "I've shifted. There's no way I can vote for Hillary now."[10]

Earlier, in an interview with CBN News, Rodriguez was asked if he thought Trump was a racist. "That's just hyperbole," he said. "That's hyperbole from the liberal media for the purpose of attempting to paint a fascist sort of racist moniker on Donald Trump that I do not believe is accurate whatsoever." He did say, however, that Trump's tweets about illegals were counterproductive. Many of those who have entered the country illegally are attending NHCLC churches and are "born-again Christians, committed to biblical orthodoxy, or very staunch conservative Catholics," he said.[11] Later Sam expressed basically the same thing on Fox's *On the Record* and on the Spanish-language network Univision in an interview with Jorge Ramos—who had become one of Trump's biggest media targets.[12]

Rodriguez's comments came to Trump's attention, and in June 2016, when Trump met with a group of one thousand evangelical leaders in New York, Rodriguez was pulled into a pre-meeting with thirty others.[13] The focus of the discussion soon centered on Rodriguez, who told Trump respectfully that Christian Hispanics were apt to vote for him, but his rhetoric about illegals and building a wall was working against him. Trump asked him what issues were most important to Hispanics. There are five priorities, Rodriguez said, and he had preached on them many times: the Supreme Court, religious liberty, educational quality, racial unity, and immigration reform, in that order.[14]

Paul Manafort, Trump's campaign director, exchanged telephone numbers with Rodriguez and said he and his colleagues wanted more discussions with him. Even though he did not endorse Trump, he began giving advice to the campaign. During that time there was also a pivot, and the rhetoric was scaled down. Thanks to the input he was getting, Trump began showing more concern for the interests of the Hispanic community, emphasizing many of the priorities that Rodriguez brought up.[15]

The day after the election one of Trump's campaign staff members called to tell Rodriguez they were pleased to report that more Hispanics, percentage-wise, voted for the Republican candidate than in any previous election. While the majority of Catholic Hispanics followed the traditional pattern and voted for the Democratic candidate, Trump overwhelmingly won the evangelical Hispanic vote.[16]

Two months later Rodriguez was invited to pray at Trump's swearing-in ceremony. He would be the first member of his Assemblies of God denomination to be invited to pray at a presidential inauguration.[17]

When he came forward to speak, he recited Christ's words from the beatitudes about serving the poor and oppressed:

> God blesses those who hunger and thirst for justice, for they will be satisfied. God blesses those who are merciful, for they will be shown mercy.... God blesses you when people mock you and persecute you and lie about you and say all sorts of evil things against you because you are my followers.... You are the light of the world—like a city on a hilltop that cannot be hidden. No one lights a lamp and then puts it under a basket. Instead, a lamp is placed on a stand, where it gives light to everyone in the house. In the same way, let your good deeds shine out for all to see, so that everyone will praise your heavenly Father.
>
> —MATTHEW 5:6–7, 11, 14–16, NLT

The reading was both a touching tribute to the new president, particularly in light of the mockery he was enduring at the time, and also a reminder of the high calling we've all been given to "love the Lord your God" and to "love your neighbor as yourself."

HEALING THE RACIAL DIVIDE

In the black community Trump had to convince pastors almost one by one that he wasn't the racist the Left made him out to be. Pastor Darrell Scott said on *The Jim Bakker Show* that Trump can't be a racist because "if he was a racist, what would he be hanging with me for?"[18]

In a podcast with me a week before the election, Scott told me about his odyssey to becoming a Trump supporter. He began by relaying how his attitude had changed from his initial meeting with Trump and other Christian ministers at the meeting described earlier, convened by Paula White Cain in 2012 with Christian friends who "know how to pray."[19]

Scott said he was surprised Trump didn't ask for support, but rather he asked for prayer. He said he was looking for godly counsel on whether or not to run against Obama in 2012. Never one to kiss up to politicians, Scott asked in that meeting why he should vote for Trump because the word in the black community was that he was a racist. Trump answered, as he had done in other settings, saying, "I am probably the least racist person you know." He said he couldn't work in business with as many people of all races and creeds as he does if he were actually a racist.[20]

Scott told this story to the podcast audience, saying that Trump impressed him by not arguing the point or saying he wasn't racist because he had a black friend in the third grade. Apparently Trump was impressed with Scott as well. After the meeting a Trump aide exchanged cell phone numbers with him and said, "The boss was interested in your boldness, and he wants to keep in touch."[21]

During his outreach to African American voters Donald Trump was interviewed by apostle Wayne T. Jackson at Great Faith Ministries International in Detroit, Michigan, on Saturday, September 3, 2016. The interview was broadcast on the Impact Network, which reaches some seventy million homes and is one of the fastest-growing faith-based television networks in the country and the only one run by African Americans. Jackson had agreed to interview the candidate on his magazine-style program, *Miracles Do Happen*, and a miracle is precisely what candidate Trump was hoping for.[22]

Jackson, a Democrat, was under enormous pressure not to invite Trump. He had also extended an invitation to Hillary Clinton, but she did not respond. He hadn't intended for Trump to say anything in his church but only to have him sit through the service. When Trump's motorcade arrived, Jackson went to greet him and felt the Lord tell him, "He's the next president." Then he told me he felt led to invite Trump to speak to his congregation while the secular media's cameras rolled.

The most striking moment of that interview was the moment when Trump was presented with a Hebrew prayer shawl, known as a tallit. Explaining that the shawl represents a very special spiritual anointing, Jackson told Trump, "There are going to be some times in your life that you are going to feel forsaken. You are going to feel down, but the anointing is going to lift you up."

He then draped the shawl over the candidate's shoulders and presented him with a "Jewish" Bible that has notes and commentary about Jewish feasts and observances, among other things. Then he said, "We have it especially for you, and we have one for your wife. Because when things go down, you can study the Word of God." Even though Trump didn't fully understand the symbolism of the moment, he was clearly moved by the presentation, as one can see in the picture of the event in the photo section of this book.[23]

Dr. Alveda King, the niece of Dr. Martin Luther King Jr., was also a

Trump supporter, although she told me she had to speak up when his daughter Ivanka said that her father was racially colorblind.[24] "If white privilege makes you colorblind," Alveda said, "then you need glasses." Alveda has a policy of not endorsing candidates but rather praying God's will be done. At the beginning of the primaries she backed Dr. Ben Carson, who, like her, is politically conservative. When Carson endorsed Trump, Alveda began actively supporting Trump and was photographed with him several times, sending signals for all to see whom she hoped would win.[25]

The crucial issue for her, she told me, was Trump's strong antiabortion position. She calls pro-life activism a civil rights campaign for the unborn.[26] She works closely with Priests for Life, a Catholic group that hopes to get more blacks to reject the abortion option. She quotes her famous uncle, who said, "The Negro cannot win as long as he is willing to sacrifice the lives of his children for comfort and safety." She adds, "How can the 'Dream' survive if we murder the children? Every aborted baby is like a slave in the womb of his or her mother. The mother decides his or her fate."[27]

Alveda believes that Planned Parenthood targets the black community for abortion. In the United States blacks make up approximately 13 percent of the population yet account for 37 percent of all abortions. This compares with about 19 percent for Hispanics and 38 percent for whites.[28] She constantly preaches this in the black community and has found a willing audience among African Americans who are Roman Catholic. She says these votes helped push Catholic numbers to be 52 percent for Trump compared with 45 percent who voted for Clinton. In some of the key states Alveda says as much as 18 percent of the black community voted for Trump, although I could not verify that statistic.[29]

The problem of identity politics remains a fact of life in most of America and something we will have to live with for some time, no doubt. While there are scores of black Evangelicals and pro-family Catholics striving to restore balance and respect between ethnic groups, the political Left embrace groups such as Black Lives Matter, blasts so-called "white privilege," and foments violence in order to drive a wedge between the blacks and whites.

Newt Gingrich says in his book that Donald Trump is doing his best to address the problem of identity politics that has been dividing the country for decades. "He called for all Americans to celebrate their differences," Gingrich writes, "but to never forget we are one people under God."[30]

In his inaugural address Trump said, "At the bedrock of our politics will be a total allegiance to the United States of America, and through our loyalty to our country, we will rediscover our loyalty to each other. When you open your heart to patriotism, there is no room for prejudice. The Bible tells us, 'How good and pleasant it is when God's people live together in unity.' We must speak our minds openly, debate our disagreements honestly, but always pursue solidarity."[31] Gingrich believes this part of Trump's message is vitally important because "it expresses an aspect of President Trump's personality that is completely overlooked by the media. To Trump," he says, "bigotry cannot exist within a patriotic heart. To be racist—to hold any other American in low regard based on their gender, religion, race or heritage—is to be completely unpatriotic."[32]

My good friend Bishop Harry Jackson, senior pastor of Hope Christian Church in Beltsville, Maryland, and a frequent Fox News contributor, made the same point when he was invited by the National Religious Broadcasters to participate in a public debate with a former Bush administration staffer who had taken the position of "anybody but Trump." Bishop Jackson began the second round of that debate by saying that Trump "may be the only one who's able to bring some substantive healing to the racial divide."[33]

In his view, Jackson said, Trump could help the country by advancing practical answers on educational and economic opportunity. Black and Hispanic voters have too often settled for "the politics of grievance." But Trump has made advancement for minority communities a priority of his campaign. There's no denying that people in these communities have been failed by both parties, but Jackson said he was convinced Trump could be a "change agent" to move America forward by addressing race and class issues in "pragmatic ways."[34]

Jackson went on to list priorities that echoed what Sam Rodriguez had said: issues that would be of particular interest to Christians in these large minority communities, such as educational reform, economic development in urban areas, and family-oriented tax policies. And with each of these leaders, high on their list of priorities were a commitment to religious liberty, the appointment of strong pro-life justices to the Supreme Court, and strong support for the nation of Israel—all of which were equally high on Trump's list of platform promises.[35]

UPHOLDING THE COVENANT

The Jewish minority in America exists in a different category from other ethnic groups, and Jews occupy a special place in Christian theology. There has been a substantial bedrock of support for Israel among evangelical Christians since the modern nation was established in 1948, but the Hebrew roots of both Christianity and Judaism are as ancient as the Bible itself. Two of the most visible Christian groups supporting the interests of the Jewish state are the International Christian Embassy in Jerusalem and Christians United for Israel, headed by megachurch pastor John Hagee. Despite this country's connections with the nation of Israel, America's support was seriously eroded under President Obama. Liberal Christians tend to favor the Palestinian cause, but most Evangelicals were horrified by the disparaging remarks made to and about Israeli Prime Minister Benjamin Netanyahu by the former president.

Most faithful Evangelicals are familiar with the words of Genesis 12:3, in which God says to Abraham, the father of the Jewish race, "I will bless them who bless you and curse him who curses you, and in you all families of the earth will be blessed." The promise of the passage is simple enough: The nation of Israel is sacred in God's eyes, and His blessings have preserved the Jewish people through destruction and disaster countless times over the centuries. He has blessed the nation and its people and has promised to bless those who uphold the Jewish nation and to curse those who harm His chosen people. Evangelical Christians believe this to be one of the most fundamental promises of Scripture.

Chuck Pierce, the charismatic prophet we met in chapter 2, predicted Obama's two terms in office, and during those eight years he focused his prayers on the nation of Israel. "The Lord told me that if I would pray for Netanyahu and that if he could remain in office, America would be OK. So instead of getting bogged down in all the issues of America," Pierce told me, "I would journey to Israel and lead prayer and worship gatherings."[36] This was all going on at the same time Obama was working behind the scenes to defeat Netanyahu's reelection campaign.[37] Pierce and other ministers flew to Israel specifically to intercede and pray that Netanyahu, who was trailing badly in the polls, would win. Fortunately he did.

In May 2017 Vice President Pence invited about one hundred rabbis, Israeli diplomats, a few congressmen, and about thirty Evangelicals to the White House to celebrate Israel's Day of Independence. "He made a public decree that as long as this administration was in place, Israel would be our best friend, and we would be their best friend. That was the first time in history, since Israel had become a nation, that the White House had done that," Pierce told me. "All of the media covering the event at the White House were there when the decree was made, but it was not publicized, and that shows you how there is such a strategy in this nation not to align with God's covenant."[38]

From Pierce's perspective, aligning with God's purposes is infinitely more important than temporal issues such as taxes, education, or immigration reform. While support for Israel is not usually perceived as swinging elections, among Evangelicals it is almost always a huge factor. And among those who identify as Christian Zionists, that issue trumps all others. So Pierce, who has never been actively political, did what he felt he could do "in the spiritual realm." He felt the Lord tell him to fly to Israel and pray for three days.[39]

"We were on our way to negating our relationship as a nation with the God of Israel," he said. "I knew that was really my intercession, that we had to remain in covenant with God, who had sovereignly chosen Israel. And if we would do that as a nation, we would prolong our status in the world. So we were on the verge of negating that covenant alignment." Pierce told me he watched the US election from Israel on November 8. It was incredibly important for America to realign with Israel, he said, adding that he believes Trump will align with Israel and reestablish this nation's covenant with that ancient land.[40]

Author, minister, and longtime friend Mike Evans is someone who understands the bond between evangelical Christians and Israel. He told me he raised more than thirty-five million dollars to build an impressive state-of-the-art museum called Friends of Zion in Jerusalem, which I have visited twice. It shows in creative ways what most Israelis do not know—that some of the earliest Zionists were Christians, as far back as the nineteenth century. One of the Christian Zionists featured in the museum was George Bush—not either president. This man was the cousin of an ancestor of the Presidents Bush.[41] In 1844, more than a century before the modern state of Israel was born, he published a book titled *The Valley of Vision; or The Dry Bones of Israel Revived*.[42] In it he denounced "the thraldom and oppression which has so long ground [the Jews] to the dust, and elevating them to a rank of honorable repute among the nations of the earth" by restoring the Jews to the land of Israel.[43]

Evans is the oldest Christian friend of the Israeli prime minister. As one of the highest-profile Christian Zionists, he understands Pierce's spiritual meaning, but Evans sees things more politically. "Not only has Prime Minister Netanyahu scored his greatest victory with the Trump presidency, so has Trump with Netanyahu," he told me. "Israel's finest days are yet to come with the Netanyahu-Trump alliance. Ultimately Trump will have a naval base in the Port of Haifa, where US troops can be protected and special ops forces can move in and out to decapitate radical Islam." Evans believes Trump has no interest in nation building in the region and no interest in fighting a conventional war. He stands adamantly opposed to the Iraq war and understands that the wars of the twenty-first century will be proxy battles, on economic, media, and ideological fronts rather than old-fashioned battlefields.[44]

Radical Islam has labeled Israel "The Little Satan," while calling America "The Big Satan," he said. When Menachem Begin was prime minister of Israel, he showed Evans a strategic plan he was going to present to the president of the United States. Israel had concluded that America could not effectively win wars in the Middle East.[45] Most of America's wars were fought over a lengthy period of time, but Israel's wars happened much faster. By the time the United States could reach the region to fight a war, it would be over. In reality, during the Communist era Israel was a US proxy and strategically deterred the spread of Communism in the Middle East. Today, thanks to the Jewish nation's strong connection with the United States, Israel is becoming a proxy against the spread of radical Islam.

ONE NATION UNDER GOD

Trump has been clear about his support for Israel. In an interview with the Israeli newspaper *Israel Hayom*, published February 26, 2016, Trump said, "My friendship with Israel is stronger than any other candidate's." When asked about his plans regarding a possible compromise agreement with the Palestinians, he said, "I want to make one thing clear: I want to strike a peace agreement between Israel and the Palestinians. It's what I aspire to do. Peace is possible, even if it is the most difficult agreement to achieve." But, he stressed, "It is a little difficult to reach an agreement when the other side doesn't really want to talk to you."[46]

More than eight months before his election, Trump sent a goodwill message to the people of Israel, saying, "Don't get confused there in Israel: I am currently your biggest friend. My daughter is married to a Jew who is an enthusiastic Israel supporter, and I have taken part in many Israel Day Parades. My friendship with Israel is very strong." Trump also said he likes the idea of moving the US embassy from Tel Aviv to Jerusalem and added that the Obama administration's nuclear deal with Iran is the "worst deal that Israel could have gotten."[47]

His daughter's conversion to Judaism is, nevertheless, an issue that has raised concerns among Christians and Jews on both sides of the Atlantic. Although she was raised Presbyterian, Trump's daughter Ivanka converted to Judaism in an Orthodox rabbinical court in July 2009 at age twenty-seven and not long before her marriage to Jared Kushner. Today the couple are Orthodox Sabbath and Jewish holiday observers. Her father, Ivanka told reporters, had to get used to the fact that from dusk Friday until nightfall on Saturdays she and her husband are inaccessible by phone, text, or e-mail. Despite serving as executive vice president in the Trump organization, she puts everything else aside and follows traditional Jewish customs and religious practices.[48]

In a February 2015 interview for *Vogue* magazine, Ivanka said, "It's been such a great life decision for me. I am very modern, but I'm also a very traditional person, and I think that's an interesting juxtaposition in how I was raised as well. I really find that with Judaism, it creates an amazing blueprint for family connectivity." She said, "We observe the Sabbath. From Friday to Saturday we don't do anything but hang out with one another. We don't make phone calls." And she added, "It's an amazing thing when you're so connected, to really sign off."[49]

On April 12, 2016, during an interview with Donald Trump and several family members, Ivanka answered questions from CNN host Anderson Cooper about her conversion to Judaism. When asked about her father's reaction to her conversion to Judaism, Ivanka said, "My father was very supportive. He knows me. He knows and he trusts my judgment. When I make decisions, I make them in a well-reasoned way. I don't rush into things." She added that her father's close relationship with her Jewish husband helped ease the process. "He loves my husband," she said. "They're incredibly close, which I think was obviously helpful. And he has been very supportive with me in that decision, as in many others I've taken throughout the years."[50]

Her husband was an active member of Trump's campaign team and now serves as special adviser to the president. He helped write Trump's speech to the American Israel Public Affairs Committee (AIPAC) conference in March 2016.[51] During a 2015 event Trump said in an off-the-cuff remark, "I have a Jewish daughter. This wasn't in the plan, but I'm very glad it happened."[52]

During his interview with James Robison, pastor Jack Graham offered an insightful assessment of Kushner's Jewish faith: "Being an orthodox Jew, Jared is full of the Old Testament. He speaks Hebrew, and he can even lead the teaching in the synagogue. He is very bright. We had a sweet time of prayer and he was moved and profusely thankful. I saw something in him that I told him after we prayed. I looked at him and said, 'Jared, I see in you the spirit of Joseph in the Old Testament. It says that Joseph had an excellent spirit...' I believe he was thankful for that analysis. He's got an excellent spirit about him like Joseph in the Old Testament. He said, 'My son's name is Joseph and my grandfather's name was Joseph.'"[53]

For many Christians it may be a little difficult to think through the implications of Ivanka's conversion. Evangelicals love the nation of Israel but pray that the Jewish people will come to know and love their Messiah as we do. However, another aspect may have longer-term significance, in that Ivanka's conversion and Trump's amiable acceptance of the marriage assures Israelis who are often skeptical of America's commitment that they can trust this Christian president to defend their interests.

Trump has made this promise repeatedly. When he made his first international diplomatic tour, Trump visited Saudi Arabia, the Vatican, and Jerusalem, the homes of the three great Abrahamic religions. In Jerusalem he did what no other sitting US president has ever done: he visited the Western Wall of the Temple Mount, standing at the holiest place where Jews are permitted to pray, and said a few words before inserting a note between the stones. He said later he prayed for wisdom as he reached out and touched the walls.[54]

As reported by the Reuters news agency, "(Trump) said that he understands the significance of the Western Wall for the Jewish people, and that's why he decided to visit here during his first trip to Israel," said Shmuel Rabinowitz, the rabbi of the Western Wall. "He is certain he will come here again, perhaps many times. He was very moved." The president was joined on the trip by his son-in-law, Jared Kushner. Both men wore black kippahs, the skull caps worn by religious Jews. While Trump and Kushner visited the area set aside for men, Melania Trump and Ivanka visited a separate section where women are allowed to pray.[55]

Whether or not the national media can perceive it, President Trump has assured the American people of his commitment to unity and to restoring the sense of community among all ethnic groups that has been missing for so long in America. At the national Celebrate Freedom event hosted by Dallas pastor Robert Jeffress at the Kennedy Center on July 1, 2017, Trump concluded his remarks by saying, "Whether we are black or brown or white, and you've heard me say this before, we all bleed the same red blood. We all salute the same great American flag, and we are all made by the same Almighty God. We face many challenges. There are many hills and mountains to climb, but with the strength and courage of the patriots assembled in this room tonight…we will get the job done. We will all prove worthy of this very important moment in history, and we will prove worthy of the sacrifice that our brave veterans have made. As long as we have pride in our beliefs, courage in our convictions, and faith in our God, we will not fail."[56]

So what kind of man is Donald Trump, and what led to his election? The next section seeks to answer these questions.

PART III

TRUMP
THE MAN

★★★★★

CHAPTER 8

THE ROLE OF FAMILY

★★★★★

WHEN I INTERVIEWED Donald Trump before the election, one of my questions was, "What is the most important thing in your life?" In a split second he said it was his family, adding that religion was also important. So knowing what he believes about his family—including the family he grew up in—is important to understanding this very complex man.

Many noticed the admirable qualities of Donald Trump's children during his campaign, and I'll touch on some of that in this chapter. In the second presidential debate even his staunch rival Hillary Clinton said that one thing she admired about Trump was his children. "His children are incredibly able and devoted, and I think that says a lot about Donald."[1]

So who are the members of Donald Trump's family tree? He has been married three times and has five children and eight grandchildren. Before starting such a big family of his own, Trump came from a large family himself as one of the five children born to Fred and Mary Trump in Queens. In his 1987 best-selling book *The Art of the Deal* Donald Trump writes, "The most important influence on me, growing up, was my father, Fred Trump. I learned a lot from him." But he quickly adds, "At the same time, I learned very early on that I didn't want to be in the business my father was in."[2] Frederick Christ Trump—whose middle name comes from his German-born mother's maiden name, pronounced with a soft *i*—was a real estate developer who built and managed thousands of apartments in Queens and Brooklyn. It was a profitable business, but it required a lot of hands-on interaction with builders, suppliers, and tenants who didn't always pay their bills on time.[3]

Born in New York in 1905, Fred discovered very early that he had a talent for construction. He loved building things, learned to read architectural plans, and spent hours in the workshop learning to use carpentry tools.[4] He was just thirteen when his father died, leaving behind a wife and three children. His father had been a boardinghouse owner in Seattle, Washington, starting in the 1890s, renting rooms to Yukon gold miners. But when the gold boom trailed off around the turn of the century, the elder Trump relocated to the borough of Queens, New York, where he made a comfortable living investing in real estate.[5]

Although the family wasn't left penniless, Fred knew he would have to find a way to help his mother, Elizabeth, and his two siblings. Two years later he and his mother decided to open a small construction company. Since he was still a minor, Fred couldn't do business under his own name, so they filled out the official documents under his mother's name, calling the business E. Trump & Son. Eventually the name would be changed to Trump Management Company.[6]

Automobiles were a new luxury in the 1920s, and homes didn't come equipped with garages. Drawing on his carpentry skills and his entrepreneurial aptitude, Fred designed and built a simple carport for a neighbor, for which he charged fifty dollars. When other neighbors saw it, they lined up to have Fred build them carports of their own. By the time he graduated from high school, Fred was already a successful businessman. Before long he was building small homes and duplexes and handling the financing himself.[7]

As the business expanded during the 1930s and 1940s, he was able to secure government contracts for Navy barracks and apartments for military families during the Second World War. After the war he began building large housing blocks for returning soldiers and their families in Brooklyn, restoring bankrupt properties, and acquiring apartments and other buildings in foreclosure. By the time of his death in 1999 the family-owned business had more than twenty-seven thousand apartment units under management.[8]

DONALD TRUMP'S SCOTTISH MOTHER

Fred met his future wife in the 1930s, as the family legend goes, at a dance. Mary Anne MacLeod had grown up speaking Scots Gaelic in her native Scotland, and Fred was enchanted by her accent. She had made at least two trips to the United States before finally gaining resident status in the early 1930s. Her older sister, Catherine, who had arrived in New York a few years earlier, invited Mary to come for a visit in 1928, and not long after her arrival Catherine found Mary a job as a nanny for a wealthy family in the New York suburbs.[9]

Unfortunately the job didn't last long. Her employers lost most of their fortune in the Wall Street Crash of 1929, and new positions were hard to come by. Mary returned to Scotland before finding a permanent position, but by 1934 when the Depression was beginning to ease, she was back in New York where she met "the most eligible bachelor in New York." After a lengthy engagement, Fred and Mary were married in 1936.[10]

"Looking back," Donald Trump has said, "I realize now that I got some of my sense of showmanship from my mother. She always had a flair for the dramatic and the grand. She was a very traditional house-wife, but she also had a sense of the world beyond her. I still remember my mother, who is Scottish by birth, sitting in front of the television set to watch Queen Elizabeth's coronation and not budging for an entire day. She was just enthralled by the pomp and circumstance, the whole idea of royalty and glamour."[11]

Mary Trump's love of royal pageantry, the Queen, and all things British was only natural. She had been born in 1912 in the tiny fishing village of Tong on the island of Lewis in the Outer Hebrides of Scotland, where her father worked as both fisherman and postmaster. She was brought up a devout Presbyterian by her Gaelic-speaking parents, who belonged to the Reformed "free church" movement within the Church of Scotland known as the "Wee Frees."[12]

We don't know how religious Fred Trump's German ancestors may have been or how faithfully he followed the teachings of the churches his family attended in New York, but Fred attended church regularly throughout his life and maintained a friendship with Dr. Norman Vincent Peale until Peale's death in 1993. Fred and Mary were sup-porters of their church and several Christian organizations, and Mrs. Trump was well known for her charity work and philanthropy until her death in 2000 at age eighty-eight. Much of her philanthropy was cen-tered in Queens, where the family lived. She supported the Women's Auxiliary of Jamaica Hospital and the Jamaica Day Nursery, and there was plenty of money to give. At the time of his death in 1999 Fred's net worth was estimated to be more than three hundred million dollars.[13]

The island of Lewis, where Mary Trump grew up, holds a place of renown and important in church history because of the Holy Spirit revival that broke out there in the late 1940s. From 1949 to 1953 the island of Lewis, the Hebrides islands, and other parts of the United Kingdom were powerfully touched by an evangelistic fire known as the Hebrides Revival, and thousands of men and women in Scotland

and the western isles were brought into the body of Christ through those events.[14] All this transpired more than a decade after Mary MacLeod had emigrated to the United States, but it's safe to say that the depth of devotion that was awakened later was there in some measure during her childhood. Donald Trump's mother was serious about her faith and would often say to her children, "Trust in God and be true to yourself."[15]

Donald John Trump was the fourth of five children born to Fred and Mary Trump. By the time Donald was born, on June 14, 1946, Fred was quite wealthy and the most successful real estate developer in Queens. In addition to the thousands of homes he had built and sold during his career, he was able to build an elegant mansion for his family in the upscale Jamaica Estates section of Queens. Thanks to several expansions and renovations, the home would eventually grow to twenty-three rooms.[16]

Donald Trump told one of his biographers that he grew up in a warm, close-knit household, but it was a highly charged, competitive home and his father was often away on business. If he and his brothers, Fred Jr. and Bob, wanted to spend time with their dad, they would have to go with him to the job site. During summer vacations the boys would work for their father collecting rents or grabbing a hammer and joining the carpentry crew on one of Fred's projects. Unfortunately Fred Jr. (known as Freddy) could never live up to his father's expectations, and the two men had a rocky relationship.[17]

To escape his father's criticism and disappointment, Freddy decided to opt out of the family business and become a commercial airline pilot, flying for TWA. The future president had been close to his brother, but he could see that Freddy didn't have a head for business. "I think Freddy became discouraged," Trump said in his book, "and he started to drink, and that led to a downward spiral." He has often said that Freddy was really the best one. He was handsome and outgoing. He had a warm personality and a zest for life, but his demons never let him relax.[18]

Freddy smoked and drank heavily but warned Trump to stay away from those habits, and he took the advice to heart. Trump could see what those addictions were doing to his brother, and Trump has been a nonsmoking teetotaler his whole life. "At the age of forty-three, [Freddy] died. It's very sad, because he was a wonderful guy who never quite found himself," Trump wrote years later. "In many ways he had it all, but the pressures of our particular family were not for him." He added, "I was devastated when he died."[19]

A POSITIVE TRANSFORMATION

Donald Trump's younger brother, Robert, followed him into the real estate business and later became supervisor of Fred Sr.'s real estate portfolio at the end of his life. Their sister Maryanne Trump Barry earned degrees from Mount Holyoke and Columbia and a law degree from Hofstra University and became a federal judge. Another sister, Elizabeth, went to work for Chase Bank.[20] Donald's sisters don't hesitate to say that he was always a handful. "He was a brat," Maryanne told one of Trump's biographers, and that behavior ended up with Donald being shipped off to the New York Military Academy (NYMA) at age thirteen to have the rough edges knocked off.[21]

"I was very bad," Trump admitted. "I was rebellious. Not violent or anything, but I wasn't exactly well behaved." Military school transformed the spoiled rich kid in remarkable ways, thanks mainly to the strong discipline he received from his coach and instructor, Ted Dobias. Trump remembers that "those guys were rough. If a guy did today what they did then they'd have them in jail for twenty-five years." His coaches and teachers weren't afraid to lay down the law and to use corporal punishment as needed. "They'd get into fights with you," he said.[22]

Dobias was a tough coach, counselor, and teacher, but after a rough start Trump responded to his discipline and went on to become the top cadet, a top athlete who was scouted by the pros, and cadet commander of his senior class.[23] He is pictured in an iconic photo in full military uniform marching before the NYMA band in New York City's Veterans Day Parade.[24] After military school Trump became more focused academically and professionally. He attended Fordham University for two years before transferring to the Wharton School of Finance at the Ivy League University of Pennsylvania during the tumultuous 1960s, where he earned a bachelor's degree in business. He has said that the time at Wharton transformed him.[25]

Trump lived in Queens until he was twenty-five, in 1971, when he moved into Manhattan for the first time. He said, "I used to stand on the other side of the East River and look at Manhattan." He was eager to take the next step in his life and career, so he rented a one-room apartment on East 75th Street near Third Avenue and commuted to Brooklyn, where he helped manage his father's business affairs.[26]

Trump grew up in the mainline Presbyterian Church (USA) and still says he's a Presbyterian.[27] When asked about his participation in worship services, he is said to have shown people copies of his childhood confirmation photo and said the Bible is the best book ever written.[28] In January 2017 he released a video that showed him holding the Trump family Bible. "It's just very special to me," he said, showing his mother's worn Bible to the camera. On one of the early pages she had written a personal inscription. "In fact, it's her writing, right here," he said. "She wrote the name and my address, and it's just very special to me."[29]

Donald Trump was twenty-eight years old when his parents transferred their membership from First Presbyterian Church in Jamaica, Queens, to Marble Collegiate Church, pastored by Norman Vincent Peale. He never transferred his membership but attended church there with his family and used the services of the church for baptisms, marriages, and funerals. Trump was especially attracted to Peale's message that faith in Christ was beneficial not just spiritually but psychologically and could contribute to success in life.[30]

Of the forty books Peale authored, *The Power of Positive Thinking* was by far the most successful and one of the best-selling books of all time. In fact, Peale's own title for the book had been *The Power of Faith*, but his publisher thought that was a bit too pious and chose a title with a more commercial spin.[31] From a business standpoint, it was a smart decision, and today there are more than five million copies of the book in print.[32]

I've long admired Peale and have read several of his books. He was mentor to my late mentor Len LeSourd, whom Peale hired as editor of *Guideposts* magazine when it was fledgling. He built it to the several-million-circulation publication it is today.[33] Len used to tell me stories when I was just starting *Charisma* about those early days working with Peale. I met Peale only once at a Christian Booksellers Convention with his wife, Ruth Stafford Peale. I remember how gracious they both were and how much energy they had even though they were both over eighty years old.

I knew Peale's story because it was background for his many books. He wrote that he had once been a shy and insecure young man. But one of his college professors took him aside and told him he needed to start thinking of himself in a better way. He assured Peale he was as intelligent and capable as any of his students, but he was too withdrawn. He could accomplish a great deal more in life, he was told, if he could stop being so shy. What he needed was a positive attitude. Those words were hurtful, Peale said, but the more he thought about it, he realized the professor was probably right, so he began speaking up and doing things that would have intimidated him before. That was the beginning of his transformation.[34]

Donald Trump has never needed much encouragement to feel good about himself, but he took Peale's message to heart, and the two men remained good friends for many years. In his autobiography Peale made a remarkable assessment of the qualities of Donald Trump. He said, "Positive thinkers are bound to be positive doers. They are achievers and winners, and I have noted that they also have non-irritating though strong personalities.... I had an opportunity to be in on some church negotiations in which Donald was firm but polite and considerate in pursuing the goals he had set. In his quiet, somewhat low-key, but persistent, way he attained for the church one of the greatest assurances of long-term financial stability in its history.[35]

"Characteristically Fred Trump, his father, acclaimed this contribution to the ongoing welfare of the church by saying, 'Donald knows how to do it.' And Donald said, 'All I know, Father taught me,' adding his usual admiring remark, 'My father is a very great gentleman.'" Peale then mentioned several of Donald Trump's business successes and concluded, "Donald Trump's career has only just begun, but what a beginning. Surely he is one of America's top positive thinkers and positive doers."[36]

THE TRUMP FAMILY PORTRAIT

Throughout his campaign Donald Trump emphasized his close relationship with his children, and that's when many of us got our first look at the future first family. I recently spoke with Frank Amedia, whom I mention throughout this book. He knows the family, especially Eric, and I asked him to share any insights he has on Trump's children. He said the first thing we need to understand is that there's a "myth" of the Trump family that sometimes is a little too critical of them. "They are a typical family," he said, "albeit a family that has enjoyed wealth. They've had to learn how to stick together as a family in spite of some of the different criticisms throughout their life together. But this is a family that you can see from the moment you're with them is very tight-knit, very close. They truly, genuinely love one another, respect one another, and there is no doubt that the head of that family, the patriarch, is Donald Trump."[37]

We all know that Donald Trump has two sons, Donald Jr. and Eric, and a daughter, Ivanka, with his first wife, Ivana Zelnickova, a former model, whom he married in 1977. He has a daughter, Tiffany, with his second wife, Marla Maples, whom he married in 1993, and a son, Barron, with his current wife, the former Melania Knauss. Like many people, I was struck by the character and values he seems to have instilled in each of his children, and I wanted to highlight some things about them in this chapter.

In addition to being his namesake, Donald Jr., born in 1977, has followed in his dad's footsteps in a number of ways: he married a former model, is the father of five children, earned a degree in finance and real estate from the Wharton School of the University of Pennsylvania, and joined his father's business as executive vice president.[38]

He is a huge outdoorsman who hunts deer with a bow and arrow. He says his love for hunting is what kept him on the straight and narrow in his younger days, leaving him little time to get into trouble.[39]

Don Jr. was twelve when his parents divorced and old enough to understand the circumstances of his father's affair with Marla Maples, whom he later married, but the family remained close.[40] Even after his parents divorced, the children continued to live in Trump Tower with their mother, so his father was never more than an elevator ride away.[41]

Don Jr. was also close to his maternal grandfather, Milos, who lived with the family for a number of years, and he named one of his sons Tristan Milos after him. Don Jr. spent his childhood summers in Prague and is fluent in Czech.[42]

His wife is the former Vanessa Haydon, whom he reportedly met when his father set them up. They married in 2005 at Trump's Mar-a-Lago estate, and they have two daughters, Kai (2007) and Chloe (2014), and three sons, Donald III (2009), Tristan (2011), and Spencer (2012).[43]

Ivanka, born in 1981, is Donald Trump's second child with Ivana, and she grew up in the spotlight like her brothers, Eric and Don Jr. She's the most famous of the Trump offspring and is considered in some ways to be the most successful, having worked as a runway model, launched her own jewelry and fashion line, and written a *New York Times* best-selling book, in addition to serving as executive vice president of The Trump Organization.[44]

She credits her dad's influence as the reason she avoided alcohol and other vices. "I've never been interested in being a wild party girl," Ivanka has said. "My dad feels very adamantly about no drugs, no drinking, no smoking, because his brother died of alcoholism, which is a horrible, horrible thing."[45]

She's an informal adviser to her father in his role as president, but she's said to have been her father's confidant for a long time. In many ways she seems to know him best and have the greatest access to him. She traces their tight bond back to her parents' divorce. "Bizarrely," she said in a 2004 interview, "it made us closer to Dad.... We didn't take his presence for granted anymore."[46]

Ivanka is also a Wharton grad, and she served as a judge on her father's TV show, *The Apprentice*, as did her brothers. I find it interesting that she's friends with Chelsea Clinton, and that friendship stayed intact throughout the election.[47]

Ivanka has three children, Arabella (2011), Joseph (2013), and Theodore (2016), with her husband, Jared Kushner, a Jewish real estate developer and now President Trump's senior adviser, whom she married in 2009.[48]

Eric Trump, born in 1984, is the third child of Donald and Ivana, and he says he prefers to "fly under the radar" when it comes to recognition and celebrity. At six-foot-five, he's often been media shy and says that Don Jr. and Ivanka were both big influences on him growing up. He and Ivanka are especially close, and he told *New York* magazine that Ivanka was like a second mother to him.[49]

In 2012 Eric proposed to his wife, Lara Yunaska, with a ring from Ivanka's fine jewelry collection, and they were married at Mar-a-Lago at a ceremony officiated by his brother-in-law, Jared Kushner.[50] They had their first child in September 2017. Eric "Luke" is Donald Trump's ninth grandchild.[51]

My friend Frank Amedia knows Eric best of all the Trumps. Of his time with Eric he recalls, "I found Eric to be very deliberate, discerning, and thoughtful. He would listen. He would ask very few questions, but they were very good questions. And he was always polite, always gentle, and always very respectful of the office of the pastor."[52]

Reportedly named after the famous jewelry store on Fifth Avenue, Tiffany Trump, born in 1993 shortly before her parents' wedding, is Donald's only child with actress Marla Maples, but she didn't grow up in Manhattan like her half-siblings. Instead, her mother raised her near Los Angeles after divorcing Donald Trump in 1999 when Tiffany was six years old.[53]

Older sister Ivanka used her connections in the fashion world to help Tiffany land an internship at *Vogue*, and she dabbled in the fashion and music industries before graduating from the University of Pennsylvania. She plans to attend Georgetown Law School in Washington, DC.[54]

Barron Trump, Donald's youngest son and only child with wife and First Lady Melania, might be the most like his father of all the Trump children. Melania once told reporters, "He loves to build something and tear it down and build something else....Sometimes I call him little Donald."[55] The nickname "Mini-Donald" appears to have stuck, possibly because Barron is said to prefer suits and ties to sweatpants and he enjoys golfing frequently with his dad.[56]

Frank Amedia recalled a recent period when he got to spend time with Melania and Barron. "I call him little Barron, but I shouldn't because this young boy, who just turned eleven, has got to be five-foot-eight, I believe...and because he's so big [for his age], I think the news media's been very harsh in trying to figure him out. And we need to remember that this is just a little boy that's been thrown into the spotlight."[57]

Amedia went on to say, "He has the same personality as his father and [Eric]....He would bow his head. He was very humble and very well behaved. He listened well, and when he spoke, he was articulate. He said exactly what he wanted to say and didn't mince any words." Amedia said that afterward he was so impressed by Barron that he looked at his wife and said, "Look at what has been done with this young man by his parents."[58]

Barron finished his school year in New York before moving to the White House where he'll be the first son in residence since John F. Kennedy Jr.[59] He is fluent in Slovene like his mother, Melania, who is of Slovenian descent.[60]

Melania is also a former model who worked in Milan and Paris before moving to New York in 1996. She met Donald Trump two years later, and they were married in 2005. Baron was born in 2006, the same year Melania became a US citizen.[61]

Frank Amedia says that "Melania is extremely intelligent. She speaks five languages. She has piercing eyes, and she gets the grip of what's going on right away." He said he has no doubt that she's a compelling force behind the presidency, and from everything he can tell, she is very moved by the things of faith, adding, "She is first and foremost a committed wife and mother."[62]

THE BEST ENDORSEMENT

During my interview with Donald Trump, I had asked him about his child-rearing priorities, his secret of having such a close relationship with his children, and their obvious respect for him. He told me he worked hard to rear them right including telling them, "No Drugs, no alcohol, no cigarettes." As I've mentioned, throughout the course of the election campaign many people commented that the best endorsement of Donald Trump as president was the character of his children, who supported their father every step of the way. His oldest son, Donald Jr., was an especially articulate spokesman. He spoke on behalf of his father's candidacy and defended him against unfounded charges by the media. He was a very capable speaker, and on several occasions he stumped for his father and made a strong impression when he spoke to Christian groups.[63]

Two days before the election, Don Jr. spoke at two Virginia churches, addressing issues of faith and values and speaking about his family's commitment to America. At the Ekklesia USA Hispanic church in Reston, Virginia, he said, "What we hold most dear in our country is in jeopardy—our faith, our freedom, our dreams, our families. I am here to reiterate how important this moment in American history is— and both parties are responsible for the mess we're in."[64]

Thanks mainly to the candidate's very intentional outreach to evangelical and charismatic pastors, Trump and his advisers understood the concerns of conservative Christians who feel they have been marginalized by the left-leaning secular culture, and Trump's son spoke to those concerns. "We as Christians shouldn't be afraid to express our faith, or say 'Merry Christmas,' or stand for our right to free exercise of our religious rights," he said. "These sacred rights are in jeopardy now by politicians who defended the status quo of decline for decades."[65]

After Don Jr.'s remarks at Heritage Baptist Church in Woodbridge, Virginia, delivered on the same day, pastor Mike Edwards told a reporter, "I felt like seeing him in person lets you know just how genuine a young man he is and tells me that his father was just as genuine in the way that he raised him." If Trump and his wife were able to instill such admirable character and strong moral values in their son, Edwards said, that ought to let people know what Donald Trump is all about. Seeing how his children turned out says a lot about how President Trump would deal with the critical concerns of the nation.[66]

"That kind of genuine character doesn't come from just anywhere," Edwards said. "It comes from both a mom and a dad who invest themselves in him. If [Donald Trump] is as real as his son is, then I think he could be well-trusted." When asked if he thought Christians would turn out to support Trump at the polls, the minister said, "What I can be sure of is that the principles that he is espousing for his administration are the principles consistent with what I believe our country needs. So if you're not comfortable voting for a person—vote for principles."[67]

In the next chapter I quote my interview with Trump. I knew I wouldn't have time to rehash what other media were asking him, so I focused on the concerns of conservative Christians, and we talked about the role of faith and family. Trump made it clear that faith was important to him, saying, "Our religion is a very important part of me, and I also think it's a very important part of the country." But then he added that family, for him, is always "number one."[68]

Since little has been written about where Donald Trump stands spiritually, we must look at what he says and does to show the importance of faith in his life. As documented elsewhere in this book, his lifestyle until the past decade was secular and not what evangelical Christians look for in a leader. But I believe as he began to think about life and what he has to accomplish with the time he has left, he gravitated to Christian leaders whom he watched on television, such as Paula White Cain, and as he began to campaign, he surrounded himself with godly counselors and began to articulate a more conservative Christian approach to issues such as protecting the unborn.[69] Evangelical preachers love to use the quote* "Preach the gospel and if necessary use words." With this quote they emphasize that a Christian's actions are all important and, I might add, provide an authentic way to look at what's in a person's heart even if he or she doesn't verbalize it. In this chapter I've tried to show that Trump's children are a reflection of his core values. Next we will examine what Trump believes on numerous issues.

---

* This quote is wrongly attributed to Francis of Assisi, "FactChecker: Misquoting Francis of Assisi," The Gospel Coalition, July 10, 2012, accessed September 8, 2017, https://www.thegospelcoalition.org /article/factchecker-misquoting-francis-of-assisi.

CHAPTER 9

WHAT TRUMP BELIEVES

★★★★★

WHEN THEN-CANDIDATE TRUMP began responding to his critics at all hours of the day and night on Twitter, he surprised and embarrassed a lot of his detractors, tweeting strongly worded comments no one had expected. He had already waged highly publicized verbal battles with Meryl Streep and other celebrities such as Rosie O'Donnell and Oprah Winfrey, but this would be an altogether different kind of war.

With a level of technical savvy uncommon for a man of his generation, Trump was able to counterattack within minutes whenever his opponents made scurrilous charges against him. This was something new, and it delighted his fans and the public at large, even as it infuriated the increasingly volatile resistance. Before long Trump was a serial tweeter, and he provided the media with some riveting sound bites.

Not everyone, of course, was thrilled by this new development. Liberal news organizations such as National Public Radio, the *New York Times*, and the political news company POLITICO compiled exhaustive catalogs of Trump's tweets to show how insensitive, ignorant, and wrongheaded he could be. But they couldn't ignore them, and they followed his tweets faithfully, hoping to catch him in some word or deed that would be his undoing.[1]

Some of his comments and counterattacks were tactless and crude, that's true, often attacking his detractors with salty schoolyard taunts. But Trump's use of Twitter gave him a way around the mainstream media and his political opponents who had been getting free access to the media and were able to insult and demean him with impunity. Suddenly those same people were being held accountable in real time, and news hawks on both sides didn't want to miss a word of it.

Fox News media analyst Howard Kurtz concluded in an online commentary that Trump's use of Twitter had turned out to be "an incredibly valuable tool for him to reach his 31 million followers, amplified by endless media coverage." That was as true during the run-up to the election as it is today, because Trump hasn't slowed his Twitter storm since moving into the White House. At one point he had said there would have been "ZERO chance of winning WH" if he had relied on the "Fake News" being churned out by the mainstream media. But his candid and unfiltered Twitter feeds helped turn the tables on his foes.[2]

Columnist James Lewis notes in the *American Thinker*, an Internet publication, that Donald Trump is the only Republican president since Ronald Reagan to be able to bypass the hostile mainstream media to reach directly into the hearts of the American people. Lewis writes that "conservatives have been under constant assault ever since the 1970s, when the Boomer Left conducted its infamous 'Long March Through the Institutions' guided by Saul Alinsky's little red book."[3]

Alinsky, with whom Hillary Clinton had worked closely early in her career, referred to the American middle class as "the enemy."[4] He preached a virulent form of sedition, more devious and dangerous than anything Machiavelli ever conceived. Leading Democrats, including Barack and Michelle Obama, Hillary Clinton, and Bernie Sanders, were students of Alinsky's methods. They studied his *Rules for Radicals* and took his anarchist philosophy to heart. Yet despite the patently anti-American views of Alinsky and his acolytes in the administration, the media gave them all a pass. And Donald Trump was determined to overcome this.

So, you might ask, if this is what the president is going to be up against, how could he hope to wage a successful campaign against them? How could he possibly succeed in what is clearly a spiritual battle of supernatural proportions? And more to the point, what does this president actually believe?

TRUMP'S CONSERVATIVE AGENDA

At least a partial answer to that question can be found in the planks of the 2016 Republican Party platform, which Donald Trump would affirm and approve. Before the general election every four years delegates from every state and region of the country gather in a central location to declare what the party believes and to outline the issues they wish to pursue and defend when their candidate is elected. The platform committee of the Republican Party met from July 18–21, 2016, in Cleveland, Ohio, to hash out the major issues of the upcoming campaign. Attempting to address the concerns of all 2,742 delegates would not be easy, but there was a broad sense of unity among them on what the delegation and their candidate believed.

Under the chairmanship of Sen. John Barrasso of Wyoming, the draft took a strong traditionalist view of the family, child rearing, and human sexuality and referred to pornography as "a public menace" that is especially harmful to children.[5] It called for a strong military, greater supervision and accountability in the Veterans Administration, as well as a ban on women in combat. As the media were quick to announce, this platform was much more conservative than those of either the McCain or Romney campaigns—as if there was something wrong with that.

The platform proposed that lawmakers look to religion as a guide when making weighty decisions affecting the well-being of the nation and stated that "man-made law must be consistent with our God-given natural rights." It called for a restoration of devotionals and Bible reading in the schools because, as the Founding Fathers had argued, "a good understanding of the Bible" is "indispensable for the development of an educated citizenry."[6]

In one section entitled "A Dangerous World," the language followed Trump's campaign remarks regarding the foreign policy failures of the previous administration. This included a reference to the failings of "the secretary of state"—who, in this case, was Trump's opponent, Hillary Clinton. There were also planks dealing with the need for fair-trade agreements between the United States and major trading partners, such as Canada, Mexico, the European Union, and China. And of course there was language calling for immigration reform, deportation of criminal aliens, and building a wall along the southern border. The basic principles supported by Donald Trump and the party platform can be summed up in a few bullet points:

- Reduce government spending, but take steps to protect Social Security and Medicare.
- Use the reach and influence of government to help create a strong business climate.
- Repeal Obamacare, and develop a more practical and affordable alternative.

- Appoint conservative jurists to the Supreme Court who will defend the Constitution.

- Defund Planned Parenthood, and work to repeal *Roe v. Wade.*

- Grow the economy, and bring outsourced jobs and American overseas businesses back home.

- Cut or substantially reduce funding for the global-warming disaster.

- Protect gun ownership as a constitutional right, but some assault weapons may require special consideration, such as a waiting period prior to purchase.

- On immigration, deport undocumented individuals and criminal aliens.

- Increase the size and authority of the Border Patrol, Immunization and Customs Enforcement (ICE), and Homeland Security.

- Place a freeze on green cards and certain kinds of visas.

- Ban immigrants from certain Muslim-majority countries.

- Build the wall on our southern border (with Trump adding that we will make Mexico pay for it).

- Undo Obama's nuclear deal with Iran, and increase sanctions on terror-sponsoring regimes.

Regarding ISIS and Islamic terrorism—a term, as I've pointed out, Barack Obama refused to use—Trump keeps his position simple: "Wipe them off the face of the earth."[7] In addition, he believes that in combat situations where American soldiers and innocent lives are at stake, waterboarding and other forms of extreme interrogation should be allowed.[8] The lives of innocent civilians and our men and women in uniform are infinitely more precious than the comfort of terrorists.

Trump has also said that military veterans deserve exceptional support during and after their service, and Veterans Affairs must be accountable for the quality of treatment given to soldiers.[9] And finally, when asked by a CNN anchor what he would say to a married lesbian or a married gay man, Trump responded, "I really don't say anything....I'm for traditional marriage."[10]

My Interview With President Trump

I have interviewed a number of presidential candidates, governors, and other politicians in my forty-five-year media career. But interviewing Donald Trump in the midst of his unlikely campaign was markedly different. With Trump, what you see on television is not what you get behind the scenes. There was a humility about the Republican nominee we don't see in the liberal media sound bites. He was still a straight shooter, but his sincerity was far more striking than I would have expected. I asked the kinds of questions I thought most of my readers would want to ask. His answers revealed a confident, determined man who is truly committed to making America great again through principles that honor God rather than defy Him. I am including here a transcript of that interview.

> STRANG: Evangelicals and Catholics have been under attack from the Obama administration for their pro-life convictions and for their desire to be left alone and not forced by the government to accept that which violates their biblical views on marriage. How can you reassure them that you will respect religious liberty?

> TRUMP: Religious liberty is the foundation. Without religious liberty you don't have liberty. I feel that so strongly, and so many other people do, and plenty of politicians do, but they don't express it. Religious liberty is something that I cherish, and you will never be disappointed.

> STRANG: You have said that you would support repealing the Johnson Amendment so that churches and ministries could maintain tax exemption. How would you do that?

> TRUMP: I have started it already because I put it in the platform. You know, a lot of people didn't even know what it was, and now a lot of the pastors and ministers have seen it and can't even believe it. How did this happen in the first place? It's shocking how they were able to take it away. So this is not something that was written from the beginning. This was something written by a strong politician; that's all it is. It

silences people we want to hear. They are afraid to talk about it because they could lose everything.

One of the first things I would do, if I win, is lobby very strongly to have this terminated, and I will tell you something, it won't be hard because your lobbyists are so powerful. Even Democrats can all approve it because it is bigger than men, bigger than women because of the numbers of people, and I'll be able to get it done. I have absolute confidence that I'll be able to get it done.

STRANG: As president, whom will you reach out to for spiritual counsel, and why? Do you feel the president needs God's wisdom and guidance?

TRUMP: I have many friends within the community. One of them who's been so incredible is Franklin Graham—he's been amazing, really terrific. So we're close to Franklin. Pastor [Robert] Jeffress has been terrific. Paula White has been incredible. So many, so many.

I really like to stay with people who have been loyal because they were here in the beginning when this was a very, very little, tiny flame, and they were here when everyone else was saying, "Well, you can't beat seventeen [Republican candidates]." The actual number was eighteen if you include Gilmore. How do you beat sixteen seasoned politicians? So they were there at the beginning.

STRANG: You talked about the rough-and-tumble campaign against seventeen candidates and so forth. Yet you have won over the evangelical vote. How has this whole process changed you spiritually?

TRUMP: Well, I can tell you I've always been spiritual, but I really appreciate the Evangelicals because they really support me. When somebody supports you, you feel pretty good about it, and I would go into a very evangelical state and people say, "Oh, gee, I won't win that state." I ended up winning in a landslide because I had tremendous support. Did you see the polls that people are leaving and supporting Trump over other people whom, in theory, they could have supported very easily? They didn't. So I think the fact that I had the tremendous support from the Evangelicals meant a lot to me and will mean a lot to me in the future.

STRANG: You've said that you supported Israel's claim that Jerusalem is the capital. Many Evangelicals are very strong supporters of Israel. How would your policies toward Israel differ from your opponent's?

TRUMP: Well, for one thing, I support Israel. I don't think Obama supports Israel. I think he's the worst thing that's ever happened to Israel. The Iran deal is a disaster for Israel, and I'm very supportive of Israel and have tremendous relationships in Israel and have a son-in-law who's Jewish, married to my daughter. I will be very strongly in favor of Israel.

STRANG: In the Book of Deuteronomy it says to be kind to the stranger in the land. How would that scripture guide policy in your administration?

TRUMP: Well, I think that's good, but I think we have to be careful at the same time. We are allowing people to come into the country, and we don't know anything about them. There is no paperwork; there's no documentation. You see what's going on in Germany, France, and many other places where they have an open-door policy, and it could go on here too. We've allowed thousands and thousands of people into our country, and we have no idea who they are.

At the same time, we want to build safe havens, and we want to get the Gulf states to fund the money because it's a tremendous amount of money. So we want to take care of people, but we can't allow them in because we just don't know who they are. You see what happened in San Bernardino; you see what happened in Orlando, right here; you see what happened with the World Trade Center. We can look all over to see what has happened in France, Nice, Germany. We have enough problems. We can't do that.

STRANG: Many believe our nation was founded on Judeo-Christian values. In our secular society a lot of people now discount that influence. Do you believe that America was founded on Judeo-Christian principles?

TRUMP: I think it was. I think when I look at football coaches who were fired because they held a prayer on the field, it's absolutely terrible. I think it is terrible to see so many things happening that are different from what our country used to be. So our religion is a very important part of me, and I also think it's a very important part of the country.

STRANG: What is the most important thing in your life?

TRUMP: Well, you always have to say family. Family is the most important thing from that standpoint. Religion is very important, but I'm assuming you are not talking about religion or family, but those two things are very important. Belief is very important, but you would always have to put family as number one.

STRANG: You have a very strong bond with your children. What has been the secret of your having such a close relationship with your children and their obvious respect for you?

TRUMP: I worked very hard when it came to my children, and one of the things I would tell them all the time is, "No drugs, no alcohol, no cigarettes." I have friends who have very smart children. But their children are hooked on drugs or alcohol. I added cigarettes because of the health thing. It's just easier if you don't smoke. I was lucky enough not to smoke. I have friends that can't get off, and they're strong people, but if you've never started, it's not a problem. That's a big factor, the fact that they're not hooked, but you never know; it's a fragile world, so who knows what happened.

STRANG: Give us some advice as we tell your story. Talk to our readers like you're encouraging the crowd, except in front of the church.

TRUMP: Well, I'm going to do a great job. I'm going to get the job done. I'm going to do a great job for religion and for

The election of Donald Trump was not expected, and some thanked God for answering their prayers (page 17). I was in the crowd in Washington, DC, on January 20, 2017, when he took the oath of office with his hand on two Bibles—one given to him by his mother two days before his ninth birthday and one used by Abraham Lincoln when he took the oath of office in 1861.

Don Hogan Charles / The New York Times / Redux

Dr. Norman Vincent Peale wrote this about the young businessman: "Donald Trump's career has only just begun, but what a beginning. Surely he is one of America's top positive thinkers and positive doers" (page 97).

ZUMA Press Inc. / Alamy

ABOVE: Dr. Norman Vincent Peale (far right) was once Trump's pastor and greatly influenced him through his sermons and book *The Power of Positive Thinking* (page 96). In this 1988 photo Trump is also shown with his first wife, Ivana, and Peale's wife, Ruth Stafford Peale.

LEFT: Donald Trump greatly admired his father, Fred (page 97). His mother, Mary Anne, ensured all her children were raised Presbyterian. This 1992 photo also includes Trump's siblings Maryanne (far right), Robert (far left), and Elizabeth. Fred Jr. died in 1981.

President Trump is close to his family (page 97). This photo, taken when Trump announced his presidential bid, in June 2015, shows (from left) son Eric and his wife, Lara; nine-year-old son, Barron; wife, Melania; Vanessa and son Don Jr. with their two oldest children, Kai and Donald III; daughter Ivanka and her husband, Jared Kushner; and daughter Tiffany.

Dr. Jerry Falwell Jr., president of Liberty University, was an early Trump supporter. He is shown here with President Trump when he visited Liberty University on May 13, 2017 (page 138).

Donald Trump found friends in the black community, such as Apostle Wayne T. Jackson of Great Faith Ministries International in Detroit, Michigan, who gave Trump a Jewish prayer shawl (page 80). After his victory Trump invited Jackson to pray at his inauguration.

Trump generated massive crowds such as the one at this rally at the US Bank Arena in Cincinnati, Ohio, on October 13, 2016, four weeks before he carried Ohio. At a similar rally in Youngstown, Ohio, before Super Tuesday, Frank Amedia gave Trump a prophetic word that he would win the Republican nomination (page 127).

Mark Wallheiser / Getty Images

Some Evangelicals believed that God was raising up Trump, implied by this sign held at a rally on August 21, 2015, that drew thirty thousand people to Ladd-Peebles Stadium in Mobile, Alabama (page 154).

Official White House photo / Shealah Craighead

Dr. Alveda King, niece of Dr. Martin Luther King Jr., says she prays for but does not endorse candidates. However, she was often photographed with Trump and said publicly she was glad he won (page 80).

I took this selfie with Amy and Robert Jeffress at the election night party in New York to send to my wife, Joy, who loves his television program—never thinking I'd publish it. Jeffress was one of the first evangelical leaders to back Trump (page 21).

After President Trump nominated Judge Neil M. Gorsuch to the Supreme Court, he is shown praying with Gorsuch and his wife, Marie Louise; Trump's sons Donald Jr. and Eric; Vice President Mike Pence and his wife, Karen; Reince Priebus; Maureen Scalia, widow of Antonin Scalia; and her son Paul, a Catholic priest (page 138).

Trump enjoys a light moment with a few members of his Faith Advisory Board (from left): pastors Robert Jeffress, Mark Burns, Ronnie Floyd, and Rodney and Adonica Howard-Browne, and author Johnnie Moore (page 64).

This photo, taken by pastor Rodney Howard-Browne in the Oval Office on July 10, 2017, went viral. Leaders say Evangelicals must lift up the president in prayer so he will be able to withstand the enormous opposition he has received (page 64).

President Trump and the First Lady, pictured here with Israeli President Reuven Rivlin and his wife, Nechama, showed support for Israel during his visit to the nation in May 2017 (page 87).

Trump contacted Paula White Cain in 2003 after watching her television show, and a friendship developed. In 2012 he asked her to assemble a group of ministers who "know how to pray" (page 79), as he was deciding whether to run for president. Paula connected him to other evangelical leaders (page 61). She also prayed at the inauguration.

On the National Day of Prayer, just three months into his term, President Trump chose to announce an executive order to help neutralize the effect of the so-called Johnson Amendment and promote free speech and religious liberty (page 41).

On Donald Trump's first international trip he showed his support for Israel by visiting Jerusalem and becoming the first sitting US president to visit the Western Wall, where he placed prayers into the cracks and reportedly prayed for wisdom from God (page 87).

During the Trumps' visit to the Vatican on May 24, 2017, Pope Francis blessed a rosary belonging to First Lady Melania Trump, who is Roman Catholic (page 130).

Before attending the G20 summit in Germany, President Trump visited Poland, where his remarks were met with warm applause and chants of "Donald Trump! Donald Trump!" (page 140). He and the First Lady pose here with Polish President Andrzej Duda and his wife, Agata Kornhauser-Duda.

The epilogue (page 179) tells of a Catholic holy man in Loreto, Italy—the late Thomas Zimmer—who predicted in the 1980s that God would use businessman Donald Trump to turn America to God. The book documents four other prophecies back to 2007 that Donald Trump would be elected president (page 83).

Evangelicals. I am going to do a great job, and that's why we got a standing ovation from the pastors who don't give much for standing ovations because they've heard a lot of people speak, so that was a great honor, but I will do a great job. I will get the job done, and I'll get it done properly, and it will be a great thing for the Evangelicals.

FOR SUCH A TIME AS THIS

After that interview I understood that Donald Trump believes America remains a great country even though we've drifted away from the clear vision of the founders. He possesses an undeniable faith in America, and I realized that a big reason for that is his lifelong faith in God.

The week before Florida's Super Tuesday on March 15, 2016, my dear friend Frank Amedia told me he was meditating on all these things prior to the election and "seeking the Lord's instructions" concerning whether or not Donald Trump was the man God had chosen as our leader. As he was praying, Frank felt the Lord speak to him and realized he was being given what Charismatics call "a prophetic word." Since he was participating in a rally the next day, he believed the Lord would give him an opportunity to give it to the candidate. But that didn't happen. Trump was whisked off to his next campaign stop before Frank could hand him the written "word." He was disappointed but kept believing that if the Lord wanted Trump to receive the message, a way would open up.

The next day Trump's campaign called to say Trump had canceled a planned trip to Florida and would deliver his final speech before Super Tuesday in Frank's hometown of Youngstown, Ohio, and Frank was asked to open the rally as he had done before. "You can imagine my awe of the wonder and fear of the Lord as I realized that almighty God had intervened to change the schedule so that the word could be delivered," Frank told me in an interview for this book. This time he texted Corey Lewandowski, Trump's national campaign manager at the time, and told him he had good news that he needed to put into the hands of Trump. So Lewandowski arranged to meet Frank offstage during the rally. As Trump took the stage, Frank handed Lewandowski two envelopes—one with his own name on it and one with Donald Trump's name, with the words: "Please open and read this on your way home to Palm Beach when you are alone and quiet."

I know this to be true because Frank told me at the time, emphasizing that it should be kept confidential until after the election. Here's what the word said: "Mr. Trump, you will surely win the Republican nomination. That is a foregone conclusion even as the Lord has spoken." Mind you, this was before Super Tuesday. "And Sir," the word continued, "if you humble yourself before the Lord, not man, but before the Lord, you shall become the next president of the United States. Mr. President, what will make this a great nation again, is if we make God great again in our nation." Then Frank cited Zechariah 4:6 (KJV), which says, "Not by might, nor by power, but by my spirit, saith the LORD of hosts."

Did Trump read the word in the quietness of his own airplane? We may never know, but Frank believes he did because a shift took place shortly after that. Months later when the *Access Hollywood* tapes came out and many felt Trump's chances of winning were lost, Frank said he knew God used that message to humble the man who once said he'd never done anything for which he needed to ask forgiveness.

A surprising episode that was briefly discussed on the Biography Channel's hour-long documentary about the life of Donald Trump related that a helicopter crash on October 10, 1989, took the lives of three of Trump's senior executives. Alan Greenberg, a banker with Bear-Stearns and a Trump associate at the time, said, "He also talks a lot about fate. I think that he was supposed to go on that trip and he didn't at the last minute, for whatever reason. So I think he appreciated how lucky he was. He also, of course, appreciated how unfortunate it was for those people and their families. But he was shaken by it."[11]

Hearing about that event, my first thought was that this tragic accident in 1989 was a warning to Donald Trump at a time when everything around him was falling apart. His casinos, one of his hotels, his marriage to Ivana, and other things were crashing all around him, and the chaos would last well into the 1990s.[12] Those tragedies were surely a wake-up call, reminding Mr. Trump that he was mortal, but it was also clear that he had been miraculously spared. Today I believe that event was also part of God's plan, not only to wake him up but also to prepare Donald Trump for the momentous task he would be given at a later time as president of the United States.

I'm convinced the policies we see unfolding now, both here and abroad, are a working out of President Trump's belief that he has been put here at this time for a special purpose. But more important than simply fulfilling a list of campaign pledges, he understands that the United States of America is a unique and a uniquely privileged nation. Our national motto proclaims, "In God We Trust," which first appeared in 1864 on a two-cent coin and has appeared on every coin and every piece of our currency since 1964. Our founders never hesitated to affirm their belief that God brought us to this continent for a reason, and I believe that's why this president made the spiritual interests of the American people such a major focus of his campaign.

Trump's campaign literature said "Putting America first means special interests no longer get to sell out our country for their own personal gain. It means we no longer enter multinational agreements that surrender our sovereignty. It means we no longer funnel billions of American dollars to countries that hate us. It means we no longer let just anyone pour over our border."[13] Strong language, but the president made no apologies for those words. He believes in America, and he believes that God has a purpose and a plan for America.

The boldness of Trump's message was something that appealed to actor Stephen Baldwin, the brother of the outspoken Hollywood actor who has caricatured Trump on *Saturday Night Live*. Unlike his brother, Baldwin supports Donald Trump because he believes Trump is honest and he's unafraid to say what he believes, regardless of the consequences. Even though Trump fired him on *Celebrity Apprentice* in 2013, Baldwin believes Trump's war on political correctness is good for the country. Politicians are so afraid they may offend some minority, he says, they refuse to speak about issues that need to be debated. "I honestly really think voters and Americans are looking at this guy saying it's refreshing to hear somebody not be a wuss, not be a politician and really say what they think."[14]

In February 2017 the president said what he meant to a joint session of Congress, repeating the general theme of his Ohio speech. He said, "My job is not to represent the world. My job is to represent the United States of America."[15] During the hour-long address the president outlined policy issues he had talked about throughout the campaign. He spoke about revising our policies on global trade in order to give greater support and leverage to American companies.

He asked for Congress to deal with the problems of illegal immigration and pass legislation to build the wall on our southern border. "We've defended the borders of other nations," he said, "while leaving our own borders wide open for anyone to cross." And he called on Congress to repeal Obamacare, which had become an unsustainable drain on the economy. He spoke about defeating "radical Islamic terrorism" and rebuilding the military, and he is taking that message abroad.[16]

Trump said he wanted to begin his presidency with a series of one-on-one conversations with world leaders, particularly heads of state in Europe and the Middle East. He wanted to solidify relations with America's allies and clarify the priorities of US foreign policy. When he made his first international diplomatic tour to those nations, from May 19–27, 2017, he chose to make his first three stops at the capitals of the world's three great religions. Not only are these some of the most volatile hot spots in the world today, but they are the birthplace of the three Abrahamic religions.

His first stop was the Muslim summit in Saudi Arabia, where the president was greeted by leaders from fifty Muslim countries and applauded for his statements about Iran—the world's number one supporter of Islamic terrorism. On the second leg of the tour Trump met with Israeli Prime Minister Benjamin Netanyahu in Jerusalem, and the following day he made the short trip to Bethlehem, where he spoke with Palestinian leader Mahmoud Abbas.[17]

Trump has said on numerous occasions that the US Embassy ought to be in the capital city of Jerusalem rather than Tel Aviv, but that conversation would not happen on this trip. He did, however, make a visit to the Church of the Holy Sepulchre in Jerusalem's Old City, where Jesus was crucified, and went to the Western Wall, where he prayed and placed a written prayer in a crack of the wall, as described in chapter 7.[18]

From there the entourage flew to Vatican City for an audience with Pope Francis. While there his wife, Melania, spoke about her own Catholic faith and received a papal blessing.[19] In Brussels Trump attended a NATO summit and made a visit to the European Union headquarters, and he met the newly elected French president, Emmanuel Macron. From there they flew south to Sicily, where the president attended the G7 summit, and then wrapped up the trip with a speech and warm personal greetings from both Donald and Melania Trump for the American and allied military personnel serving at Signoella air base.[20]

We know for sure as we look at the life of this man that he is an extraordinary and remarkably capable individual. He hardly sleeps. His aides can barely keep up with him. He has never smoked, he doesn't drink alcohol, and he has never used drugs. He is driven to achieve great things, to build great buildings, and he is determined to make America great again. These are not small ambitions, and he is not a small man by any measure. He towers over almost everyone, and he is the center of attention whenever he enters the room. But in person, as I learned during my interview with him, he is kind and gentle and genuinely interested in what people have to say. He even offered to get me a bottle of water as we were beginning the interview.

I discovered that Donald Trump is not the overwhelming personality we've seen on the evening news. Yes, he's passionate, he's outspoken, and he's a dynamic achiever, but he is also smart, sincere, and a man of faith. We've examined how that came to be and how he has stood up to the storm of controversy that surrounds him. Now let's look at what he calls American values and how he has articulated his political priorities.

CHAPTER 10

POLITICAL PRIORITIES

★★★★★

ONALD TRUMP WAS swept into office by an electorate who were deeply dissatisfied with the direction the country had been going for a very long time. Evangelical Christians, in particular ,wanted a president who would take their concerns seriously. They wanted someone who understood their issues, and they wanted a president who would not just talk the talk, boasting of his or her religious beliefs on the campaign trail, but walk the walk when it was time to defend our interests in Congress, the courts, and the media.

Barack Obama had never done any of those things, and his flip-flop on gay marriage was a perfect example of the kind of dishonesty that was energizing Evangelicals who wanted things in Washington to change. During two national political campaigns Obama had claimed to believe in traditional marriage. In his 2004 campaign for the US Senate he told an audience in Springfield, Illinois, "I have been very clear on this. I have said I am not a supporter of gay marriage. I think the term *marriage* itself has strong religious roots and a strong tradition that means something special to people in this country."[1]

Four years later during his 2008 presidential campaign he said essentially the same thing. Speaking at a Civil Forum on the Presidency sponsored by pastor Rick Warren's Saddleback Church, he said marriage is a sacred bond between a man and a woman. "Now, for me as a Christian," Obama said, "it is also a sacred union. God's in the mix."[2] Over the next four years as the issue was being hotly debated and discussed in the press, Obama was less clear, often indistinct, seeming to shift one way and then the other. Then during an interview on ABC's *Good Morning America* on May 9, 2012, he told the world, "I've been going through an evolution on this issue....I've just concluded that for me personally it is important for me to go ahead and affirm that I think same-sex couples should be able to get married."[3]

In fact, this was just one more example of the Obama administration's policy of deception. Obama campaign adviser David Axelrod, in his autobiography published in 2015, reported that the president had deliberately misled the country about his views on this issue because it was politically expedient to appear to be pro-family. He had been in favor of gay marriage all along, but knowing that a large percentage of his core constituency in the black community was opposed to it, Obama decided he would claim to support traditional marriage for a while, knowing he could claim to have a sudden change of heart later on.[4] So he did, and it was precisely the sort of duplicity conservative voters were sick and tired of from their so-called leaders.

Although the president stressed that he had reached a purely personal decision on the matter, almost immediately the debate seemed to be settled. The gay community and the mainstream media declared victory, and the federal government made a complete pivot to the left, transforming codes and regulations to show that homosexual marriage was legal and in every way compatible with traditional marriage. Laws would be altered in every city and town, and before long open war was declared on any business or individual who refused to serve gay couples. Bakers, florists, and wedding planners who had moral or religious scruples were threatened, sued, driven out of business, and mocked in the media as bigots and homophobes.

STANDING FOR AMERICAN VALUES

When actor Jon Voight introduced Donald Trump at the 2016 Values Voter Summit in Washington, DC, he said he had come to introduce a candidate who may not be everybody's first choice for president, but he believed Trump was someone who spoke the truth and stuck by his word. Voight told the crowd about the joy he had felt on receiving a blessing from Mother Teresa and later playing the part of Pope John Paul II in a television miniseries. He compared the sense of hope he felt then with the darkness and depression the country had experienced over the previous eight years.[5]

We know the difference between good and bad, right and wrong, he said. But too many politicians seem to have lost their ability to tell the difference. He said, "I feel there is a dark cloud over the country now. And we are all witness to Hillary Clinton's lies and corruption. We are witness to President Obama covering every false move that she makes and making them appear right. And we are witness to our so-called football heroes, that are supposed to set examples for our young children, that mock our national anthem."[6]

Then he went on to say, "My heart aches watching Donald Trump day after day, pouring his heart out, telling the American people what he wants to do to save the nation. How can anyone doubt his sincerity? I can only feel, if God allows truth to be said and heard, that we will see Donald Trump the next president of this great America. And he will lift the dark cloud that hovers over us now."[7]

When then-candidate Trump went to the platform, he thanked Jon Voight, and he thanked the men and women who had come out to support his campaign, saying, "Our media culture often mocks and demeans people of faith. All the time I hear from concerned parents how much harder it is for a Christian family to raise their children in today's media environment.

"Your values of love, charity, and faith built this nation," he said. "So how can it be that our media treats people of faith so poorly? One of the reasons is that our politicians have really abandoned you to a large extent.... So let me state this right up front: A Trump administration, our Christian heritage will be cherished, protected, defended... and that includes religious liberty." At that point the crowd erupted with cheers and applause. He also said that "it will be our faith in God and His teachings, and in each other, that will lead us back to unity."[8]

In the course of his speech Trump said he would make four promises to people of faith. First, he said he would repeal the Johnson Amendment, which he called a "massive penalty" that must be reversed. "The first thing we have to do," he said, "is give our churches their voice back." Second, he said his administration would allocate $130 billion for school choice. School choice offers poverty-stricken children, primarily African American and Hispanic, alternatives to failing inner-city schools. He promised to create a $20 billion federal block grant, then work with the states to reallocate funds from existing education budgets for school choice. This would be the cornerstone of "a new civil rights agenda for our time," he said. Funding would then be available to private schools, religious schools, charter schools, and magnet schools, as well as home schools.[9]

Third, he would appoint conservative justices such as Antonin Scalia to the Supreme Court. The next president would be positioned to appoint Scalia's successor, and possibly as many as four more, which Trump called one of the most important issues any president could face, second only to military defense. He said, "We reject judges who rewrite the Constitution to impose their own personal views on three hundred million–plus Americans." He said, "You pick the wrong people, and you have a country that is no longer your country."[10]

Fourth, he said his administration would stop the genocide of Christians in the Middle East. "ISIS is hunting down and exterminating what it calls 'the nation of the cross.'" He said, "ISIS is carrying out a genocide against Christians in the Middle East. We cannot let this evil continue." His administration, he said, would use all the resources at its disposal, including our military forces, cyber warfare, financial pressure, and other assets to create "safe zones in the region" for Christians and then to destroy "radical Islamic terrorism." Those are words President Obama had never spoken, he pointed out, "and words that Hillary Clinton won't use."[11]

AN APPEAL TO PROVIDENCE

Our next indication that Donald Trump's administration would be very different from that of Obama came on Inauguration Day. The tradition of prayers during inaugural ceremonies dates back to the very beginning of this country when President George Washington prayed with the members of his cabinet during post-inaugural worship at St. Paul's Chapel in New York.[12] Now, and ever since the inauguration of Franklin Roosevelt in 1937, ministers are invited to offer prayers for divine guidance for the nation's presidents during the swearing-in ceremony.[13] At Donald Trump's inauguration, on January 20, 2017, four evangelical ministers, a Jewish rabbi, and a Catholic archbishop prayed for the president and the United States of America. As an indication of his support for religious diversity, the president invited ministers representing diverse racial and ethnic communities.[14]

Cardinal Timothy Dolan, the archbishop of New York, was the first Catholic priest to participate in an inaugural ceremony since the Jimmy Carter presidency in 1977. He was followed by Rev. Samuel Rodriguez, an ordained Assemblies of God minister and president of the National Hispanic Christian Leadership Conference, and then Paula White Cain, pastor of the New Destiny Christian Center near Orlando and also one of Trump's spiritual advisers. As I mentioned earlier, she is the first female minister to lead a prayer at an inauguration.[15]

Next was Rabbi Marvin Hier, the founder of the Simon Wiesenthal Center, a Jewish human rights organization, who provided an invocation. Rev. Franklin Graham, president of the Billy Graham Evangelistic Association and Samaritan's Purse and son of the beloved evangelist Billy Graham, offered his comments just as a light rain began to fall. He noted that rain is considered a blessing in the Bible, and he expressed the possibility that the rain this day was a sign of God's blessing on the inauguration. Bishop Wayne T. Jackson, pastor of Great Faith Ministries International in Detroit, Michigan, gave the benediction.[16]

Several prayers specifically ended "in the name of Jesus," something often excluded in these kinds of settings.[17] This was the largest number of prayers ever offered at an inauguration- and an indication that the new president understood the importance of faith to the people of this country. He wanted the occasion to be a statement of his administration's support for religious freedom.

In his tribute to America's peacekeepers, he said, "We will be protected by the great men and women of our military and law enforcement and, most importantly, we are protected by God."[18]

Addressing the importance of national unity, he said that "we all salute the same great American flag. And whether a child is born in the urban sprawl of Detroit or the windswept plains of Nebraska, they look up at the same night sky, they fill their heart with the same dreams, and they are infused with the breath of life by the same almighty Creator." Then, at the end of the speech, he concluded with the words that have now become a tradition, saying, "God bless you, and God bless America."[19]

Clearly Donald Trump had tapped into the heartfelt beliefs and emotions of his supporters. He understood their concerns, and he was listening to their cries for help. As a result, his ratings were over 80 percent with evangelical voters during the election, and they have remained high ever since. Despite speculation from some quarters that Trump's evangelical support doesn't reflect actual churchgoers, a Pew poll confirms that the Christian community was the difference in this election.[20]

Three-quarters of poll respondents said they intended to vote for him. Among white Evangelicals, regular churchgoers are the most supportive of Trump, and fully 77 percent of white Evangelicals who are registered to vote and who attend church at least once a month say they support the president. Among those who attend church weekly, his support is 78 percent. At the one-hundred-day mark of his presidency, 78 percent of white evangelical Protestants approved of the way Donald Trump was handling his job.[21]

When he spoke to the graduates of Liberty University in May 2017, Trump had said, "In America we don't worship government, we worship God." He also said, "We don't need a lecture from Washington on how to lead our lives." Then he promised, "As long as I am your president, no one is ever going to stop you from practicing your faith or from preaching what's in your heart."[22] By that time he had already signed the "Religious Liberty" executive order, which included the Johnson Amendment and conscience protections for organizations such as the Little Sisters.[23] He had also nominated and gained the successful appointment of a conservative, pro-life Supreme Court justice—Judge Neil M. Gorsuch, who was sworn in on April 10, 2017.[24]

Four times during his commencement address Trump made reference to Scripture and faith in God.[25]

KNOWING WHO YOUR FRIENDS ARE

To make good on his promises and begin the process of undoing the disastrous policies of the Obama administration, the new president would have to tackle some of the most intractable foreign policy challenges the nation has ever faced. How do we deal with a rogue nation such as North Korea and threats of a nuclear holocaust engineered by a certifiable madman? How do we untangle the diplomatic and military mess created by Obama's policies in Syria, Iraq, and Afghanistan?

Perhaps most challenging would be mobilizing the political and military resources needed to neutralize the malignant growth of ISIS and radical Islamic terrorism that has destabilized the entire world. America had been taking a beating in all these areas for years, but Trump was convinced we could handle them all once we began operating from a position of strength rather than the weak-kneed approach the government had taken over the previous eight years.

Since taking office in January 2017, President Trump has begun that process by taking a position of strength with the European Union (EU). The president demanded that either members of the North Atlantic Treaty Organization (NATO) pay their fair share of the military and administrative costs of the organization or the United States would pull out of the agreement. There was immediate blowback from EU officials and the press in both Europe and America, but within weeks every NATO member nation announced plans to comply. Trump also said the United States would review terms of our partnership in the North American Free Trade Agreement (NAFTA), which had put American business interests in a weakened posture when dealing with the neighboring nations of Mexico and Canada. We would continue the relationship, he said, so long as American businesses are allowed to compete on an open and fair basis.

On June 16, 2017, the president unilaterally closed the open-door policy with Cuba the Obama administration established in 2014. In doing so, he made it clear that America would no longer provide financial or political cover for the Communist dictatorship. While Cuban Americans would be allowed to travel to the island, Trump pointed out that human rights abuses under Cuban president Raúl Castro had not improved since the Obama thaw began. Cuban dissidents in Miami enthusiastically supported Trump's announcement, saying he was right to apply pressure to the Castro regime.[26]

More troublesome, however, would be the challenge of dealing with the ongoing conflict between Israel and its neighbors in the Middle East. Trump's long friendship with Prime Minister Benjamin Netanyahu and his commitment to Israeli autonomy would be a dramatic change from what the *Washington Post* called "the frosty relationship, sometimes devolving into outright hostility, between former President Barack Obama and Netanyahu." But that in itself would not be enough.[27]

Michael Makovsky, chief executive of the Jewish Institute for National Security of America, has said that Trump's Israel policy is a sea-change from Obama's hostility toward Israel, sending a strong signal of "a new, far better bilateral political relationship."[28] During his five-nation international tour in May 2017, Trump took steps to build on that relationship, but also to maintain the region's delicate balance by meeting with Palestinian leader Mahmoud Abbas in the Muslim-controlled town of Bethlehem, to make it clear that America would listen to all sides.

Trump has made it clear he understands the depth of Christian commitment to the nation of Israel. That ancient land is the soil where our spiritual heritage was conceived. My friend and *700 Club* host Pat Robertson provided a memorable perspective on the Christian view of the Holy Land in a speech he delivered at the Herzliya Conference in Jerusalem back in 2003. He said, "Mere political rhetoric does not account for the profound devotion to Israel that exists in the hearts of tens of millions of evangelical Christians." The Bible makes it clear, he said, that the land of Israel is a sacred place. "The Holy City of

Jerusalem is our spiritual capital." He added that "the continuation of Jewish sovereignty over the Holy Land is a further bulwark to us that the God of the Bible exists and that His Word is true."[29]

While Christian support for Israel remains strong for all the reasons Robertson explained to the Israeli audience, political decisions concerning the region are always volatile, which is why President Trump promised the leaders of both Israel and Palestine that the United States would strive to forge a workable compromise. Any agreement, he said, must begin by unraveling the Obama administration's nuclear deal with Iran, which not only would be beneficial for both Arabs and Jews, but it was the main concern expressed by Prime Minister Netanyahu in his conversation with the American president three months earlier.

DEFENDING WESTERN CIVILIZATION

During the week of July 5, 2017, while anticapitalist thugs and anarchists were attempting to wreak havoc on the G20 Summit of world leaders and finance ministers meeting in Hamburg, Germany, President Trump made a visit to the historic Krasiński Square, in the heart of Warsaw, Poland. He had come to one of the most heroic and war-torn nations in Europe to deliver a powerful address in support of faith, freedom, and the survival of Western civilization. Before a crowd of several thousand citizens and scores of diplomats and government officials, the president said the people of Poland and the West are proclaiming today, as they have done for centuries, "We want God!"[30]

As the president spoke, it was immediately apparent that this was not going to be a routine political address. He spoke forcefully with no hesitation and no off-the-cuff remarks. "Through four decades of communist rule," he said, "Poland and the other captive nations of Europe endured a brutal campaign to demolish freedom, your faith, your laws, your history, your identity—indeed the very essence of your culture and your humanity. Yet through it all you never lost that spirit. Your oppressors tried to break you, but Poland could not be broken." The Poles refused to bend to Nazi occupation and Soviet tyranny, buoyed by their fearless national pride and unflagging faith in God. Throughout his remarks the crowds chanted continually, "Donald Trump, Donald Trump," and, "USA, USA," in loud and enthusiastic support of the president's message.[31]

Trump recalled some of the most dramatic episodes of Polish history, including the events of June 2, 1979, when Poles gathered in Warsaw's

Victory Square for Mass with the first Polish Pope, John Paul II. The turmoil that brought the Polish labor leader and hero Lech Walesa to international fame was first and foremost a spiritual revolution aimed at freeing the Polish people from the iron shackles of Communism. The enormous crowds that assembled for that Mass were sending a message to their Soviet oppressors and the whole world, Trump said, and the world was listening. "They must have known it at that exact moment during Pope John Paul II's sermon when a million Polish men, women, and children suddenly raised their voices in a single prayer. A million Polish people did not ask for wealth. They did not ask for privilege. Instead, one million Poles sang three simple words: 'We want God.'"[32]

Lech Walesa, who was seated in the front row just a few yards from where Trump was speaking, rose and saluted the president, and the crowds roared their gratitude. "For Americans," Trump continued, "Poland has been a symbol of hope since the beginning of our nation. Polish heroes and American patriots fought side by side in our War of Independence and in many wars that followed. Our soldiers still serve together today in Afghanistan and Iraq, combating the enemies of all civilization."[33]

Then, speaking directly about the threat of Islamic terrorists, he said, "We are fighting hard against radical Islamic terrorism, and we will prevail. We cannot accept those who reject our values and who use hatred to justify violence against the innocent. Today the West is also confronted by the powers that seek to test our will, undermine our confidence, and challenge our interests. To meet new forms of aggression, including propaganda, financial crimes, and cyber warfare, we must adapt our alliance to compete effectively in new ways and on all new battlefields."[34]

In one of his most impassioned statements, the president reminded his audience around the world of the great achievements of Christian Europe and Christian America, saying, "Americans will never forget. The nations of Europe will never forget. We are the fastest and the greatest community. There is nothing like our community of nations. The world has never known anything like our community of nations. We write symphonies. We pursue innovation. We celebrate our ancient heroes, embrace our timeless traditions and customs, and always seek to explore and discover brand-new frontiers."[35]

As the audience thundered their appreciation, the president

continued, "We reward brilliance. We strive for excellence, and cherish inspiring works of art that honor God. We treasure the rule of law and protect the right to free speech and free expression." The president paused briefly, but the roar continued as he said, "We empower women as pillars of our society and of our success. We put faith and family, not government and bureaucracy, at the center of our lives. And we debate everything. We challenge everything. We seek to know everything so that we can better know ourselves. And above all, we value the dignity of every human life, protect the rights of every person, and share the hope of every soul to live in freedom. That is who we are. Those are the priceless ties that bind us together as nations, as allies, and as a civilization."[36]

"What we have, what we inherited from our—and you know this better than anybody, and you see it today with this incredible group of people—what we've inherited from our ancestors has never existed to this extent before. And if we fail to preserve it, it will never, ever exist again. So we cannot fail." Then, with cheers resounding all around him, he said, "As I stand here today before this incredible crowd, this faithful nation, we can still hear those voices that echo through history. Their message is as true today as ever. The people of Poland, the people of America, and the people of Europe still cry out 'We want God.'"[37]

This was undoubtedly the most powerful speech Trump has given, and the mainstream media took notice. While the liberal *Washington Post* called it a "dark and provocative address with nationalist overtones," the editors of the conservative Breitbart news website called the speech "The Emerging Trump Doctrine: The Defense of the West and Judeo-Christian Civilization." And no one who heard those words and saw the reaction of the crowds could doubt that's exactly what it was.[38]

For anyone who has ever asked the question "What does Donald Trump really believe?" this was the answer millions had been hoping for. For too long the forces of darkness have tried to destroy the emblems of our Christian history, to silence the voice of God, and drive the faithful underground and out of sight. But on this day the president of the United States was saying to the voices of insurrection and hatred, "You will fail." And he said, "Our values will prevail, our people will thrive, and our civilization will triumph."[39]

AMERICA'S PLACE IN THE WORLD

The president has said repeatedly that the policy of his administration will be focused on American interests and America's national security. The terrorist bombings in Paris, London, Berlin, and cities all across Europe awakened the world to the face of evil, and terrorist incidents in this country have made it clear that the politically correct approach of the last eight years can no longer be tolerated.

Trump prioritizes defeating ISIS and radical Islamic terrorists, and his administration has taken steps to work with our allies to cut off funding for terrorist groups, to expand intelligence gathering, to use cyber warfare to disrupt and disable the enemy's propaganda and recruiting efforts, and to annihilate enemy combatants on the battlefield. Supporting all these efforts, the president has brought new leadership on board to begin the process of rebuilding the American military.

According to Pentagon sources, the US naval fleet has been cut nearly in half under Obama, from more than 500 ships in 1991 to just 275 in 2016. The US Air Force is roughly one-third smaller than it was in 1991, and contracts for essential aircraft and material were canceled under Obama. Meanwhile the US Army has undergone a 25 percent reduction in forces and suffered draconian cuts in its budget. President Trump has used the expression made popular during the Reagan years, "Peace through strength," and he has begun the process of undoing Obama-era orders and restoring America's military dominance in the world.[40]

He has also promised a renewed focus on jobs, business, and creating a more favorable trade balance for US manufacturing. For too long blue-collar communities have seen their factories closed down and their jobs shipped overseas. America's mounting trade deficit and destabilized manufacturing base have impoverished entire regions of the country. Once proud coal-mining communities have been devastated, and families have been ripped apart.

For many voters, the promise of a new focus on jobs and infrastructure was the number one reason for supporting Donald Trump. With his record of success in the business world, they trusted his ability to revise the tax code, reduce burdens on employers, strengthen the business climate, and put Americans back to work.

A big part of that commitment was withdrawing from the Trans-Pacific Partnership (TPP) and making certain that all international trade deals would be in the best interest of American workers. Since the recession of 2008 American businesses have suffered through the slowest economic recovery since World War II. The United States lost nearly three hundred thousand manufacturing jobs during this period, while the share of Americans in the workforce plummeted to levels not seen since the 1970s. At the same time, the national debt doubled, and the middle class got smaller. Trump's plan to get the economy back on track creates twenty-five million new jobs in the next decade and returns us to a 4 percent annual economic growth.[41]

It begins with pro-growth tax reform and lower rates for Americans in every tax bracket. Congress would simplify the tax code and lower the corporate tax rate, which is one of the highest in the world. As a job creator and businessman himself, the president knows the importance of getting Washington out of the way and letting business owners do what they do best.[42]

Federal regulations cost our economy more than two trillion dollars in 2015 alone. In response Trump proposed a moratorium on new federal regulations while also ordering all heads of federal agencies and departments to identify job-killing regulations that ought to be repealed.[43] As a small-business owner myself, I am well aware of the mountains of needless paperwork the Obama administration required and some of the onerous labor regulations that were passed, so I'm happy to see the Trump administration moving in a more business-friendly direction.

Energy is a staple of American life and the world's economy. Trump is committed to increasing energy production, which will free the United States from dependence on foreign oil, and increasing availability, which will lower energy costs for American homeowners. The Obama administration did everything in its power to increase regulations on energy producers. Obviously the aim was to weaken the industry and give government support to a long list of failed schemes that bureaucrats claimed would help the environment. Trump has said he is committed to eliminating those dangerous and unnecessary policies and freeing up America's energy producers to get the country up and running again.[44]

These new energy policies are designed to exploit the vast untapped domestic energy reserves in this country, including shale, petroleum, and natural gas. The energy department has reported that there is an estimated fifty trillion dollars in untapped shale, crude oil, and natural gas reserves in the United States, with much of it on federal lands that belong to the American people. Revenues from energy production can be used to rebuild roads, schools, bridges, and other public facilities.[45]

CLIMATE CHANGE AND THE PRINCIPLE OF STEWARDSHIP

In addition to being good for the economy and good for business, the wise use of energy and other natural resources seems a smart move from many points of view. It's a practical move since scientists have shown that the United States produces the largest amount of oil and gas in the world.[46] US production now surpasses both Saudi Arabia and Russia[47] and promises to be a mainstay of our economy for the long term. But responsible management of these vital resources also involves the principle of stewardship, which is very much a biblical concept and an imperative that Christian leaders ought to understand.

When President Trump made his speech in the White House Rose Garden on June 1, 2017, withdrawing the United States from the Paris Accord on climate change, he was not speaking in biblical terms or reciting Scripture, but he was elaborating a principle that reflects a scriptural view of stewardship and accountability. The Old Testament principle of dominion (Gen. 1:26, 28) and the New Testament parable of the wise steward (Luke 12:42–43) tell us that God has entrusted us with the riches of the earth and He cares how we use them. We're not to waste or abuse them but to safeguard our treasure and use it wisely.

The president's speech lasted only a few minutes, but it was a clear and well-developed presentation of ideas he had talked about throughout the campaign. Ending the Paris Accord would prevent foreign nations from draining the US treasury in the name of the fraudulent "climate change" agenda. It would protect millions of American jobs, and it would provide a major boost to the nation's overall economy for years to come.

During that speech the president said, "One by one, we are keeping the promises I made to the American people during my campaign for president, whether it's cutting job-killing regulations; appointing and confirming a tremendous Supreme Court justice; putting in place tough new ethics rules; achieving a record reduction in illegal immigration on our southern border; or bringing jobs, plants, and factories back into the United States at numbers which no one until this point thought even possible....[48]

"On these issues and so many more," he said, "we're following through on our commitments. And I don't want anything to get in our way.... Thus, as of today, the United States will cease all implementation of the non-binding Paris Accord and the draconian financial and economic burdens the agreement imposes on our country. This includes ending the implementation of the nationally determined contribution and, very importantly, the Green Climate Fund, which is costing the United States a vast fortune.... [49]

"We have among the most abundant energy reserves on the planet, sufficient to lift millions of America's poorest workers out of poverty. Yet, under this agreement we are effectively putting these reserves under lock and key, taking away the great wealth of our nation...and leaving millions and millions of families trapped in poverty and joblessness." Then he added, "As the *Wall Street Journal* wrote this morning: 'The reality is that withdrawing is in America's economic interest and won't matter much to the climate.'[50]

"The United States, under the Trump administration," he said, "will continue to be the cleanest and most environmentally friendly country on earth. We'll be the cleanest. We're going to have the cleanest air. We're going to have the cleanest water. We will be environmentally friendly, but we're not going to put our businesses out of work, and we're not going to lose our jobs.... Foreign leaders in Europe, Asia, and across the world should not have more to say with respect to the US economy than our own citizens and their elected representatives.[51]

"Thus, our withdrawal from the agreement represents a reassertion of America's sovereignty. Our Constitution is unique among all the nations of the world, and it is my highest obligation and greatest honor to protect it. And I will." The president concluded his remarks to sustained applause that day, as he had done many times before, saying, "It is time to make America great again."[52]

PART IV

THE
POLITICAL
OUTSIDER

★★★★★

CHAPTER 11

FRIENDS AND SUPPORTERS

★★★★★

WHEN THE 2016 presidential campaign began, few Republican voters were willing to resurrect dead horses like Romney and McCain. Both men were tarnished by their losses, and comments each had made since their campaigns surprised many people and reflected attitudes the voters could no longer support. Even the idea of a former governor with a presidential pedigree wasn't enough to arouse the electorate. Instead, after eight years of the most confrontational and disruptive administration in history, conservative and evangelical voters were looking for new blood, fresh faces, and an energetic candidate who could energize the base and attract support from as many communities as possible.

Among the early favorites was a group of outspoken Evangelicals who had already won important races, including Sen. Ted Cruz of Texas, Gov. John Kasich of Ohio, Sen. Marco Rubio of Florida, and Gov. Mike Huckabee of Arkansas. The GOP brain trust poured millions into the campaign of former Florida governor Jeb Bush, but the voters weren't impressed. The last thing they wanted was a Bush family retread. Eventually a total of seventeen candidates made their pitch to the people, and debate platforms looked more like a Brooks Brothers showroom than a contest for the nation's highest office.

When Donald Trump suddenly appeared on the scene, nobody really thought he would have a chance. The outspoken late-night host David Letterman, who had invited Trump on his television show many times, assured his audience, "There's not a chance...that this man will be elected president."[1] New Yorkers knew Trump. He was one of their own, and so long as he seemed to be just another New York liberal and reality-TV celebrity, the media adored him. He was harmless. But the minute he declared his intention to run for the presidency as a Republican, he suddenly became a pariah.

Actually many people on both sides had their doubts about Trump. The evangelical frontrunners had a strong appeal to Christian voters, but there were doubts whether any of them could stand up to the fury of the Clinton machine. No one really expected the Vermont socialist Bernie Sanders to become the Democrat nominee; as an avowed socialist he was too far out of the mainstream. But Hillary Clinton, who would have the unquestioned support of the White House, enormous financial resources, and a long-standing history of cheating in every way possible, would chew up anyone who showed the slightest sign of weakness. And many conservatives were afraid the evangelical candidates were, well, too nice. Furthermore, the mainstream media were staunch allies of the Democrats, and they could be counted on to pile on and destroy a vulnerable opponent.

The main thing in Trump's favor when he entered the race was the fact that he was a total outsider. He was brash. He wasn't afraid to speak his mind. He would be able to pour millions of his own dollars into the campaign, but there was something else in the mix that hardly anyone would have expected. As I have tried to explain in this book, there was a supernatural element to the campaign, and a small group of Christian prayer warriors were convinced Donald Trump was the right man at the right time, and they fully expected a miracle.

I discussed in chapter 6 Trump's surprising early backing by charismatic Christian leaders. Also among his early supporters were old friends such as celebrity coaches Bobby Knight, Bill Belichick, Lou Holtz, Rex Ryan, and Mike Ditka, along with quarterback Tom Brady of the New England Patriots, and NASCAR CEO Brian France. Former New York mayor Rudy Giuliani was one of the most influential supporters. Many people had urged Giuliani to run, but he couldn't be persuaded. He had made a brief run for the Senate against Hillary Clinton during the 2000 election, but he dropped out after being diagnosed with prostate cancer. During that race Giuliani came face-to-face with the Clinton war machine, and he never trusted either of them, Bill or Hillary, after that.

While Trump and Giuliani were never fast friends, they had a long-standing relationship. Trump had been a guest in the mayor's box at Yankee Stadium, and Giuliani spoke at the funeral of Donald's father, Fred Trump, in 1999, calling him a giant and a great benefactor to the citizens of New York.[2] In the aftermath of the September 11 attacks on the World Trade Center, when the mayor had spoken so eloquently about the heroes and victims of that horrendous tragedy, Trump called to thank him and made his private plane available to Giuliani to fly to Washington for President Bush's televised address to Congress. Giuliani's support had been hesitant at first, "but once Mr. Trump won the nomination," as the *New York Times* reported, "Mr. Giuliani's tentative embrace became a bear hug."[3]

AN IMPERFECT INSTRUMENT

Before long Trump's list of celebrity endorsements looked more like the cover of a supermarket tabloid, featuring the likes of Clint Eastwood, Jon Voight, Stephen Baldwin, Charlie Sheen, Stacey Dash, Willie Robertson, Loretta Lynn, Scott Baio, Gary Busey, Kanye West, Omarosa Manigault (whom I met on November 8, 2016, at the election night party), and even the rockers Kid Rock and Gene Simmons. As the list continued to grow, the early supporters were joined by public figures who made their fame on radio and TV, including Fox News personality Sean Hannity, talk show host Laura Ingraham, and the firebrand columnist and Fox News contributor Ann Coulter.

Trump's longtime friend and top-rated cable commentator Bill O'Reilly was slower to come around, playing hard to get, while conservative icon Rush Limbaugh held back in order to appear "fair and balanced." On his June 21, 2017, radio broadcast Limbaugh said he knew Trump would be the Republican nominee from the moment he saw him coming down the escalator at Trump Tower on June 16, 2015, with the sound of Neil Young's 1989 hit "Rockin' in the Free World" blasting in the background.[4] Limbaugh would become a full-fledged Trump supporter, defending the nominee even when close friends seemed to be backing away, but he held off his support until the nomination was settled.

Unlike so many of the candidates who preceded him, Donald Trump refused to run from controversy and seemed to enjoy a well-publicized spat. He has used his Twitter account as a handheld weapon, provoking Twitter cofounder Evan Williams to apologize for giving Trump the tools to wage war on his critics.[5] But Trump showed that he could also be conciliatory and sympathetic, as he did in October 2016, apologizing for lewd comments he had made about women. He said, "I've never said I'm a perfect person nor pretended to be someone that I'm not. I've said and done things I regret, and the words released today on this more than a decade-old video are one of them. Anyone who knows me, knows these words don't reflect who I am. I said it, I was wrong, and I apologize."[6]

For many people Trump remains an enigmatic figure. Liberals can't imagine how anyone could support the man, while many conservatives see him as a game changer, a scrapper, and someone who has an irresistible sense of purpose. He has an undeniable love for his country and the ability to fight for the country's values and beliefs, and that means a lot even if it's sometimes hard to defend his behavior. As teacher and author Lance Wallnau has pointed out, "Figures like Churchill, Lincoln, and George S. Patton don't step out of cathedrals onto the stage of history, yet we canonize them later as instruments God raised up to meet a singular crisis."[7] None of these men were conventional Christians, and they had many detractors in the clergy, yet each played a pivotal role in history. They stood strong against the enemies of freedom and helped safeguard our way of life and our Christian heritage.

Wallnau makes a great point. If you've ever seen the movie *Patton*, you know you wouldn't want to be around an abrasive military commander like Gen. George Patton. He was often rough and rude, but he had a strong sense of destiny and felt he'd been called to lead men in combat to defeat the Nazi war machine. When rain and cold and overcast skies prevented Allied planes and artillery from firing on the advancing enemy lines during the Battle of the Bulge, Patton sent for an Army chaplain and demanded that he write a prayer imploring God for clear skies and an end to the rain. When the prayer was delivered, Patton read it aloud and commanded the entire Third Army to read it as well. The following morning the skies were miraculously clear, the American Army surged into Germany, and the Allied rout of Nazi forces went into overdrive.

Patton was no choirboy, but he was a strong-willed and powerful man who trusted in the authority and compassion of a powerful God. Donald Trump, with his swagger, cocky self-assurance, and ruthless determination, may well be the George Patton of our age and the one man who could stand up to the leftist insurgents who have done such damage to the republic over the last fifty years. His language and behavior may be disagreeable, but he possesses an undeniable passion to make America great again, and the people have responded to his message.

TRUMP REWARDS LOYALTY

The men and women who gravitated to Trump's message from the outset would have to weather severe turbulence along the way, but if there's anything Donald Trump values more than money and fame, it's loyalty, and he was quick to repay his friends and supporters. After the election Trump called my friend Jim Bakker, the broadcaster who went to jail and rebuilt his life after he lost everything. On his new *The Jim Bakker Show* out of the Branson, Missouri, area, Bakker did everything he could to rally his very conservative audience, as I documented in chapter 6. Why did Trump call? To thank Jim for his support. Jim was dumbfounded Trump even knew about him. Like me, he supported Trump because he knew how important it was to keep Hillary Clinton out of the White House and because he recognized Trump's leadership capabilities.

Trump seems to know everyone who helped him get elected. On January 27, 2016, less than a month before the all-important South Carolina Republican primary, Trump was endorsed by Lt. Gov. Henry McMaster. As I reported in chapter 5, this primary was a turning point for Trump. But it was significant for more than just South Carolina. McMaster was the first statewide elected official in the nation to endorse the New York billionaire, and Trump did not forget. When the Clemson football team visited the White House on June 12, 2017, to be recognized for winning the national championship, McMaster was in the audience. Trump spotted him and thanked him again for his endorsement and said how important it was, not only for his victory in South Carolina but also for the nomination and ultimately the White House. Of course Trump may have already thanked him by appointing South Carolina governor Nikki Haley to be ambassador to the United Nations. Haley is well qualified, but as I pointed out when I described the South Carolina primary, my sources in that state say it's pretty accepted that at least part of the reason Haley was promoted was so McMaster could ascend to become the South Carolina governor.

Four days after the South Carolina primary Rep. Chris Collins of New York was the first member of Congress to endorse Trump for the presidency. As he said in an interview for the online news site POLITICO, he had been a successful businessman before running for office, and he understood where Donald Trump was coming from. He didn't know if Trump would want him to go public with his support, so he asked one of his DC staffers to make a call to check it out, and the response was fast. Later the same day, he received a voice message from Trump expressing his pleasure for Collins's offer of support. He told the congressman to spread the word and said he was grateful for all the help he could get.[8]

Collins soon discovered that Trump was more than grateful for his help; he also wanted to reward his early supporters for taking the risks and going public. "He absolutely values loyalty," Collins said, "particularly to those who were with him through thick and thin. Those of us who stood firm in our support, many of those are being named to some of the top posts, but they also are extremely talented people." Collins could have been named to a post in the administration, he said, but he decided to hold on to his seat in Congress, where he could serve as an informal liaison with the White House. "I made very clear that the right place for me at this stage in my life was in Congress," he told Fox News, and Trump appointed him as a liaison to his transition team.[9]

When then-senator Jeff Sessions endorsed Trump four days later at a campaign rally in Alabama, he told an audience of thirty thousand avid Trump supporters that they were participants in an important moment in history. "I told Donald Trump this isn't a campaign, this is a movement," he said. "Look at what's happening. The American people are not happy with their government."[10] Sessions was the first member of the Senate to endorse Trump, and one year later, on February 8, 2017, he was confirmed by that body as US attorney general and head of the Department of Justice.

Rep. Marsha Blackburn of Tennessee was another of the early supporters, even offering to serve as Trump's running mate, if asked. As it turned out, Mike Pence was the right person for that job, but Blackburn was steadfast in her support and agreed that loyalty is especially important to this president because he is someone who likes to make the important decisions for himself. "I see him as putting on a personal touch," she said. "This is not going to be a transition where the decisions are going to [be] delegated. This is one where the leader of the team is going to be involved in choosing a team. He wants to build a team that can work together."[11]

Blackburn added that Trump's loyalty to his early supporters did not stop him from appointing talented people to high office who had spoken against him before the Republican primary, including former South Carolina governor Nikki Haley, who had once described Trump as "everything a governor doesn't want in a president."[12] Despite their brief verbal spat, Haley was picked to serve as ambassador to the United Nations in November 2016, two months before the inauguration. In her acceptance remarks she said, "When the President believes you have a major contribution to make to the welfare of our nation, and to our nation's standing in the world, that is a calling that is important to heed."[13]

TRUMP'S CHRISTIAN DEFENDERS

Paula White Cain had known Trump since 2003 and had prayed with him many times. When Trump was thinking about running in 2012, he asked Paula to invite some of her friends to come to New York and pray he would have wisdom on whether or not to run. He decided not to enter the race that year, and as I described in chapter 6, Paula helped to lay the groundwork in the charismatic community that would be the bedrock for his strong evangelical support four years later. I also mentioned that when the president of Liberty University, Jerry Falwell Jr., endorsed Trump on January 26, 2016, it was such big news the candidate tweeted about it.[14]

In a lengthy interview for the campus magazine, *Liberty Champion*, Falwell said he understands why the entire political world was up in arms over the Trump presidency. He said, "The establishment is having a seizure. They're going ballistic because they are scared to death that they're going to lose power....They're scared to death of Trump because he's the kind of guy that will walk into Washington, kick over the tables, kick over the chairs, throw the bums out, start over, and do things that a career politician would never do." Leaders of both political parties expressed alarm that Trump had never held elective office, but this was precisely what the voters wanted. Too often they had put their faith in experienced politicians who let them down. Falwell said it's the fact that Trump hadn't held political office that made him their candidate and president of choice.[15]

"I think he is what our Founding Fathers envisioned—citizen legislators," he said, "not career politicians to run this country." The men who built the country, wrote the Declaration of Independence and the Constitution, and laid the foundation of our government were farmers, tradesmen, and business owners. Government was not a full-time job, and when they had made a substantial contribution most of them went back to their homes to participate as citizens in the society they helped build. "I think Donald Trump fits that definition better than anybody else because he has been extremely successful in the private sector," Falwell said.[16]

Trump's personal wealth ought to be a major factor in his favor, he said, because we know for sure he's not in it for the money. "He's paying for his own campaign. He's not beholden to anybody like the rest of them are. He's made a payroll with tens of thousands of employees, and nobody else on that debate stage has ever made a payroll and never will. They don't understand it. They don't know what it's like to be a businessman who is trying to survive or a businesswoman who is trying to make it.[17]

"Now I think conservatives have reached a point where they want somebody who has succeeded in the private sector, not just someone who makes the right promises in speeches," Falwell said. "That's why a large majority of them are supporting him, and I think maybe after the country is saved and restored, perhaps evangelicals will start voting in traditional patterns again." Trump's position on the issues is no secret. He is very much "What you see is what you get." Saving the country from terrorist attacks, runaway debt, and open borders, Falwell said, ought to be everyone's first priority. "All the other issues will be moot if we don't save the country." He added, "It is sad to see Christians attacking other Christians because they don't support the same candidate or the candidate who they believe is the most righteous."[18]

The university president acknowledged that many of his peers who are ministry heads, pastors, and Christian leaders, including some on his own faculty, had spoken against Trump and worked to derail his campaign. While he respects their opinions, he said, he believes Evangelicals really ought to think about the stakes in today's political climate in a new way. The issues facing this country are deadly serious. But how many times do we have to be let down by so-called evangelical candidates who promise to defend our beliefs and then turn the other way when the going gets tough?

This was also the perspective of the African American pastors who spoke for Trump during his campaign. Cleveland pastor Darrell Scott offered his support in 2015 while Trump was just thinking about running and helped organize a meeting between Trump and a group of mostly African American pastors later that fall. Among those in attendance were Texas pastor Mike Murdock and South Carolina pastor Mark Burns, along with charismatic preachers Kenneth and Gloria Copeland and TBN founder Jan Crouch, who were captured in a cell-phone photo praying with Trump around a table with a "Make America Great Again" hat in the middle. When that picture appeared in print, a number of black pastors were critical of the event and accused their fellow preachers of caving in to the Republicans.

But Scott never wavered. He became not only one of Trump's strongest supporters but also one of his most articulate spokesmen. In gratitude for his support Trump invited Scott to speak at the Republican National Convention, and it was no ordinary speech. He articulated a strong argument for why Donald J. Trump should be the next president of the United States, but his message was delivered in a way few could do—with all the passion of an African American sermon, ending with an emotional crescendo that brought a roar of approval from the crowd.

Four days before the November general election, Rev. William Owens, the president of the Coalition of African American Pastors who had marched with Martin Luther King Jr. in the civil rights movement of the 1960s, entered the arena to give Trump a personal endorsement. "Donald Trump has humbly asked the African American community to give him a chance. After witnessing fifty years of failure from the Democratic Party, compounded by a growing hostility to religion in their platform, I feel that it is definitely time that we give Mr. Trump that chance to prove he can be a great president."[19]

There was a reason Trump garnered all this support. Despite the negative depictions in the left-leaning media, Donald Trump is, as I learned in my interview with him, a sincere and generous person, as we will see in the next chapter.

CHAPTER 12

FAITH, HOPE, AND CHARITY

★★★★★

O N FEBRUARY 2, 2017, almost two weeks after being sworn in as president of the United States, Donald Trump spoke to a crowd of thirty-five hundred at the sixty-fifth annual National Prayer Breakfast at the Washington Hilton hotel. During his remarks he said, "I was blessed to be raised in a churched home. My mother and father taught me that to whom much is given, much is expected. I was sworn in on the very Bible from which my mother would teach us as young children, and that faith lives on in my heart every single day.

"The people in this room," he said, "come from many, many backgrounds. You represent so many religions and so many views. But we are all united by our faith in our Creator and our firm knowledge that we are all equal in His eyes. We are not just flesh and bone and blood. We are human beings with souls. Our republic was formed on the basis that freedom is not a gift from government, but that freedom is a gift from God."[1]

Referring to the words of Jesus in Luke 12:48, the president was affirming that he understood that his gifts and his good fortune were not an entitlement but a responsibility to use his advantages to bless others. This was what his mother had taught him, he said, and it was a principle he had chosen to live by. Whether or not you were for him in the 2016 election, you must admit that Donald Trump believes in the importance of faith and he takes his vow to serve the best interests of the American people very seriously.

As I've said throughout this book, he doesn't fit neatly in any category, especially when it comes to his closely held beliefs. But he has made a commendable effort to learn about Christian principles and beliefs, and he has brought together men and women from many denominations and religious expressions to give him counsel and guidance. I have had the privilege of talking to him about such things in my 2016 interview, which I quoted in chapter 9. But how do you evaluate something like that? How do you know what's in a person's heart? What a person says about his or her faith is one thing, but we can learn a lot by how the person invests his or her their time and treasure.

One measure of the values and beliefs of President Trump can be found in the executive orders he has given and the ones he has overturned or reversed from Obama's eight years in office. Under terms of the Congressional Review Act enacted in 1996, an incoming president has a short window, usually no more than three or four months after the inauguration, to review and undo executive orders and regulations imposed by his predecessor that could interfere with his legislative agenda. The new orders can become law with simple majority votes from the members of Congress.

In a flurry of executive action the *New York Times* referred to as "a historic reversal of government rules,"[2] President Trump used the provisions of the review act as "a regulatory wrecking ball," signing thirteen bills in record time and effectively erasing executive orders signed by Obama in his last few months in office concerning labor, finance law, Internet privacy, funding for Planned Parenthood, drug testing, education standards, coal mining, and gun rights. One news report said Trump's executive action was the most substantial legislative achievement of his first hundred days in office, and the long-term effect would be to boost small business and take the handcuffs off of America's energy producers.[3]

His critics claimed Trump was merely deleting Obama's legacy, but Trump made it clear throughout his campaign that he believes in free-market capitalism, and he wasted no time overturning policies he and his team believed would impede economic development or be an inappropriate invasion of privacy. In his book *Great Again*, originally published as *Crippled America* in 2015, Trump offered a fast-paced review of the policy proposals and initiatives he would be discussing in the presidential campaign, and he wrote that a strong and growing economy is essential for a safe and free America.

In a chapter on economic issues he says, "I've spent my entire life not just making money but, more importantly, learning how to manage my resources and share them with the thousands who have worked for me. To hear our left-wing critics tell it, we need socialism to make this country move forward, and we need a president who can make up the rules as he goes along. If he can't get Congress to do something, he needs to rule by executive order." And then he writes, "I say that's complete nonsense."[4]

As a small-business owner I know that during the Obama presidency business and industry were almost always penalized by regulations that put employers at a disadvantage. The administration focused more on social issues, gender policy, climate change, and reversing America's long-standing partnerships in Europe and the Middle East than on policies to make life easier for American workers and their employers.

Evidence of Obama's anticapitalist bias could be seen in a talk he gave in March 2016 to a group of young people in Argentina. In his candid remarks Obama told the students they shouldn't worry about the differences between capitalism and Communism—as if there were no difference between them. He said, "just choose from what works,"[5] ignoring the history of Communist oppression over the past century— including the murder of more than one hundred million men, women, and children[6]—compared with the unparalleled prosperity that free-market capitalism had given the world. Obama's words had more relation to Saul Alinsky's *Rules for Radicals* than to anything one would expect to hear from an American president.

SUPPORT FOR WORTHY CAUSES

Obviously speeches and public statements can be helpful in assessing the policies of a president, as well as the person's character, but there are other ways, and the kinds of charitable contributions an individual makes can be revealing. The Donald J. Trump Foundation was established as a family charity in 1988. According to a report in *Forbes* magazine, the foundation gave away $10.9 million between 2001 and 2014, with donations to more than four hundred separate charities. During that time the main beneficiary was the Police Athletic League (PAL), a New York City charity that works with local police officers to provide summer camps, pre-K programs, and after-school activities for children. According to *Forbes*, donations from the Trump Foundation totaled more than $832,000 during that period.[7]

Another report based on IRS records indicated that 36 percent of the foundation's donations went to approximately one hundred organizations promoting health care. More than $465,000 went to the Dana-Farber Cancer Institute and Operation Smile, which offers free surgeries to children born with cleft palates in developing countries. The foundation gave at least $326,000 to New York Presbyterian Hospital and $250,750 to its sister institution, the Hospital for Special Surgery, also in New York.[8]

A story in the *New Yorker* magazine, despite its overall critical tone, reported that many of the foundation's biggest contributions went to charities such as the Red Cross, the American Cancer Foundation, the United Way, and several hospitals. There were also donations to charities associated with golfers such as Tiger Woods, Jack Nicklaus, and Arnold Palmer. In addition, the Trump Foundation made large donations to political and religious organizations. In 2012 the Billy Graham Evangelistic Association received $100,000 from the foundation. In 2013 $50,000 was donated to the American Conservative Union Foundation, part of the conservative lobbying group founded by the late William F. Buckley Jr. In 2014 the foundation gave $100,000 to the Citizens United Foundation, headed by conservative activist David Bossie.[9]

The gifts and grants provided by the foundation board covered a wide range of interests. For example, the foundation gave money to charities that put on galas, including the Celebrity Fight Night Foundation, which hosted an event honoring Muhammad Ali that Trump attended. They supported major golf outings, and the foundation donated $135,000 to charities of past presidents, including $25,000 to the Ronald Reagan Presidential Foundation in 2005 and $110,000 to the William J. Clinton Foundation in 2009 and 2010, just as Hillary Clinton was beginning her term as secretary of state. Meanwhile Trump's son-in-law and senior adviser, Jared Kushner, an observant Jew, oversaw a foundation that donated more than $500,000 to Jewish causes, including the Museum of Jewish Heritage and the Jewish National Fund.[10]

Between 2001 and 2008, before Trump stepped down as an officer of the foundation, an estimated 29 percent of its gifts were to healthcare causes. That increased to an estimated 42 percent from 2009–2014 when the foundation began making grants from funds contributed by other organizations. During that time foundation grants to "arts and culture" organizations dropped from 11 to 4 percent. Even though at this time Trump wasn't contributing his own cash to the foundation, he directed $100,000 in 2010 to the foundation headed by his son Eric. Eric Trump's foundation directs most of its giving to the St. Jude

Children's Research Hospital in Memphis, Tennessee. St. Jude was founded and funded for many years by the late television personality Danny Thomas, and his daughter, Marlo Thomas, serves today as the organization's national outreach director.[11]

CHARITY WITH A PERSONAL TOUCH

His detractors like to say Trump is greedy and miserly, but the people who know him best often speak of his generosity. At the Republican National Convention in July 2016, former New York mayor Rudy Giuliani said, "I have known Donald Trump for almost thirty years. And he has created and accomplished great things. But beyond that, this is a man with a big heart. Every time New York City suffered a tragedy, Donald Trump was there to help."[12] Jerry Falwell Jr., president of Liberty University, told Fox News host Sean Hannity, "I got to know Donald Trump after he spoke [at Liberty] in 2012." He said, "Right after he visited here last time…I called him about a large Christian ministry in another state that needed some help. I learned within a day or two he had donated $100,000 of his own money."[13]

Falwell then recounted the story of an inner-city basketball tournament Trump rescued from financial disaster. "He learned about Clyde Frazier Jr. who ran the Harlem Hoops tournament in the inner city and was killed in the 9/11 attacks," Falwell said. "He searched down the family and he donated the money to keep that tournament going."[14] There are also many stories of Trump's unsolicited generosity, including the story reported by Fox News and other media outlets about Sgt. Andrew Tahmooressi, who was grabbed by Mexican authorities at the border after making a wrong turn at the Tijuana Port of Entry.

The marine was taken into custody and held in a Mexican jail for seven months before a series of commentaries by Fox host Greta Van Susteren, who publicized the case on her nightly news program for several weeks, forced US and Mexican officials to reach a compromise. Shortly after his release, Tahmooressi reported that he had received a gift of $25,000 to help with medical care and treatment for post-traumatic stress disorder brought on by his two tours in Afghanistan. That gift came from Donald Trump.[15]

In the wake of the devastating floods that ravaged southern Louisiana in August 2016, Tony Perkins, the president of the Washington-based Family Research Council, told the *Christian Post* that Donald Trump had made a donation of $100,000 to relief efforts in Baton Rouge, Louisiana. Trump and his running mate, Mike Pence, made the trip to the Bayou State to show their support for the families whose lives had been turned upside down. Perkins said he was grateful for their show of support. "I'm grateful Donald Trump visited Louisiana," he said. "He helped turn the attention of the nation to a devastated region that faces a very long road to recovery." At the time, Perkins was serving as interim pastor of Greenwell Springs Baptist Church, which was a hub for distributing supplies and hot meals to displaced residents.[16]

More than twenty-six inches of rain fell on the area, flooding the low-lying terrain and damaging more than sixty thousand homes. At least thirteen people lost their lives, and more than ten thousand individuals were left homeless. Franklin Graham, who spearheaded relief efforts of his organization, Samaritan's Purse, was on hand as well, providing meals, clothing, and other essentials for the victims. Graham expressed gratitude for Trump's visit and led the two candidates on a tour of the area.[17] Along the way they were greeted at several points by groups of people yelling, "Thank you, Mr. Trump," and, "We knew you would not forget us!"[18]

A well-known urban legend, allegedly reported by *Forbes* as true, was about Trump's generosity that began with an incident on the New Jersey Turnpike back in 1995. But to me, the fact an urban legend was created shows his reputation for generosity. The story is that one day the limo in which Trump was riding had a flat tire and was forced to the side of the busy multi-lane highway. A passing motorist, seeing what had just happened, pulled over quickly and jumped out of his car to offer assistance. The man helped Trump's driver mount the spare tire so the limo could get back on the road, and when the job was finished, Trump asked how he could repay the good Samaritan. The man said, "Just send my wife a bouquet of flowers." Trump agreed, and true to his word, a beautiful bouquet arrived a few weeks later with a note saying, "We've paid off your mortgage."[19]

While that story may not be true, there are many that are true. One of the most touching, which was reported by the *Atlanta Journal-Constitution*, happened back in 1986 when farmers in Burke County, Georgia, were suffering through the worst farm disaster since the Great Depression. Through the long drought, crops had failed, and after struggling to make ends meet, Leonard Dozier Hill III realized he was going to lose the farm where his family had lived for three generations. The property was under foreclosure and was going to be auctioned off on the courthouse steps. Hill couldn't bear the thought, and believing his life insurance would be enough to settle the debt, the sixty-seven-year-old farmer committed suicide.[20]

Unfortunately Hill's insurance policy simply wasn't large enough to cover the debt, and his death was a crushing blow to his widow, Annabel Hill, and their family. When Hill's neighbors heard what had happened, they were angry, and someone painted "Farmer Killer" on the walls of the local bank.[21] When Donald Trump saw the news reports about the incident, he got in touch with Mrs. Hill and told her he would take steps to delay the foreclosure. Then he contacted WNBC radio talk show host Don Imus and asked his friend to help the Hill family tell its story in hopes of raising the money it needed. Trump tried to keep his involvement a secret, but the news eventually leaked out, and at that point Trump decided to get more involved publicly.

As he related in *The Art of the Deal* the following year, Trump called the bank that held the Hills' mortgage and asked for relief for the Hill family. But the bank vice president told him they were going to auction off the property and said, "Nothing or no one is going to stop it." At that, Trump's tone suddenly changed. He said, "You listen to me. If you do foreclose, I'll personally bring a lawsuit for murder against you and your bank on the grounds that you harassed Mrs. Hill's husband to his death." It didn't take long for the banker to take a more conciliatory tone.[22]

Mrs. Hill and her daughter were able to raise about $20,000 through their appearances on the Don Imus radio program, which certainly helped, but it wasn't enough to cover the full amount. So Trump and another businessman pitched in, and they eventually raised over $100,000, which was more than enough to cover the remaining amount of the mortgage. After the account was settled, Trump brought Mrs. Hill and her daughter to New York for a Christmas Eve mortgage-burning ceremony in the atrium of Trump Tower.[23]

WHEN HOPE IS NEEDED

On January 18, 2017, two days before Donald Trump was to be sworn in as America's forty-fifth president, I was in Washington, DC, to attend the inauguration when I happened to read a story in the *Washington Post* about a young man named Shane Bouvet, a single parent from a

small town in Illinois who had been invited to attend the inauguration. There were color photos with the story, and it looked interesting,
so before leaving my hotel room to go into the District, I sat down
and began reading. The young man in the story had grown up in the
rural community of Stonington, Illinois. He said he had watched as
factories and the local mine were shut down, as jobs disappeared, and
as the hopes and dreams of his neighbors faded away. He worked as a
night watchman and FedEx driver, but it was tough making ends meet.
"I get tired of seeing people hit rock bottom," he told the *Post* reporter.
"If you go to the coffee shops, the old guys talk about the old days when
engines roared and things weren't built in China."[24]

The story went on to tell how Bouvet was drawn to Trump's message during the primary, how he volunteered to hand out signs and
stickers, and how he used his knowledge of social media to help spread
the word. He was highly motivated, and it was apparent he had an
aptitude for it. Bouvet was soon named coordinator for social media
in Illinois, and his diligence and passion were rewarded with an invitation to attend the Great American Inaugural Ball at the MGM resort
hotel near Washington, DC. The only problem was that he didn't have
clothes for an event like that. But hearing about Bouvet's predicament,
a former teacher bought him a new suit and a nice pair of shoes so
Bouvet would have a chance to shake hands with the new president.[25]

Well, it was a nice story, but what happened next came as a complete
surprise. It turns out Donald Trump had read the story as well and
arranged to have the young man join him in the green room prior to
the big pre-inauguration concert on the evening of January 19. When I
opened my copy of the *Post* the next morning, I saw the sequel to that
first article, and this time the reporter told the rest of Bouvet's story.
He spent the most memorable evening of his life, it said, as a guest of
the president-elect, hanging out with Reince Priebus, Stephen Bannon,
and Melania Trump. They posed for photos and even gave Bouvet a
round of applause. Trump said, "This is the greatest guy." Then before
leaving the green room, the president placed a hand on Bouvet's
shoulder and told an aide, "Send him a check for $10,000." After that,
the *Post* story reported, Shane Bouvet broke down and cried.[26]

I'm glad I saw those stories because they gave me a better sense
of who Donald Trump really is. But even with touching episodes like
those, the media continue to portray Trump in negative terms, often
calling him a racist and bigot. In fact, Trump has a history of helping

individuals struggling with difficult circumstances, regardless of race or gender. One example is the story of the sixty-nine-year-old homeless black woman who stepped in to try and protect Donald Trump's star on the Hollywood Walk of Fame in October 2016. When Denise Scott saw the man, identified later as James Otis, pulverizing Trump's star on Hollywood Boulevard with a pickax, she demanded that he stop what he was doing. But it was too late, and the star was damaged beyond repair.[27]

Nevertheless, Scott said, "I'm gonna stay here and watch this and make sure nobody touches it." But as a crowd of young people and loud anti-Trumpers began gathering around her, a man grabbed the hand-printed signs she had been carrying that said Obama had failed the homeless and "Vote for Trump," and he ripped them to pieces. While tourists, locals, and the media looked on, Scott was shoved, punched, and cursed, and she eventually threw herself on the ground, covering Trump's star to protect it from further damage.[28]

When a cell-phone video of the incident showed up on YouTube, many people were outraged. Before long word about what had happened reached Donald Trump, and he said he wanted to give Scott a special gift. Trump's lawyer, Michael Cohen, went to work and said Scott would have "the last laugh on these thugs."[29] But first they had to find her somewhere on the streets of Los Angeles because Scott had no known address. Eventually the director of an outreach program for the homeless located her, and a GoFundMe page was set up to help Scott improve her circumstances. Assistance began pouring in, and the GoFundMe page reported, "Denise is safe and healthy and is very excited about all the tremendous support!"[30]

WHERE OTHERS HAVE FAILED

In his inaugural address President Trump outlined his vision for America and made promises concerning the goals he hoped to accomplish during his tenure. He said, "At the bedrock of our politics will be a total allegiance to the United States of America, and through our loyalty to our country, we will rediscover our loyalty to each other. When you open your heart to patriotism," he said, "there is no room for prejudice." He added, "The Bible tells us 'how good and pleasant it is when God's people live together in unity.'"[31]

But it was painfully clear, even as he spoke those words, that this is a divided nation and the dream of unity is still a long way off. Perhaps the greatest threats to unity are not the challenges from abroad but threats from men and women in our own country who are determined to dismantle our democracy and deconstruct our heritage of freedom and self-determination. Among them are the teachers and professors in America's universities who proudly declare themselves to be Marxists or anarchists, indoctrinating impressionable students and undermining the hope of peaceful coexistence.

President Abraham Lincoln said in his Lyceum address in 1838 that America's power and unity of purpose had made this country an invincible force. No foreign power would have the slightest chance of defeating us, he said, but he warned that alien forces in our midst could be a great danger. He said, "At what point then is the approach of danger to be expected? I answer, if it ever reach us, it must spring up amongst us. It cannot come from abroad. If destruction be our lot, we must ourselves be its author and finisher. As a nation of freemen, we must live through all time, or die by suicide."[32] It would be another twenty-three years before American unity would be shattered by the Civil War, but Lincoln could hardly have imagined that social and political differences in the twenty-first century would become such a hostile battleground.

Goodwill, compassion for others, and acts of charity mean very little to men and women who repudiate our history and focus only on the dark moments of America's past. It's not surprising that so many of this country's academic and intellectual elites—including the men and women in the media—are repelled by Donald Trump's agenda. Faith, freedom, and charity are nowhere on their list of priorities, and it seems that nothing short of a miracle and a spiritual renewal will ever shake them from their skepticism and doubt.

While the president acknowledged the divisions in the country in his inaugural address, he said, "We must speak our minds openly, debate our disagreements honestly, but always pursue solidarity. When America is united, America is totally unstoppable." Then he added, "There should be no fear. We are protected, and we will always be protected. We will be protected by the great men and women of our military and law enforcement, and most importantly we will be protected by God."[33]

The applause he received for those words was sincere because it was precisely that kind of hope and faith that brought him to the White House. We can only pray that his faith will be rewarded and by some miracle what Lincoln called "the better angels of our nature"[34] will prevail.

FOR SUCH A TIME

★★★★★

OST EVANGELICALS BELIEVE our nation was founded on a love for God and reverence for His Word, and because of that we have experienced the undeserved favor of God upon our country. Robert Jeffress, pastor of the prestigious First Baptist Church, made this point on the weekend of the first Independence Day celebration of Donald Trump's presidency, when he gave a rousing introduction before the president spoke.

Addressing a packed house at the Kennedy Center in the nation's capital and an audience of millions around the world via the Daystar television network, Jeffress said that while it's true the founders gave us a nation built on Christian principles, "it is also an indisputable fact that in recent years there have been those who have tried to separate our nation from its spiritual foundation. And that reality has caused many of us, many Christians, to despair and to wonder, 'Is God finished with America? Are our best days over? Has God removed His hands of blessing from us?' But in the midst of that despair," Jeffress said, "came November the 8th, 2016. It was on that day, November the 8th, that God declared that the people, not the pollsters, were gonna choose the next president of the United States. And they chose Donald Trump."[1]

In these few words Jeffress summed up the point of this book. My aim in taking on this project has not been to write Donald Trump's spiritual biography—that would have been a fairly short book. Rather, it was an attempt to look at the dramatic events of the 2016 election, and perhaps the most extraordinary candidate in our nation's history, not through the lens of what happened politically but through the lens of what happened spiritually. I know there are those who will disagree with my premise, but there are many people who are more than a little curious about how this whole episode happened. And it's for them that I've written this book.

Few people outside the four walls of a church pay much attention to what God is doing in the world. To them, acts of God are what you call tornadoes and hurricanes. But is it possible God has a plan for this nation? Is it possible He has a plan for His people? I've tried to make the case that President Trump won the evangelical vote by the largest margin in history because, as Jeffress said, Christians understood that he alone had the leadership skills and the unwavering persistence to reverse the death spiral of our nation.

In his remarks Jeffress referred to the surprise and enthusiasm of the people he has encountered since the election. He said, "Everywhere I go I find that people are even more excited about President Trump than they were on Election Day. And it's easy to understand why. President Trump has not only met but he has exceeded our every expectation, in reviving the economy, rebuilding our military, respecting our veterans, and restoring our greatest freedom of all, the free exercise of our faith. President Trump has done more to protect religious liberty than any president in United States history, and we are grateful to him for that."[2]

When the president took the podium, he affirmed what Jeffress said. "My administration will always support and defend your religious liberty. We don't want to see God forced out of the public square, driven out of our schools, or pushed out of our civic life. We want to see prayers before football games, if they want to give prayers." Before he even finished the sentence, the Kennedy Center audience members were on their feet with loud and resounding applause. They had seen too many examples of secular schools stamping on the beliefs of religious students. Then Trump added, "We want all children to have the opportunity to know the blessings of God.....As long as I am president, no one is going to stop you from practicing your faith or from preaching what is in your heart."[3]

As I listened to those words, I wondered if people were asking themselves why Donald Trump was saying such things. For most of his life, as I've pointed out, he has not been very religious. He was more interested in making money—lots of money—than defending religious liberty. But just as millions of Christians were praying for someone to stand up and help turn things around, here came Donald Trump, seemingly out of left field. At first most Christians didn't think much of him. Perhaps they didn't believe him. But now they're happy to know he has their back.

Not everyone appears so happy about this new Donald Trump, however. If you're secular, you see the world through a different lens. You may not even believe God exists. And if that's the case, you feel there's no reason to be concerned with such things. While people such as Jeffress decry "the downward spiral," calling for restoration and renewal of the culture, Hillary Clinton and her supporters have been saying that everything is just fine. When Trump raised concerns about the moral decline in America, he was lampooned by the media as a hypocrite.

Leftists, meanwhile, were marching in the streets for abortion on demand and celebrating the right to take the life of an unborn child right up to the moment of birth. They were glad same-sex marriage has been validated by the Supreme Court and that marijuana is being legalized in state after state. And when it comes to old-fashioned morality, the mantra of the secular culture these days is simply "anything goes." But most Americans recognized the problems; they didn't have to be religious to perceive that something is wrong with the way this country has been going.

WHERE THERE IS LIBERTY

For a very different view of Donald Trump and his faith, you need to go no further than a feature on CNN's website published a couple of weeks before Trump's inauguration called "God and the Don." The article is somewhat less biased than most of the reporting we've come to expect from CNN, but it was a typical elitist, dismissive interpretation of the faith of Donald Trump and bore the subtitle "Presidents often turn to faith in times of crisis. That seems unlikely for Trump."[4]

In the story the writer reported on a meeting between Trump and a couple of Presbyterian pastors in New York City: Rev. Patrick O'Connor, senior pastor at the First Presbyterian Church in Jamaica, Queens, where Trump was confirmed as a child; and Rev. Scott Black Johnston, senior pastor of Manhattan's Fifth Avenue Presbyterian Church, located within sight of Trump Tower. During the conversation Trump made the comment, "I did very, very well with Evangelicals in the polls," at which point both ministers informed him that neither of them is an Evangelical.[5]

"Well," Trump responded, "what are you then?" The pastors told him they were mainline Protestants, Presbyterians, from the same tradition in which Trump had been raised and in which he still claims membership. The unstated assumption of the article, of course, was that Trump was so clueless he didn't know the difference between an Evangelical and a mainline Protestant. There were several examples in the piece aimed at catching Trump on little things in order to undermine his Christian credentials.[6]

In this book I have tried to report on the miraculous way Donald Trump became president and what that means for America. I haven't tried to analyze his spiritual condition—only God knows the heart. Yet I've been told that the way of salvation has been explained to him, and if he believes in his heart that Jesus Christ is risen and the only begotten Son of God, then he is a Christian—and an evangelical Christian at that since that's what evangelical Christians believe. Maybe Dr. James Dobson was right when he said during the campaign that Trump is "a baby Christian."

Johnston made the same point to the writer of the CNN article: "It just clicked into place in my head, where I was like, 'Oh, this is a new Christian,' He is a Christian who's what I would call a young Christian. He is early on this journey. He has not spent a lot of time exploring the faith."[7] Very likely true, but a more insightful perspective comes from Professor David L. Holmes, professor emeritus of religious studies at the College of William and Mary, in an interview for *U.S. Catholic* magazine.

"Journalists are often secular and consider religion relatively unimportant," he said. "But virtually every president of our lifetime would tell you that religious faith does matter. Most presidents would tell us that they actually prayed in the Oval Office. Presidents are required to make decisions daily that affect millions of lives. They are often uncertain about what is the right thing to do. In those cases, they draw on their religious background."[8] Holmes summed up his assessment of Trump's religious beliefs by quoting the words of political scientist David Innes and said, "Trump's religion 'seems to be a sincerely held, vague, nominal, but respectful form of old-school Protestantism.'"[9] And that's about right. But the emphasis ought to be on the words "old school."

Like many segments of the mainstream culture, and many Christian denominations for that matter, the mainline Presbyterian church has drifted leftward over the years. The faith Donald Trump grew up in was more conservative, believed in biblical inerrancy, and would likely be considered "fundamentalist" by today's standards. The Presbyterian

Church (USA) hardly resembles the early expression of that denomination, which is why denominations such as the Presbyterian Church in America (PCA), the Orthodox Presbyterian Church (OPC), the Evangelical Presbyterian Church (EPC), and others have broken away from their mainline roots to embrace a more traditional understanding of the faith.

Historically all of America's presidents have turned to their faith in moments of crisis. Bill Clinton, a Southern Baptist, called on Rev. Jesse Jackson to counsel his family during the Monica Lewinsky scandal. The night before announcing his resignation, President Richard Nixon, a Quaker, is said to have wept and prayed on his knees in the Lincoln Sitting Room of the White House.[10]

Well-informed students of American history know that George Washington prayed when it looked as if the American Patriots were losing to the British. And Abraham Lincoln turned to prayer again and again and spoke about it often, calling the nation to prayer during the darkest days of the Civil War. President Franklin Roosevelt read a powerful and moving prayer over the radio while all of America listened on the night before the climactic D-day Invasion of June 6, 1944. All of this suggests that President Trump is in very good company.

SPEAKING FROM THE HEART

Many Bible-believing Christians who feel they're being bombarded by an avalanche of godlessness hardly know where to turn these days. At one time many Evangelicals believed that if they could just put a born-again president in the White House, everything would be fine and the nation would return to its former glory. However, Jimmy Carter and George W. Bush both claimed to be born-again, but not much changed. For that matter, Bill Clinton and Barack Obama talked about "my Christian faith" with little evidence to support the claim.

Christian author Lance Wallnau, interviewed in part 2 of this book, quotes the late Chuck Colson, who went to jail for his part in the Watergate scandal of the 1970s. After his born-again experience Colson went on to found a dynamic prison ministry and a Christian worldview institute, and he became one of the world's most respected evangelical thinkers. Colson wrote that most Christians are familiar with the doctrine of "saving grace," which is the mercy extended by God to all who believe in the death and resurrection of Jesus. But

Colson explains that there is also an even broader form of mercy known as "common grace."

Wallnau told me on a podcast before the election that "common grace" is the way the Reformers grappled with how the Word of God applies to all of life, not just to church reform. A key aspect of the concept holds that secular leaders are raised up in times of great historical consequence to protect God's agenda and His purposes. Such leaders are chosen for a unique role, whether or not they may actually know God or even care about doing His will. They are people, as Cyrus mentioned earlier, who have the capacity and the motivation to fulfill a divine plan.

"This is the proposition I give to Christians who are dispirited by the failure of their favorite candidate to capture the nomination," Wallnau said. "Don't ask, 'Who is the most Christian candidate?' Instead, ask, 'Who is the one anointed for the task?'" As an example, in 1860 the pious evangelical Salmon Chase was a better Christian than the men he ran against, but the wily outsider Abraham Lincoln ended up with the nomination. Chase couldn't understand why God had denied him the privilege of leading the nation, but in the end the country lawyer from Springfield, Illinois, proved to be the vessel God had chosen for the coming chaos.[11]

R. T. Kendall, a respected theologian and author who is also a long-time friend, dealt with common grace in a blog shortly after the election. In his witty style he told how his seven-year-old grandson, Toby, had asked out of the clear blue, "Grandpa, is Donald Trump a Christian?" Kendall replied, "I don't really know for sure." "Well, then, Grandpa, can God use someone who is not really a Christian to do His work?" Toby asked. Kendall replied, "Yes, through God's common grace."[12]

Kendall explains: "Common grace is God's goodness to all humankind. John Calvin called it 'special grace in nature.' We call it 'common grace' not because it is ordinary but because it is given commonly to all people of all ages in all places in the whole world. It is a creation gift not a salvation gift. It is what keeps the world from being topsy-turvy. It is why there is a measure of law and order in all countries. It is why we have traffic lights, hospitals, firemen, policemen, nurses and doctors. It is the basis of one's IQ, their ability for poetry, science, botany, astronomy. It is what gave Albert Einstein what is (perhaps) the highest IQ in history. It is what gives an Arthur Rubenstein an ability to play the piano, Yehudi Menuhin to play the violin, Rachmaninoff to write a concerto. It has nothing to do with whether you are a Christian. Being a Christian is not what gives you your IQ; you would have had the same IQ whether saved or lost."[13]

He continued: "Perhaps Donald Trump is a Christian. I have heard rumors of this person or that person who led him to the Lord Jesus Christ. I hope they are true. But if not, one should have a theological rationale for God using people like him to be used of God in this wicked world of ours. Yes, Toby, God can use someone who is not a Christian to do His work in the world. And if Donald Trump is truly born again, all the better for us all!"[14]

Wallnau surprised me when he said that Donald Trump is more prophetic than most people realize. "In fact," he said, "he is Churchillian in this regard. He sees the threat nobody else has courage to talk about until it's too late. He sees it with radical Islam; he sees it with the soaring nineteen-trillion-dollar debt; and he sees it in America's tinderbox of the inner city."[15] Trump accurately described Brussels as no longer being the same city he knew years before. The press was picking apart his statement at the very moment Brussels became the epicenter of a shocking round of organized terror and death. Likewise, Trump predicted that English voters would pass the contentious "Brexit" referendum, separating Britain from the European Union. When that actually happened as Trump had predicted, government officials and the media's expert commentators were stunned.

After the Republican National Convention in Cleveland, July 18–21, 2016, the media quickly described Trump's message as "dystopian"—meaning dark and pessimistic about America's future. Those who agreed with Trump's vision for America, on the other hand, found his words encouraging, largely because someone was finally speaking the truth. When a full 70 percent of Americans believe the country is on the wrong track, it can be very encouraging to have a candidate who shares their opinion and has the courage to speak about it.

In that respect Trump resembles the indefatigable British Prime Minister Winston Churchill, who often went against convention, decorum, and his own party to badger the people of Great Britain into defending their country against Hitler's Third Reich. Churchill was viciously attacked by the media in his day. Today Donald Trump invites the same kinds of bitterness and resentment by raising alarms about the unraveling of America's society at a time when our political elites, buttressed by the media, are denying that anything is wrong. Like Churchill, Trump is the target of opposition forces seeking to silence him for his bluntness and to stop him from speaking from the heart about problems the political establishment has been sweeping under the carpet for generations.

A NEW AWAKENING

Pastor Robert Jeffress said in his July 1 remarks that "millions of Americans believe the election of President Trump represented God giving us another chance—perhaps our last chance to truly make America great again. And how grateful we are. We thank God every day that He gave us a leader like President Trump."[16] But Todd Starnes, a popular Fox radio host and blogger, says that getting another chance may not be enough. In an article for *Charisma* magazine, Starnes writes that America is engaged in a war of worldviews.

"In 2008," he said, "President Barack Obama promised to fundamentally transform the United States of America. And ladies and gentlemen, he fulfilled that campaign promise. In less than eight years, our former president turned the most exceptional nation on earth into a vast wasteland of perpetually offended snowflakes." Then Starnes said, "You would think at some point in this story, the church would stand up and shout, 'Enough!'... [but] these days some churches resemble the Cowardly Lion more than the Lion of Judah."[17]

In his book *The Deplorables' Guide to Making America Great Again* Starnes wrote about how to be a Christian citizen in a nation under attack by secularists. "If you and I don't do something, there's nothing the White House can do by itself. If we don't get on board and row—hard—we could find ourselves drifting back to where we were. These opportunities don't come along often. It's time to call this what it is: a historic moment in the life of our country."[18] I believe Starnes is right, but I also believe that Christians are waking up. The evidence we've seen in these pages tells me that there is a new optimism and a new spirit rising all across the land. Many Christians believed they had to vote for Donald Trump, or the downward spiral of the past eight years would continue. There is no doubt that things would have gotten worse under Hillary Clinton's administration.

If you're old enough to remember the difficult days of the 1960s, you may remember the race riots, the protests against the Vietnam War, and the violence at the Democratic National Convention in 1968. Who can forget the assassination of President John F. Kennedy in 1963, followed five years later by the assassination of his brother Robert as well as civil rights leader Dr. Martin Luther King Jr. In the midst of all the mayhem, the younger generation was turning to sex, drugs, and rock and roll as the antidote to the pain in their lives. But what happened next was surprising. Two of the greatest revivals of our lifetimes took place, involving, of all people, the same young people who were part of the tune-in and dropout youth culture.

Many of those same hippies and dropouts suddenly found Jesus and got so turned on to Him that they were called "Jesus People." In fact, many of today's Christian leaders, including me, trace their spiritual roots to the Jesus movement of the 1970s. While I was raised in a Pentecostal home, I had strayed from the Lord at a secular university, but I gloriously saw my life transformed as a result of the revival that swept hundreds of thousands of young people into the kingdom of God.

Even though our own culture and all of Western civilization remains in a downward spiral, there is at least a hope that we may be in a similar moment of history. Two years ago I would never have suspected that God would raise up a brash billionaire from Queens, New York, to undertake the transformation of America, not only politically but also spiritually. I expected to vote for Ted Cruz in November, but when he left the race, I had to reconsider my options. Now I have a better understanding of why that reorientation was necessary.

Could it be that this intersection of God and Donald Trump as well as the simultaneous shifts in the United States of America and the kingdom of God are much more than random anomalies of coincidental occurrences? Is it possible that Donald Trump was raised up suddenly out of the obscurity of a business and entertainment environment with what Frank Amedia called a "breaker anointing" that was activated to make a way for our nation to return to God? Is it the Creator's plan that the diverse factions of the Christian church be united in a way to take back our country for God?[19]

The prophet Amos declared, "Surely the Lord God does nothing without revealing His purpose to His servants the prophets" (Amos 3:7). What also makes this election unique is that the declarations of a few Christian prophets were remarkably accurate and bold to declare that Trump would win. That is past. What's the future, and how can you be involved? Frank and other faith leaders decided the day after the election to organize a group of prophets and intercessors who could speak to power in our country and who could also be a spiritual shield for this new president. They called it POTUS Shield after

Prophetic Order of the United States. A potusshield.org website and regional conferences are ways you can be involved.[20]

Not everyone is happy with this. Already voices from the Left, specifically People for the American Way and Right Wing Watch, complained in August 2017 that POTUS Shield was trying to establish a prophetic order to continue to be a spiritual force in the nation, adding they have never seen anything similar in terms of an organized Pentecostal prayer shield for a sitting president before![21]

It was as if the prophetic word gained momentum throughout the election process, but pundits and critics mocked the word that declared Trump was similar to Cyrus and that he would win by an electoral college majority.

In various places in this book I've written about my conversations with Mark Taylor, Frank Amedia, Lance Wallnau, Chuck Pierce, and others who prophesied that Donald Trump would be the next president. I know each of those men, and I trusted their insights, but I'm not a prophet. I wouldn't begin to forecast what will happen tomorrow, but I am convinced that God has a plan for America, and I'm equally convinced that, for this moment in our history, He has lifted up one of the most unlikely leaders anyone could imagine to guide the nation. Knowing that, the very best thing I can do now is pray for the safety and success of President Trump and hope that millions will join me.

THE HERMIT OF LORETO

★★★★★

IHAVE TOLD WHAT I believe is the "God story" of Donald Trump's election from my evangelical perspective. I have reported that several modern-day charismatic prophets believe God showed them that He had raised up Donald Trump and he would win the presidency. I even went out on a limb and reported this in *Charisma* before the election, knowing if it didn't happen, I would be embarrassed. But it did come to pass.

In my research I came across a video from a Roman Catholic priest that is so incredible I hardly know whether to believe it—and it doesn't really fit into the narrative of this book. Yet I am compelled to share it, if only to make you wonder if it might be true and if it's one more confirmation—from a very different perspective—that somehow God raised up Donald Trump.

The remarkable prophecy came to light around the time of the election that a Catholic "holy man" named Thomas Zimmer prophesied in the 1980s that Donald Trump "would lead America back to God."[1]

Zimmer, who died on September 10, 2009, was known as the "Hermit of Loreto." An American, he moved to Loreto in the early 1990s after living for two decades in Rome. He lived there until 2008, when he returned to America to die. Besides being very devout, he coauthored the *Pietà* prayer book, which sold millions of copies, and he is said to have attended mass many times a day.[2]

The month after Trump's inauguration, an American priest from Rhode Island named Fr. Giacomo Capoverdi posted a video on YouTube with this amazing story. A few weeks later Bret Thoman, SFO, a Catholic pilgrimage leader and author, wrote about the story. He told about the video and how Capoverdi says he met the hermit. The priest said it was around 2000 when a friend of his, an American doctor named Claude Curran of Bristol, Rhode Island, told him he had to meet this holy man. Capoverdi took the train from Rome to Loreto the next time he was in Italy and went to the basilica and saw an old man sitting on the floor hunched over in prayer at the "Holy House"—also called Santa Casa—which Catholics believe was the home in Nazareth where the angel Gabriel appeared to Mary. Three walls of the house were brought to Loreto by Crusaders named DeAngelo to save it from being destroyed by Arabs. (This apparently gave rise to the story that it was transported by angels.)[3]

Capoverdi asked the old man in English if he were Thomas. The hermit acknowledged that he was, and Capoverdi said they had a delightful conversation.[4] Sixteen years later, when Trump ran for president, Curran mentioned Zimmer again to Capoverdi, remembering that back in the 1980s Zimmer said he had a "premonition" and that "a certain man would lead America back to God. And that man would be none other than Donald J. Trump." "The millionaire playboy from New York?" the incredulous doctor is said to have asked. "Yes," responded Zimmer, adding he was so sure that Donald Trump would become a great spiritual leader of America that he wrote his name on a brick and had it placed in the reconstruction of St. Peter's Holy Door after the Jubilee so that Trump would receive blessings from the many masses that would be said in the Vatican.[5]

Thoman writes: "After interviewing a number of people around Loreto who knew Tom Zimmer, the 'Hermit of Loreto,' when he was living there, I have no reason to doubt Fr. Capoverdi's statements that Thomas Zimmer communicated to his friend that he received a 'premonition' that Donald Trump would 'lead America back to God.' They all confirmed that Tom was a holy and virtuous man and that he prayed constantly and sought to help people in need. Further, some even recounted personal stories they witnessed regarding Tom's supernatural gift of 'foreseeing the future.'"[6]

He then writes what the church says to do in order to determine whether a prophecy is true or false. First, one must ask if the prophet is a good and virtuous person—Zimmer was certainly that. Next the prophecy must not contradict Scripture or church doctrine. Here too, "there is nothing scriptural or in church teachings that would suggest that a political leader cannot lead people to God; on the contrary," Thoman writes, "Scripture indicates it as a duty."[7]

Finally, Thoman says, the prophecy must come true.[8] And of course there is also the possibility of locating the brick at St. Peter's door with Donald Trump's name inscribed on it—to see if Zimmer really did it. "It does seem extraordinary that an elderly, prayerful man would have had such an intuition about Donald Trump as being a Christian leader when he was, indeed, living a life quite the opposite at that moment," Thoman wrote.[9] How this could happen became clearer when I verified this story by contacting Curran. He explained he met Zimmer in Rome when he was a medical student in Italy. A friendship ensued, and Zimmer told him many things over the years. For example, he said that God sees the good in people even when we don't—so we must look for the good. He said in 1988—a year Curran remembers because his mother died that year—that God wanted the Berlin Wall torn down. Zimmer persuaded a priest to say 101 masses for the wall to come down. A short time later the wall was torn down.[10]

As to the brick, Curran says he knows Zimmer placed other names on bricks to be prayed over. One woman claimed to have seen the brick with Donald Trump's name and left a message on Capoverdi's YouTube video that she assumed Trump had placed it there. My Italian contacts doubt this story, but it's possible. Besides, Curran says the Vatican never throws anything away, so there's a list somewhere showing that Zimmer paid for a brick bearing Donald Trump's name.[11]

As a Protestant I don't understand all these Catholic connections, but I also know I don't understand many mysteries of God. I believe if God could speak to Chuck Pierce and Frank Amedia and others whom I know, He could speak to a man like Thomas Zimmer, who devoted his life to prayer.

Whether or not Trump will actually lead America back to God, he has reawakened the national conversation about faith, religious liberty, and the dangers of moral decline. Capoverdi said in this way he has already moved America toward God by changing regulations via executive orders to make abortion more difficult and so Little Sisters of the Poor don't have to distribute contraception at their hospitals, and slowing the serious moral collapse advocated by the Left.[12] That's something to be thankful for.

ACKNOWLEDGMENTS

★★★★★

MANY PEOPLE PLAYED a part in putting this book together, and I would like to express my gratitude to each of them for their assistance, working at such a high level with a very short deadline. First, I want to give a heartfelt thank-you to all the team at Charisma House for their enthusiasm and professionalism, starting with the publisher, Marcos Perez, who saw the possibility for this book and worked tirelessly to help bring it to fruition. Special thanks also to Debbie Marrie, our vice president of product development, for her skill and dedicated work as the main editor on the manuscript. In her seventeen years at Charisma Media I've come to know and respect Debbie as a truly outstanding editor.

Thanks to Justin Evans, who captured the vision for what the book is about in his elegant cover design. I'm grateful to Frank Hefeli and his team, who took the project through the manufacturing and printing process and worked hard to make it the best book it could be. And thanks to the Charisma House marketing team and the firm of Hamilton Strategies, who always do such a fantastic job helping to spread the message far and wide.

Rarely do I have an opportunity to publicly thank my administrative assistant of seventeen years, Bob Cruz, for his tireless help and support. A retired Air Force master sergeant, Bob's military job was taking care of generals—which I like to think was good preparation for this job. He helped me with myriad details, including correspondence with friends such as Evan Tinkle, Tom Ertl, Ray Moore, and Gary McCullough, whose input has been invaluable.

Our great executive team made certain the business operated smoothly while I took time off for writing, and I'm deeply grateful to each one of them. In particular, special thanks to Dr. Steve Greene, executive vice president of the media group; and to Ken Hartman, our controller, who works closely with Joy Strang, our CFO. I also want to thank Joy publicly for her love and support, not only during this writing project but for forty-five years as my wife and thirty-six years as co-owner of the company we began together. And while I'm at it, I want to acknowledge my two wonderful sons, Cameron and Chandler. Although they had no active role, I had them in mind throughout the research and writing process. I knew it was important to keep younger readers in mind who may not be as conservative as I am.

Although I began my career as a newspaper reporter at the *Orlando Sentinel*, I mainly write a monthly column and blogs these days, not book-length projects. And because of the short timetable we were on, I knew I would need help with research and writing and was fortunate to enlist the assistance of Dr. Jim Nelson Black, who has worked with us on several previous projects and has written a half dozen books of his own. In my forty years as a publishing executive and editor, I don't think I've ever worked with an editor I've enjoyed or respected more than Jim. But I also want to thank Jim's wife, Connee Black, who came up with the title, *God and Donald Trump*. I had considered other titles, but I knew this was the right one the moment I heard it. Thank you, Connee.

Last, but certainly not least, I want to thank the Lord for the leading of the Holy Spirit as I wrote. I wanted this to be more than just a political book. I wanted to tell the story of how God intervened in this election, answering our prayers for a dramatic shift in the nation. If I've been able in these pages to connect the dots for a few readers and cause you to see that God is involved in the affairs of men, then I want to give the Lord all the glory for that.

ABOUT THE AUTHOR

★★★★★

STEPHEN E. STRANG graduated with a journalism degree from the University of Florida in 1973. While a student he won the William Randolph Hearst Award for journalistic excellence, considered to be the highest award in collegiate journalism.

He began his career at the *Orlando Sentinel,* where he was a general-assignment reporter. While at the newspaper he started a small church magazine called *Charisma,* which began to grow and has become a major Christian magazine. *Charisma* also became the basis for founding what is now Charisma Media in 1981 with his wife, Joy.

His company has grown over the years, adding other magazines, such as *Ministry Today, Christian Retailing,* and *SpiritLed Woman.* In the 1980s Charisma Media expanded into publishing books, and it later began publishing in Spanish. The book group has published thousands of books, including thirteen *New York Times* best sellers, by authors such as John Hagee, Dr. Don Colbert, and Jonathan Cahn. In 2014 Charisma House released an important new Bible translation called the Modern English Version. Today Charisma Media is recognized as the leading Charismatic/Pentecostal publisher in the world.

During his four-decade-long journalism career he has traveled the world covering the fast-growing charismatic movement. He has interviewed or met virtually every American evangelical leader. He has also interviewed four US presidents: George H. W. Bush, George W. Bush, Barack Obama, and Donald Trump.

During his career he has received many awards from secular and religious organizations, including an honorary doctorate from Lee University. In 2005 *Time* magazine listed Strang as one of the twenty-five most influential Evangelicals in America.

ENDNOTES

★★★★★

FOREWORD

1.   "Full Text: Trump Values Voter Summit Remarks," POLITICO, September 9, 2016, accessed August 14, 2017, http://www.politico.com/story/2016/09/full-text-trump-values-voter-summit-remarks-227977.

INTRODUCTION

1.   Kelly Riddell, "Evangelical Pastors Descend on Las Vegas to Learn to Motivate Christians to Vote," *Washington Times*, April 22, 2015, accessed August 16, 2017, http://www.washingtontimes.com/news/2015/apr/22/evangelical-pastors-descend-on-las-vegas-to-learn-/.

CHAPTER 1—TRUMP'S MIRACULOUS WIN

1.   Sarah Posner, "Donald Trump Divides God's Voters," *New York Times*, January 28, 2016, accessed June 1, 2017, https://www.nytimes.com/2016/01/28/opinion/campaign-stops/donald-trump-divides-gods-voters.html.

2.   James Barron, "Overlooked Influences on Donald Trump: A Famous Minister and His Church," *New York Times*, September 5, 2016, accessed June 7, 2017, https://www.nytimes.com/2016/09/06/nyregion/donald-trump-marble-collegiate-church-norman-vincent-peale.html?_r=0.

3.   Don Nori Sr., "Is Donald Trump the President We Need?," Charisma News, October 2, 2015, accessed June 5, 2017, http://www.charismanews.com/politics/opinion/52384-is-donald-trump-the-president-we-need.

4.   Ibid.

5.   Ibid.

6.   Ibid.

7.   David Brody, "Michele Bachmann: 'God Raised Up' Trump to Be GOP Nominee," CBN News, August 30, 2016, accessed July 31, 2017, http://www1.cbn.com/thebrodyfile/archive/2016/08/30/only-on-the-brody-file-michele-bachmann-says-god-raised-up-trump-to-be-gop-presidential-nominee.

8.   Ibid.

9.   William J. Clinton, "Remarks to the 48th Session of the United Nations General Assembly in New York City," address: September 27, 1993,

The American Presidency, accessed July 31, 2017, http://www.presidency.ucsb.edu/ws/?pid=47119.

10. George Bush, "Address Before a Joint Session of the Congress on the State of the Union," address: January 29, 1991, The American Presidency, accessed July 31, 2017, http://www.presidency.ucsb.edu/ws/?pid=19253.

11. Donald Trump, Twitter post, January 9, 2017, 6:27 a.m., https://twitter.com/realdonaldtrump/status/818419002548568064?lang=en.

12. Meghan McCain, Twitter post, January 8, 2017, 10:14 p.m., https://twitter.com/meghanmccain/status/818294731742580736?lang=en.

13. Emily Heil, "Is Obama's 2011 White House Correspondents' Dinner Burn to Blame for Trump's Campaign?," *Washington Post*, February 10, 2016, accessed July 31, 2017, https://www.washingtonpost.com/news/reliable-source/wp/2016/02/10/is-obamas-2011-white-house-correspondents-dinner-burn-to-blame-for-trumps-campaign/?utm_term=.54640dbe5a87.

14. Rebecca Savransky, "Obama Told Friends Trump Is a 'Bulls----er,'" *The Hill*, May 17, 2017, accessed July 31, 2017, http://thehill.com/homenews/news/333782-report-obama-told-friends-trump-is-a-bulls-ter.

15. Sarah Kaplan, "George Will Exits the Republican Party Over Trump," *Washington Post*, June 25, 2016, accessed July 31, 2017, https://www.washingtonpost.com/politics/george-will-exits-the-republican-party-over-trump/2016/06/25/2b6cdcaa-3b09-11e6-9ccd-d6005beac8b3_story.html?utm_term=.d7b49fb42d1b.

16. Bill Kristol, Twitter post, February 14, 2017, 8:36 a.m., https://twitter.com/billkristol/status/831497364661747712?lang=en.

17. David Horowitz and Richard Poe, *The Shadow Party: How George Soros, Hillary Clinton, and Sixties Radicals Seized Control of the Democratic Party* (Nashville: Nelson Current, 2006), 78ff.

18. "MRC/YouGov Poll: Most Voters Saw, Rejected News Media Bias," Media Research Center, November 15, 2016, accessed August 1, 2017, https://www.newsbusters.org/blogs/nb/nb-staff/2016/11/15/mrcyougov-poll-most-voters-saw-rejected-news-media-bias.

19. "O'Reilly: At Least 3 Media Orgs Have 'Ordered Employees to Destroy Trump,'" Fox News, October 10, 2016, accessed August 1, 2017, http://insider.foxnews.com/2016/10/10/oreilly-least-3-media-orgs-have-ordered-employees-destroy-trump.

20. Tom Westervelt and Raghavan Mayur, "Media Malpractice? Media Bias and the 2016 Election," Investor's Business Daily, November 18, 2016, accessed August 1, 2017, http://www.investors.com/politics/commentary/media-malpractice-media-bias-and-2016-election/.

21. David Chalian, "Road to 270: CNN's Latest Electoral College Map," CNN, August 25, 2016, accessed August 15, 2017, http://www.cnn.com/2016/08/19/politics/road-to-270-electoral-college-map-3-august/index.html; David Chalian, "Road to 270: CNN's Latest Electoral College Map," CNN, October 10, 2016, accessed August 15, 2017, http://www.cnn.com/2016/09/22/politics/road-to-270-electoral-college-map-4-september/index.html; Josh Katz, "Who Will Be President?," *New York Times*, November 8, 2016,

accessed August 15, 2017, https://www.nytimes.com/interactive/2016/upshot
/presidential-polls-forecast.html.

22.   Jim Rutenberg, "A 'Dewey Defeats Truman' Lesson for the Digital
Age," *New York Times*, November 9, 2016, accessed June 7, 2017, https://
www.nytimes.com/2016/11/09/business/media/media-trump-clinton.html
?_r=1.

23.   Thomas E. Patterson, "News Coverage of the 2016 General Election:
How the Press Failed the Voters," Shorenstein Center, December 7, 2016,
accessed June 2, 2017, https://shorensteincenter.org/news-coverage-2016
-general-election/.

CHAPTER 2—AN ANSWER TO PRAYER

1.   David Aikman, "Does Trump Want to Remake America 'Morally'?,"
Charisma News, June 29, 2017, accessed June 29, 2017, http://www.Charisma
News.com/politics/opinion/65909-does-trump-want-to-remake-america
-morally.

2.   Ibid.

3.   Ibid.

4.   Ibid.

5.   Supreme Court of the United States, *Engel v. Vitale*, June 25, 1962,
accessed August 1, 2017, https://supreme.justia.com/cases/federal/us
/370/421/case.html.

6.   Supreme Court of the United States, *School Dist. of Abington Tp. v.
Schempp*, June 17, 1963, accessed August 1, 2017, https://supreme.justia.com
/cases/federal/us/374/203/case.html.

7.   Supreme Court of the United States, *Roe v. Wade*, Justia, January
22, 1973, accessed August 1, 2017, https://supreme.justia.com/cases/federal
/us/410/113/case.html.

8.   Supreme Court of the United States, *Obergefell v. Hodges*, Justia,
June 26, 2015, accessed August 1, 2017, https://supreme.justia.com/cases
/federal/us/576/14-556/.

9.   In communication with author.

10.   In communication with author.

11.   Aikman, "Does Trump Want to Remake America 'Morally'?"

12.   Ibid.

13.   Ibid.

14.   Ibid.

15.   In communication with author.

16.   In communication with author.

17.   In communication with author.

18.   Ibid.

19.   In communication with author.

20.   In communication with author.

21.   Ibid.

22.   Ibid.

23.   Ibid.

24.   Ibid.

25.   Ibid.

26.   Ibid.

27.   Ibid.

28.   James Robison, "Faith and Prayer in the Oval Office: James Robison Speaks With Jack Graham," The Stream, July 14, 2017, accessed August 2, 2017, https://stream.org/faith-prayer-oval-office-james-robison-speaks-jack -graham/.

29.   Ibid.

30.   Ibid.

31.   In communication with author.

32.   In communication with author.

CHAPTER 3—AFTER THE ELECTION

1.   Jonathan Allen and Amie Parnes, *Shattered: Inside Hillary Clinton's Doomed Campaign* (New York: Crown Books, 2017), 380–384; Nathan Heller, "A Dark Night at the Javits Center," *New Yorker*, November 9, 2016, accessed June 21, 2017, http://www.newyorker.com/culture/culture-desk/a -dark-night-at-the-javits-center.

2.   Steve Lohr and Natasha Singer, "How Data Failed Us in Calling the Election," *New York Times*, November 10, 2016, accessed August 2, 2017, https://www.nytimes.com/2016/11/10/technology/the-data-said-clinton -would-win.

3.   *New York Times* Video "Clinton Campaign Chairman Speaks at Javits Center," *New York Times*, November 9, 2016, accessed August 3, 2017, https://www.nytimes.com/video/us/politics/100000004708086/podesta -clinton-speech-election-day.html.

4.   "Transcript: Donald Trump Speaks at Victory Rally," NPR, November 9, 2016, accessed August 3, 2017, http://www.npr.org/2016 /11/09/500715254/transcript-donald-trump-speaks-at-victory-rally.

5.   Ibid.

6.   Elizabeth Dias, "How Evangelicals Helped Donald Trump Win," *Time*, November 9, 2016, accessed June 14, 2017, http://time.com/4565010 /donald-trump-evangelicals-win/.

7.   Ibid.

8.   Ibid.

9.   Ibid.

10.   Marcus Yam, "Trump Head Burned in Effigy Outside L.A. City Hall," *Los Angeles Times*, November 9, 2016, accessed August 3, 2017, http://www.latimes.com/nation/politics/trailguide/la-na-election-aftermath -updates-trail-trump-head-burned-in-effigy-outside-la-1478751211-htmlstory .html.

11.   Euan McKirdy, Susanna Capelouto, and Max Blau, "Thousands Take to the Streets to Protest Trump Win," CNN, November 10, 2016, accessed August 3, 2017, http://www.cnn.com/2016/11/09/politics/election -results-reaction-streets/index.html.

12.   Barbara Demick and Vera Haller, "Thousands Protest Trump in New York," *Los Angeles Times*, November 9, 2016, accessed August 3, 2017, http://www.latimes.com/nation/la-na-new-york-trump-protest-20161109 -story.html.

13.   Newt Gingrich, "Hannity: The American People Have Finally Been Heard; Newt Gingrich on President-Elect Trump's Calls for Unity," transcript, Fox News, November 9, 2016, accessed August 3, 2017, http://www .foxnews.com/transcript/2016/11/09/hannity-american-people-have-finally -been-heard.html.

14.   Bernie Sanders, "Bernie Sanders on Resisting Trump, Why the Democratic Party Is an 'Absolute Failure' and More," transcript, Democracy Now!, July 3, 2017, accessed August 3, 2017, https://www.democracynow .org/2017/7/3/bernie_sanders_on_resisting_trump_why.

15.   Ibid.

16.   Jennifer Wishon, "Bible Studies at the White House: Who's Inside This Spiritual Awakening?," CBN News, July 31, 2017, accessed August 3, 2017, http://www1.cbn.com/cbnnews/politics/2017/july/bible-studies-at-the -white-house-whos-at-the-heart-of-this-spiritual-awakening.

17.   Capitol Ministries website, accessed August 3, 2017, https://capmin .org/ministries/washington-dc/.

18.   "Statement of Faith," Capitol Ministries website, accessed August 3, 2017, https://capmin.org/about/statement-of-faith-2/.

19.   Tom Gjelten, "With His Choice of Inauguration Prayer Leaders, Trump Shows His Values," NPR, January 13, 2017, accessed June 12, 2017, http://www.npr.org/2017/01/13/509558608/with-his-choice-of-inauguration -prayer-leaders-trump-shows-his-values.

20.   "Billy Graham: Pastor to Presidents," BGEA, February 19, 2012, accessed August 3, 2017, https://billygraham.org/story/billy-graham-pastor -to-presidents-2/.

21.   Gjelten, "With His Choice of Inauguration Prayer Leaders, Trump Shows His Values."

Chapter 4—Trump and Evangelicals

1.   Marvin Olansky and the editors, "Unfit for Power," *WORLD*, October 29, 2016, accessed August 3, 2017, https://world.wng.org/2016/10 /unfit_for_power.

2.   Ramesh Ponnuru, "Clinton on Late-Term Abortions: Checking the Fact-Checkers," *National Review*, October 14, 2016, accessed August 3, 2017, http://www.nationalreview.com/article/441071/hillary-clinton-late-term -abortion-supporter.

3.   Alastair Jamieson, "Hillary Clinton: Half of Trump Supporters Belong in 'Basket of Deplorables,'" NBC News, September 10, 2016, accessed August 3, 2017, http://www.nbcnews.com/politics/2016-election/hillary -clinton-half-trump-supporters-belong-basket-deplorables-n646026.

4.   Tom Gjelten, "Evangelical Leader Under Attack for Criticizing Trump Supporters," NPR, December 20, 2016, accessed June 25, 2017, http://www.npr.org/2016/12/20/506248119/anti-trump-evangelical-faces-backlash.

5.   Russell Moore, Twitter post, October 8, 2016, 1:39 a.m., https://twitter.com/drmoore/status/784825668257316873.

6.   Gjelten, "Evangelical Leader Under Attack for Criticizing Trump Supporters."

7.   Ibid.

8.   R. Albert Mohler Jr. "Donald Trump Has Created an Excruciating Moment for Evangelicals," *Washington Post*, October 9, 2016, accessed June 25, 2017, https://www.washingtonpost.com/news/acts-of-faith/wp/2016/10/09/donald-trump-has-created-an-excruciating-moment-for-evangelicals/.

9.   Jack Jenkins, "A List of Faith Leaders Calling Out the Religious Right for Failing to Abandon Trump," ThinkProgress, October 9, 2016, accessed June 25, 2017, https://thinkprogress.org/a-list-of-faith-leaders-calling-out-the-religious-right-for-failing-to-abandon-trump-7a2ee8fb26e6.

10.   Beth Moore, Twitter post, October 9, 2016, 9:07 a.m., https://twitter.com/bethmoorelpm/status/785119502769852418?lang=en.

11.   Beth Moore, Twitter post, October 9, 2016, 9:34 a.m., https://twitter.com/bethmoorelpm/status/785126388776873985?lang=en.

12.   Stephen Moore, "The Never Trumpers Do Need to Get a Hold of Themselves," *American Spectator*, August 23, 2016, accessed June 7, 2017, https://spectator.org/the-republicans-sore-loser-caucus/.

13.   Ibid.

14.   Ibid.

15.   Gregory A. Smith and Jessica Martínez, "How the Faithful Voted: A Preliminary 2016 Analysis," Pew Research Center, November 9, 2016, accessed August 4, 2017, http://www.pewresearch.org/fact-tank/2016/11/09/how-the-faithful-voted-a-preliminary-2016-analysis/.

16.   Tim Alberta, "Inside the Secret Meeting Where Conservative Leaders Pledged Allegiance to Ted Cruz," *National Review*, December 14, 2015, accessed June 22, 2017, http://www.nationalreview.com/article/428515/conservative-leaders-ted-cruz-earns-their-allegiance-secret-meeting.

17.   Ibid.

18.   Ibid.

19.   Ibid.

20.   Ibid.

21.   Ibid.

22.   Ibid.

23.   John Stemberger, "WMFE: Radio Interview With John Stemberger on the 2016 Presidential Election," YouTube video, 2:03, October 13, 2016, posted by Florida Family Policy Council, https://www.youtube.com/watch?v=tK-wo_HOACg.

24.   "FULL TEXT: Donald Trump's 2016 Republican National Convention Speech," ABC News, July 22, 2016, accessed August 4, 2017,

http://abcnews.go.com/Politics/full-text-donald-trumps-2016-republican
-national-convention/story?id=40786529.

25.   Lance Wallnau, "Is Trump Himself a Prophet? This Businessman
Says Yes!," Charisma Media, August 18, 2016, accessed August 4, 2017,
https://www.charismanews.com/opinion/59307-is-trump-himself-a-prophet
-this-businessman-says-yes.

26.   Ben A. Franklin, "200,000 March and Pray in Washington,"
Courier-Journal, April 30, 1980, Newspapers.com, accessed August 4, 2017,
https://www.newspapers.com/newspage/109434617/.

27.   Ronald Reagan, "National Affairs Campaign Address on Religious
Liberty (Abridged)," American Rhetoric, August 22, 1980, accessed August
4, 2017, http://www.americanrhetoric.com/speeches/ronaldreaganreligious
liberty.htm.

28.   Jennifer Harper, "Franklin Graham . . . Calls for 'Christian Revolution'," *Washington Times*, November 6, 2016, accessed June 23, 2017, http://
www.washingtontimes.com/news/2016/nov/6/frankling-graham-asks-nation
-to-pray-on-election-d/.

29.   Ibid.

30.   Jennifer LeClaire, "Will We Make the Right Decision?," *Charisma*,
October 2016, 48.

31.   Ibid.

32.   "Dr. James Dobson on Donald Trump's Christian Faith," Family
Talk, accessed August 24, 2017, http://drjamesdobson.org/news/dr-james
-dobson-on-trumps-christian-faith; James Dobson, "A Conversation With
Donald Trump," Family Talk, August 2016, accessed August 24, 2017,
https://www.drjamesdobson.org/news/commentaries/archives/2016-news
letters/august-newsletter-2016.

33.   "Dr. James Dobson on Donald Trump's Christian Faith," Family
Talk.

34.   "Dr. James Dobson Endorses Donald J. Trump for President of the
United States," Religion News Service, July 22, 2016, accessed August 24,
2017, http://religionnews.com/2016/07/22/dr-james-dobson-endorses-donald
-j-trump-for-president-of-the-united-states/.

35.   OxfordDictionary.com, s.v. "epistemology," accessed August 24,
2017, https://en.oxforddictionaries.com/definition/us/epistemology.

Chapter 5—Mobilizing the Faithful

1.   David Jackson, "Republicans Hope to Find 'Missing' Evangelical
Voters," *USA Today*, October 19, 2016, accessed August 5, 2017, https://
www.usatoday.com/story/news/politics/elections/2015/10/19/2016-campaign
-republicans-evangelicals/74206060/.

2.   Jim Garlow, "Prop 8 Preserves Freedoms," jimgarlow.com, October
30, 2008, accessed August 5, 2017, http://www.jimgarlow.com/381/prop-8
-preserves-freedoms/. Controversy, endless media attacks, and a heated war
of words followed passage of the bill, and in 2013 the US Supreme Court

upheld an earlier federal court ruling blocking the amendment and allowing same-sex marriages to continue in that state.

3.   Jim Garlow, "Deciphering Hillary's Strong Delusion," *Charisma*, October 2016, 40–42.

4.   In communication with author.

5.   Lindsey Cook, "South Carolina's Key Role in the Presidential Race," U.S. News and World Report, February 17, 2016, accessed August 6, 2017, https://www.usnews.com/news/blogs/data-mine/articles/2016-02-17/south -carolinas-key-role-in-the-2016-presidential-race.

6.   In communication with author.

7.   Ibid.

8.   Leigh Ann Caldwell, "Donald Trump Wins South Carolina Primary," NBCNews.com, February 21, 2016, accessed August 6, 2017, http:// www.nbcnews.com/politics/2016-election/trump-wins-south-carolina -primary-nbc-news-projects-n522726.

9.   Paul Bedard, Twitter post, November 9, 2016, 12:30 p.m., https:// twitter.com/SecretsBedard/status/796223524528603136.

Chapter 6—Surprising Early Supporters

1.   The first woman to pray at a presidential inauguration was Myrlie Evers-Williams who offered the invocation at the second inauguration of President Obama, on January 21, 2013, but unlike Paula White Cain, she was not a minister.

2.   In communication with author.

3.   Patrick Healy and Megan Thee-Brenan, "More Republicans See Donald Trump as Winner, Poll Finds," *New York Times*, September 15, 2015, accessed August 6, 2017, https://www.nytimes.com/2015/09/16/us /politics/gop-support-for-donald-trump-rising-as-ben-carson-gains-poll -finds.html.

4.   Author personally attended this event, which was also reported by Amy Sullivan, "Obama's Play for the Faithful," *New York Times*, June 12, 2008, accessed August 6, 2017, http://content.time.com/time/politics/article /0,8599,1814206,00.html.

5.   "Paula White, Kenneth Copeland and Others Lay Hands On, Pray for Donald Trump," YouTube video, 0:59, September 30, 2015, posted by Christian News, https://www.youtube.com/watch?v=EQ18exdhR6I; "Praying for Donald Trump 9-28-2015 at Trump Tower NYC," YouTube video, September 28, 2015, posted by Donald Nori Jr Don Nori, https://www.youtube .com/watch?v=TthhM3gL3ZM.

6.   "Paula White, Kenneth Copeland and Others Lay Hands On, Pray for Donald Trump," YouTube video, 3:10.

7.   "Pastor Takes You Inside the Oval Office Prayer Meeting," CBN News, July 14, 2017, accessed August 21, 2017, http://www1.cbn.com /cbnnews/us/2017/july/pastor-takes-you-inside-the-oval-office-prayer -meeting; "The Truth Behind the Oval Office Prayer Circle," Fox News, http://video.foxnews.com/v/5508752433001/?#sp=show-clips.

8. Donald Trump's Twitter page, accessed August 19, 2017, https://twitter.com/realdonaldtrump/status/692028126189199360?lang=en.

9. Marv Knox, "Editorial: The 'Downward Death Spiral' of Hypocrisy," Baptist Standard, January 28, 2016, accessed August 16, 2017, https://www.baptiststandard.com/opinion/editorial/18753-editorial-the-downward-death-spiral-of-hypocrisy.

10. Elizabeth Landers, "Some Liberty University Students Rebel Against Falwell Over Trump," CNN, October 13, 2016, accessed August 16, 2017, http://www.cnn.com/2016/10/13/politics/liberty-university-jerry-falwell-jr-donald-trump/index.html.

11. David Weigel and Jose A. DelReal, "Phyllis Schlafly Endorses Trump in St. Louis," *Washington Post*, March 11, 2016, accessed August 16, 2017, https://www.washingtonpost.com/news/post-politics/wp/2016/03/11/phyllis-schlafly-endorses-trump-in-st-louis/?utm_term=.ef03a272e96c.

12. Julia Hahn, "Exclusive–Phyllis Schlafly Makes the Case for President Trump: 'Only Hope to Defeat the Kingmakers'," Breitbart, January 10, 2016, accessed August 16, 2017, http://www.breitbart.com/big-government/2016/01/10/phyllis-schlafly-makes-the-case-for-president-trump/.

13. Donald Trump, Twitter post, September 6, 2016, 6:00 a.m., https://twitter.com/realdonaldtrump/status/773113752271060992?lang=en.

14. "Trump Speaks at Phyllis Schlafly's Funeral," YouTube video, 0:07, posted by CNN, https://www.youtube.com/watch?v=1Bng_6HZlPM.

15. Donald J. Trump's Facebook page, accessed August 16, 2017, https://www.facebook.com/pg/DonaldTrump/about/?ref=page_internal.

16. Lance Wallnau, "Donald Trump Key to Isaiah 45 Prophecy?," Charisma News, August 17, 2016, accessed August 16, 2017, https://www.charismanews.com/opinion/59304-donald-trump-key-to-isaiah-45-prophecy.

17. "Kim Clement: 'God Says, 'Time Magazine Will Have No Choice but to Say What I Want Them to Say,'" The Elijah List, April 14, 2007, accessed August 16, 2017, http://www.elijahlist.com/words/display_word/5190.

18. Bob Eschilman, "A Prophetic [Political] Showdown," *Charisma*, October 2016, 50.

19. Ibid.

20. "TRUNEWS 04/18/16 Mark Taylor | God's Man," TRUNEWS, April 18, 2016, audio 9:09, http://www.trunews.com/listen/firefighter-prophecy-trump-mark-taylor-gods-man.

21. Bob Eschilman, "Donald Trump Is a Central Figure in This Prophecy," Charisma News, April 22, 2016, accessed August 17, 2017, https://www.charismanews.com/politics/primaries/56703-donald-trump-is-a-central-figure-in-this-prophecy.

22. Eschilman, "A Prophetic [Political] Showdown."

23. Steve Strang, "Pastor Darrell Scott Says It's Possible That Trump Will Win by a Landslide and Become America's Greatest President," *Strang Report*, podcast audio, MP3, accessed August 17, 2017, https://www

.charismapodcastnetwork.com/shows/strangreport/1c13dd7eeb0616d5c4964
d465d3c7cfb.

24.   Jessilyn Justice, "Frank Amedia Makes Bold Prophetic Declaration Over Donald Trump," Charisma News, September 27, 2016, accessed
August 11, 2017, http://macarthur.CharismaNews.com/politics/60182-frank
-amedia-makes-bold-prophetic-declaration-over-donald-trump0.

25.   Ibid.

26.   Steve Strang, "Is Donald Trump America's Cyrus? With Lance
Wallnau," *Strang Report*, podcast audio, MP3, 18:0, accessed May 6, 2016,
https://www.cpnshows/.com/shows/strangreport/fa261ca761fb800f76c6804
ed34998f5.

27.   Jerome Corsi, "Viral Sermon Hints at God's Hidden Purpose for
Trump," WND.com, October 18, 2016, http://www.wnd.com/2016/10/viral
-sermon-hints-at-gods-hidden-purpose-for-trump/#xO3ohq9JxlWixrTm.99.

28.   Strang, "Is Donald Trump America's Cyrus? With Lance Wallnau."

29.   Tom Horn, "Divine Providence and a Big Question: If God Was
Behind the Election of Donald Trump, Is He a Cyrus (Deliverer) or Nebuchadnezzar (Agent of Judgment)?," Charisma News, August 22, 2017,
accessed August 30, 2017, http://tinyurl.com/tom-horn-divine-providence.

30.   Ibid.

CHAPTER 7—ETHNIC ISSUES

1.   Neil Irwin, Claire Cain Miller, and Margot Sanger-Katz, "America's
Racial Divide, Charted," *New York Times*, August 19, 2014, accessed June 26,
2017, https://www.nytimes.com/2014/08/20/upshot/americas-racial-divide
-charted.html?mcubz=2.

2.   Ibid.

3.   Alan Gomez, "Another Election Surprise: Many Hispanics Backed
Trump," *USA Today*, November 9, 2016, accessed August 17, 2017, https://
www.usatoday.com/story/news/politics/elections/2016/2016/11/09/hispanic
-vote-election-2016-donald-trump-hillary-clinton/93540772/; Mark Hugo
Lopez and Paul Taylor, "Latino Voters in the 2012 Election," Pew Research
Center, November 7, 2012, accessed August 17, 2017, http://www.pew
hispanic.org/2012/11/07/latino-voters-in-the-2012-election/.

4.   Amanda Sakuma, "Trump Did Better With Blacks, Hispanics Than
Romney in '12: Exit Polls," NBC News, November 9, 2016, accessed August
7, 2017, http://www.nbcnews.com/storyline/2016-election-day/trump-did
-better-blacks-hispanics-romney-12-exit-polls-n681386.

5.   Omri Ben-Shahar, "The Non-Voters Who Decided the Election:
Trump Won Because of Lower Democratic Turnout," *Forbes*, November 17,
2016, accessed August 7, 2017, https://www.forbes.com/sites/omribenshahar
/2016/11/17/the-non-voters-who-decided-the-election-trump-won-because
-of-lower-democratic-turnout/#32de9d4453ab.

6.   Newt Gingrich, *Understanding Trump* (New York: Center Street,
2017), 152.

7.   "Presidential Candidates Videos," NHCLC, accessed August 7, 2017, https://nhclc.org/presidential-candidates-videos/.

8.   "2016 Presidential Election Results," 270towin.com, accessed August 7, 2017, http://www.270towin.com/maps/2016-actual-electoral-map; From data collected by Ralph Reed's Faith and Freedom Coalition as shared on Monday, November 14, 2016, on a conference call meeting with the Faith Advisory Board.

9.   Samuel Rodriguez, in communication with author.

10.   Ibid.

11.   Heather Sells, "Latino Leader Samuel Rodriguez: Trump Is Not a Racist," CBN News, April 29, 2016, accessed August 7, 2017, http://www1.cbn.com/cbnnews/politics/2016/april/latino-leader-samuel-rodriguez-trump-is-not-a-racist.

12.   "Hispanic Evangelical Leader Rejects Univision Anchor's Anti-Trump Rant," NHCLC, accessed August 7, 2017, http://nhclc.org/hispanic-evangelical-leader-rejects-univision-anchors-anti-trump-rant/.

13.   Ibid.

14.   Samuel Rodriguez, in communication with author.

15.   Ibid.

16.   Ibid.

17.   "Do Pastors Belong on the Trump Inauguration Stage?," *Christianity Today*, January 19, 2017, accessed August 7, 2017, http://www.christianitytoday.com/ct/2017/january-web-only/do-pastors-belong-on-trump-inauguration-stage.html.

18.   Darrell Scott, "Trump: The Media's Portrayal Is Wrong," *The Jim Bakker Show*, November 1, 2016, accessed August 7, 2017, https://jimbakkershow.com/video/darrell-scott-frank-amedia-day-1/.

19.   Steve Strang, "Pastor Darrell Scott Tells Us What His Friend Donald Trump Is Really Like," *Strang Report*, podcast audio, MP3, November 3, 2016, accessed August 7, 2017, https://www.charismapodcastnetwork.com/shows/strangreport/23fe5a40df8d23cbd9cd5d2d93b4e6fc.

20.   Ibid.

21.   Ibid.

22.   In communication with author; David Brody, "Donald Trump Will Appear on Christian TV Courting African-American Community," CBN News, August 29, 2016, accessed August 7, 2017, http://www1.cbn.com/thebrodyfile/archive/2016/08/29/new-this-morning-donald-trump-going-to-church-will-appear-on-christian-tv-courting--community.

23.   Nikita Vladimirov, "Pastor Presents Trump With Prayer Shawl During Church Visit," *The Hill*, September 3, 2016, accessed August 7, 2017, http://thehill.com/blogs/ballot-box/presidential-races/294403-pastor-presents-trump-with-prayer-shawl-during-church.

24.   Seema Mehta, "Ivanka Trump Introduces Father as a Colorblind, Gender-Neutral Leader," *Los Angeles Times*, July 22, 2016, accessed August 19, 2017, http://www.latimes.com/nation/politics/trailguide/la-na-republican

-convention-2016-trump-ivanka-trump-introduces-father-as-a-1469156040
-htmlstory.html.

25.   Alveda King, in communication with author.

26.   Ibid.

27.   Alveda King, "Niece of Dr. Martin Luther King Speaks Out for the Future of the Yet Unborn," Priests for Life, accessed August 7, 2017, http:// www.priestsforlife.org/africanamerican/howcandreamsurvive.htm.

28.   Karen Pazol, Andreea A. Creanga, and Denise J. Jamieson, "Abortion Surveillance—United States, 2012," Centers for Disease Control and Prevention, November 27, 2015, accessed August 7, 2017, https://www.cdc .gov/mmwr/preview/mmwrhtml/ss6410a1.htm#tab3.

29.   Alveda King, in communication with author.

30.   Gingrich, *Understanding Trump*.

31.   Donald Trump, "The Inaugural Address," The White House, January 20, 2017, accessed August 7, 2017, https://www.whitehouse.gov /inaugural-address.

32.   Gingrich, *Understanding Trump*, 134.

33.   Harry Jackson, "Evangelicals and the 2016 Presidential Election," C-SPAN, September 16, 2016, accessed August 7, 2017, https://www.c-span .org/video/?415379-1/evangelical-leaders-discuss-2016-presidential-election.

34.   Ibid.

35.   Ibid.

36.   Chuck Pierce, in communication with author.

37.   "State Department Sent Taxpayer Money to Group That Attempted to Oust Israel's Netanyahu," Fox News, July 13, 2016, accessed August 7, 2017, http://www.foxnews.com/politics/2016/07/13/state-department-sent -taxpayer-money-to-group-that-attempted-to-oust-israels-netanyahu.html.

38.   Chuck Pierce, in communication with author.

39.   Ibid.

40.   Ibid.

41.   "Is the Author of a Book Critical of Islam an Ancestor of President Bush?," archived from USINFO, updated January 27, 2005, accessed August 7, 2017, https://web.archive.org/web/20081112171741/http://usinfo.state.gov /media/Archive_Index/Life_of_Mohammed_Book_NOT_Authored_by _Grandfather_or_Ancestor_of_President_Bush.html.

42.   "Professor George Bush (1796–1859)," Friends of Zion Museum, accessed August 7, 2017, https://www.fozmuseum.com/explore-foz/professor -george-bush-1796-1859/.

43.   George Bush, *The Valley of Vision; or The Dry Bones of Israel Revived* (New York: Saxton & Miles, 1844), accessed August 7, 2017, https:// books.google.com/books?id=3TbDDxRB_t4C&source=gbs_navlinks_s.

44.   Mike Evans, in communication with author.

45.   Ibid.

46.   Boaz Bismuth, "'If I Win, I Will Be Israel's True Friend in the White House,'" *Israel Hayom*, February 26, 2016, accessed August 8, 2017, http://www.israelhayom.com/site/newsletter_article.php?id=32049.

47. "Trump's 'Neutral' View on Israel Targeted by Rubio and Cruz at GOP Debate," Breaking Israel News, February 28, 2016, accessed August 8, 2017, https://www.breakingisraelnews.com/62384/trumps-neutral-view -israel-targeted-by-rubio-cruz-gop-debate-jerusalem/#KHFH8ilvQ 8fRs6EO.97.

48. Shira Schmid, "Ivanka Trump and Shabbat: Pure Family Time," *Jerusalem Post*, November 9, 2016, accessed August 8, 2017, http://www .jpost.com/Opinion/Ivanka-Trump-and-Shabbat-Pure-family-time-472181; Hannah Hayes, "Ivanka Trump Proudly Keeps Kosher," *Jewish Voice*, March 6, 2015, accessed August 8, 2017, http://www.pressreader.com/usa/the -jewish-voice/20150306/281487864811618/TextView.

49. Jonathan Van Meter, "Ivanka Trump Knows What It Means to Be a Modern Millennial," *Vogue*, February 25, 2015, accessed August 8, 2017, http://www.vogue.com/article/ivanka-trump-collection-the-apprentice -family.

50. Michele Gorman, "Transcript: Donald Trump's Family Town Hall With CNN," *Newsweek*, April 13, 2016, accessed August 8, 2017, http://www .newsweek.com/donald-trump-cnn-family-town-hall-full-transcript-new -york-city-447144.

51. Emily Flitter, "Jewish Son-in-Law Kushner Guided Trump's Triumphant AIPAC Speech," Haaretz.com, April 5, 2016, accessed August 8, 2017, http://www.haaretz.com/world-news/u-s-election-2016/1.712750.

52. Schmid, "Ivanka Trump and Shabbat: Pure Family Time."

53. James Robison, "Faith and Prayer in the Oval Office: James Robison Speaks With Jack Graham," The Stream, July 14, 2017, accessed August 8, 2017, https://stream.org/faith-prayer-oval-office-james-robison-speaks-jack -graham/.

54. Brandon Showalter, "Trump Says He Prayed for Wisdom From God While Touching Western Wall," *Christian Post*, May 24, 2017, accessed August 8, 2017, http://www.christianpost.com/news/trump-says-he-prayed -for-wisdom-from-god-while-touching-western-wall-184738/.

55. Luke Baker and Steve Holland, "In U.S. Presidential First, Trump Prays at Jerusalem's Western Wall," Reuters, May 22, 2017, accessed August 8, 2017, http://www.reuters.com/article/us-usa-trump-israel-wall -idUSKBN18I1V6.

56. "Speech: Donald Trump at Celebrate Freedom Rally—July 1, 2017," Factbase, accessed August 8, 2017, https://factba.se/transcript/donald-trump -speech-celebrate-freedom-rally-july-1-2017.

CHAPTER 8—THE ROLE OF FAMILY

1. Donald Trump, in interview with author, August 11, 2016.

2. Donald Trump with Tony Schwartz, *The Art of the Deal* (New York: Random House, 1987), 45.

3. Kaitlin Menza, "16 Things You Didn't Know About Donald Trump's Father, Fred," *Town & Country*, April 5, 2017, accessed August 9, 2017, http://www.townandcountrymag.com/society/money-and-power/g9229257

/fred-trump-facts/?slide=4; Trump with Schwartz, *The Art of the Deal*, 74–76.

4.   Trump with Schwartz, *The Art of the Deal*, 66.

5.   Catherine Holder Spude, "Trump's Grandfather Made His Fortune in the Yukon," JuneauEmpire.com, February 9, 2017, accessed August 9, 2017, http://juneauempire.com/art/art/2017-02-09/trump-s-grandfather-made -his-fortune-yukon.

6.   Tracie Rozhon, "Fred C. Trump, Postwar Master Builder of Housing for Middle Class, Dies at 93," *New York Times*, June 26, 1999, accessed August 9, 2017, http://www.nytimes.com/1999/06/26/nyregion /fred-c-trump-postwar-master-builder-of-housing-for-middle-class-dies -at-93.html.

7.   Trump with Schwartz, *The Art of the Deal*, 66–68; Rozhon, "Fred C. Trump, Postwar Master Builder of Housing for Middle Class, Dies at 93."

8.   Rozhon, "Fred C. Trump, Postwar Master Builder of Housing for Middle Class, Dies at 93."

9.   Mary Pilon, "Donald Trump's Immigrant Mother," *New Yorker*, June 24, 2016, accessed August 9, 2017, http://www.newyorker.com/news /news-desk/donald-trumps-immigrant-mother; Steven Brocklehurst, "Donald Trump's Mother: From a Scottish Island to New York's Elite," BBC, January 19, 2017, accessed August 9, 2017, http://www.bbc.com/news/uk -scotland-38648877.

10.   Torcuil Crichton, "Never Before Seen Pictures of Donald Trump's Scottish Mum Make a Mockery of His Migrant Bashing," *Daily Mirror*, August 8, 2016, accessed August 9, 2017, http://www.mirror.co.uk/news /world-news/never-before-seen-pictures-donald-8584962.

11.   Trump with Schwartz, *The Art of the Deal*, 79–80.

12.   Crichton, "Never Before Seen Pictures of Donald Trump's Scottish Mum Make a Mockery of His Migrant Bashing"; Meghan Murphy-Gill, "The Faith of Donald Trump," US Catholic, January 19, 2017, accessed August 9, 2017, http://www.uscatholic.org/articles/201701/faith-donald -trump-30910.

13.   Liz Posner, "Who Is Donald Trump's Mother? Mary MacLeod Trump Has Such an Interesting Backstory," Bustle, October 26, 2015, accessed August 9, 2017, https://www.bustle.com/articles/119550 -who-is-donald-trumps-mother-mary-macleod-trump-has-such-an -interesting-backstory; James Barron, "Overlooked Influences on Donald Trump: A Famous Minister and His Church," *New York Times*, September 5, 2016, accessed August 9, 2017, https://www.nytimes.com/2016/09/06 /nyregion/donald-trump-marble-collegiate-church-norman-vincent-peale .html; Murphy-Gill, "The Faith of Donald Trump."

14.   Colin Melbourne, "Scottish Hebrides Revival of 1949," accessed August 9, 2017, http://www.born-again-christian.info/scottish.hebrides .revival.duncan.campbell.htm.

15.   Posner, "Who Is Donald Trump's Mother? Mary MacLeod Trump Has Such an Interesting Backstory."

16.   Pilon, "Donald Trump's Immigrant Mother"; Timothy L. O'Brien, *TrumpNation: The Art of Being The Donald* (New York: Hachette Book Group, 2005), accessed August 9, 2017, https://books.google.com/books?id =VSyrCgAAQBAJ&dq=trump+nation&source=gbs_navlinks_s.

17.   O'Brien, *TrumpNation*.

18.   Trump with Schwartz, *The Art of the Deal*, 71.

19.   Ibid.; O'Brien, *TrumpNation*.

20.   Gwenda Blair, *The Trumps: Three Generations of Builders and a Presidential Candidate* (New York: Simon & Schuster, 2000), 404–405, accessed August 9, 2017, https://books.google.com/books?id=uJifCgAAQB AJ&q=robert#v=snippet&q=robert&f=false; Jane Musgrave, "Trump's Sister, the Federal Judge, 'a Little Different' From Him," PalmBeachPost.com, June 10, 2016, accessed August 9, 2017, http://www.mypalmbeachpost.com/news /national-govt--politics/trump-sister-the-federal-judge-little-different-from -him/Xmh06XLsdyCgyb17snkFXJ/; "Elizabeth Trump Weds James Grau," *New York Times*, March 27, 1989, accessed August 9, 2017, http://www .nytimes.com/1989/03/27/style/elizabeth-trump-weds-james-grau.html.

21.   O'Brien, *TrumpNation*.

22.   Ibid.

23.   Trump with Schwartz, *The Art of the Deal*, 73; O'Brien, *TrumpNation*.

24.   Hunter Walker, "Donald Trump's Classmates Share Their Memories About His 'Lord of the Flies' Days in Military School," Business Insider, October 5, 2015, accessed August 9, 2017, http://www.businessinsider.com /donald-trump-high-school-classmates-what-he-was-like-2015-10.

25.   Trump with Schwartz, *The Art of the Deal*.

26.   Ibid.; O'Brien, *TrumpNation*.

27.   M. J. Lee, "God and the Don," CNN, June 2017, accessed August 8, 2017, http://www.cnn.com/interactive/2017/politics/state/donald-trump -religion/.

28.   Jim Milliot, "Trump Signs for New Book With S&S," *Publisher's Weekly*, September 21, 2015, accessed August 8, 2017, https://www .publishersweekly.com/pw/by-topic/industry-news/book-deals/article/68124 -trump-signs-for-new-book-with-s-s.html.

29.   Donald J. Trump's Facebook page, January 30, 2016, accessed August 8, 2017, https://www.facebook.com/DonaldTrump/videos /10156583412010725/.

30.   Murphy-Gill, "The Faith of Donald Trump."

31.   Timothy L. Hall, *American Religious Leaders* (New York: Facts on File, 2003), 289, accessed August 8, 2017, https://books.google.com/books ?id=-eBX522JniwC&dq=hall+american+religious+leaders&source=gbs _navlinks_s.

32.   Norman Vincent Peale, *The Power of Positive Thinking*, Simon & Schuster Inc., accessed August 8, 2017, http://www.simonandschuster .com/books/The-Power-of-Positive-Thinking/Dr-Norman-Vincent-Peale /9780743234801.

33.   Bart Barnes, "Leonard Earle LeSourd, *Guideposts* Editor, Dies," *Washington Post*, February 7, 1996, accessed August 8, 2017, https://www.washingtonpost.com/archive/local/1996/02/07/leonard-earle-lesourd-guideposts-editor-dies/5b94e4ce-f212-4ce8-a041-7ecd7386cb15/?utm_term=.cd8d0056c73d.

34.   Norman Vincent Peale, *The True Joy of Positive Living: An Autobiography* (New York: Open Road Integrated Media, 2015), accessed August 8, 2017, https://books.google.com/books?id=BB5ZCgAAQBAJ&dq=the+true+joy+of+positive+living+%22ben+arneson%22&source=gbs_navlinks_s.

35.   Norman Vincent Peale, *The True Joy of Positive Living: An Autobiography* (New York: William Morrow & Co., special edition for the Foundation for Christian Living, 1984), 220-221.

36.   Ibid.

37.   In communication with author.

38.   April Walloga, "The Trump 5: Meet the Fabulous Offspring of GOP Presidential Candidate Donald Trump," Business Insider, July 6, 2015, accessed August 19, 2017, http://www.businessinsider.com/meet-donald-trumps-five-children-2015-7.

39.   Ibid.

40.   Ibid.

41.   Sarah Ellison, "Inside Ivanka and Tiffany Trump's Complicated Sister Act," *Vanity Fair*, February 2017, accessed August 19, 2017, https://www.vanityfair.com/news/2016/12/inside-ivanka-trump-and-tiffany-trump-complicated-sister-act.

42.   Walloga, "The Trump 5."

43.   Stephanie Dube Dwilson, "Donald Trump Jr.'s Family & Children: 5 Fast Facts You Need to Know," Heavy.com, July 12, 2017, accessed August 19, 2017, http://heavy.com/news/2017/07/donald-trump-jr-family-children-kids-wife-vanessa-parents-grandparents-milos-zelnicek/.

44.   Walloga, "The Trump 5"; Alana Abramson, "Ivanka Trump's Book Will Appear on a 'New York Times' Bestseller List," *FORTUNE*, May 11, 2017, http://fortune.com/2017/05/11/ivanka-trumps-book-will-appear-on-a-new-york-times-bestseller-list/.

45.   Kaitlin Menza, "18 Things You Didn't Know About Donald and Ivanka Trump's Father-Daughter Relationship," *Redbook*, http://www.redbookmag.com/life/g4235/ivanka-trump-donald-trump-relationship/.

46.   Ibid.

47.   Ibid.; Jamie Reysen and amNY.com staff, "Donald Trump's Family Tree: Melania, Ivanka, Tiffany, Eric and More Relatives," *amNewYork*, April 10, 2017, accessed August 21, 2017, http://www.amny.com/news/elections/donald-trump-s-family-tree-melania-ivanka-tiffany-eric-and-more-relatives-1.12039888.

48.   Ibid.

49.   Walloga, "The Trump 5."

50.   Ibid.

51.   Yaron Steinbuch, "Eric Trump and Wife Expecting First Child," *Page Six*, March 20, 2017, accessed August 19, 2017, http://pagesix.com /2017/03/20/eric-trump-and-wife-expecting-first-child/.

52.   In communication with author.

53.   Reysen and amNY.com staff, "Donald Trump's Family Tree."

54.   Walloga, "The Trump 5"; Katie Rogers, "Tiffany Trump Will Attend Georgetown Law," *New York Times*, May 8, 2017, accessed August 19, 2017, https://www.nytimes.com/2017/05/08/us/politics/tiffany-trump-georgetown -law.html?mcubz=1.

55.   Walloga, "The Trump 5."

56.   Ibid.

57.   In communication with author.

58.   Ibid.

59.   Alexandra King, "Barron Trump Will Be First Son in White House Since JFK Jr.," CNN, November 10, 2016, accessed August 19, 2017, http:// www.cnn.com/2016/11/10/politics/barron-trump-first-son-in-white-house -since-jfk-jr-/index.html.

60.   Bonnie Fuller, "Baron Trump: 5 Things to Know About Donald Trump's Youngest Son," Penske Media Corporation, accessed August 19, 2017, http://hollywoodlife.com/2016/07/21/who-is-barron-trump-donald -youngest-son-facts/.

61.   Reysen, "Donald Trump's Family Tree."

62.   In communication with author.

63.   Maggie McGlamry, "Donald Trump, Jr. Visits Milner Church on Campaign Trail," Sinclair Broadcast Group, October 28, 2016, accessed August 8, 2017, http://wgxa.tv/news/local/donald-trump-jr-visits-milner -church-on-campaign-trail; Katherine Mozzone, "Trump Jr. Rallies for Donald Trump in New Mexico," KRQE News 13, November 4, 2016, accessed August 8, 2017, http://krqe.com/2016/11/04/trump-jr-to-rally-for -dad-in-new-mexico/.

64.   Elisa Cipollone, "Don Jr. Goes to Church," LifeZette, November 6, 2016, accessed August 8, 2017, http://www.lifezette.com/faithzette/don-jr -goes-church/.

65.   Ibid.

66.   Ibid.

67.   Ibid.

68.   Donald Trump, in communication with author.

69.   Kate Shellnutt and Sarah Eekhoff Zylstra, "Who's Who of Trump's 'Tremendous' Faith Advisers," *Christianity Today*, June 22, 2016, accessed August 8, 2017, http://www.christianitytoday.com/ct/2016/june-web-only /whos-who-of-trumps-tremendous-faith-advisors.html; Jonathan Swan and Sarah Ferris, "Trump Toughens Anti-Abortion Stance," *The Hill*, September 16, 2016, accessed August 8, 2017, http://thehill.com/blogs/ballot-box /presidential-races/296254-trump-strengthens-anti-abortion-stance.

CHAPTER 9—WHAT TRUMP BELIEVES

1. For a look at one exhaustive compilation, see Jasmine C. Lee and Kevin Quealy, "The 359 People, Places and Things Donald Trump Has Insulted on Twitter: A Complete List," *New York Times*, updated August 15, 2017, accessed August 15, 2017, https://www.nytimes.com/interactive /2016/01/28/upshot/donald-trump-twitter-insults.html?_r=0; Nick Gass, "Donald Trump's Greatest 2016 Tweets," POLITICO, June 6, 2015, accessed August 8, 2017, http://www.politico.com/story/2015/06/donald-trump-best -2016-tweets-119057.

2. Howard Kurtz, "Trump Ups the Ante on Twitter, Defying Media Criticism and His Own Aides' Advice," Fox News, June 7, 2017, accessed August 8, 2017, http://www.foxnews.com/politics/2017/06/07/trump-ups -ante-on-twitter-defying-media-criticism-and-his-own-aides-advice.html.

3. James Lewis "What Does Donald Trump Really Believe?," *American Thinker*, February 28, 2016, accessed August 7, 2017, http://www .americanthinker.com/articles/2016/02/what_does_donald_trump_really _believe.html.

4. Ibid.

5. "2016 Republican Party Platform, July 18, 2016," The American Presidency Project, accessed August 7, 2017, http://www.presidency.ucsb.edu /ws/?pid=117718.

6. Ibid.

7. "Trump on the Somali Pirates," YouTube video, :39, Human Events, March 14, 2011, accessed August 7, 2017, https://www.youtube.com /watch?v=_HT-43axdgc; David Sherfinski, "Donald Trump: We will 'Eradicate' 'Radical Islamic Terrorism' 'From the Face of the Earth,'" *Washington Times*, January 20, 2017, accessed September 16, 2017, http://www .washingtontimes.com/news/2017/jan/20/donald-trump-we-will-eradicate -radical-islamic-ter/.

8. Dan Merica, "Trump on Waterboarding: 'We Have to Fight Fire With Fire,'" CNN, January 26, 2017, accessed August 7, 2017, http://www .cnn.com/2017/01/25/politics/donald-trump-waterboarding-torture/index .html.

9. "Congress Passes Long-Awaited Veterans Affairs Accountability Act," CBS News, June 14, 2017, accessed August 7, 2017, http://www.cbsnews .com/news/congress-passes-long-awaited-veterans-affairs-accountability-act/.

10. "Interview With Donald Trump," *State of the Union*, June 28, 2015, transcript, accessed August 7, 2017, http://transcripts.cnn.com /TRANSCRIPTS/1506/28/sotu.01.html.

11. "Biography Donald Trump Full Original," YouTube video, 22:32, posted by Biography Documentary Channel, March 24, 2017, https://www .youtube.com/watch?v=u4GWDJkBrXQ.

12. Ibid.; Robert Hanley, "Copter Crash Kills 3 Aides of Trump," *New York Times*, October 11, 1989, accessed August 7, 2017, http://www.nytimes .com/1989/10/11/nyregion/copter-crash-kills-3-aides-of-trump.html.

13.   Trump headquarters, GOP fund-raising letter, June 14, 2017, received by Jim Nelson Black.

14.   Latoya West, "Stephen Baldwin: Trump Would Make a Great President," *Tennessean*, July 15, 2015, accessed August 7, 2017, http://www.tennessean.com/story/entertainment/people/suburbarazzi/2015/07/15/stephen-baldwin-trump-would-make-a-great-president/30190301/.

15.   Jessica Estepa, "Trump: ' My Job Is to Represent the United States of America,'" *USA Today*, March 1, 2017, accessed August 7, 2017, https://www.usatoday.com/story/news/politics/onpolitics/2017/02/28/trump-my-job-represent-united-states-america/98560320/.

16.   "Remarks by President Trump in Joint Address to Congress," The White House, February 28, 2017, accessed August 8, 2017, https://www.whitehouse.gov/the-press-office/2017/02/28/remarks-president-trump-joint-address-congress.

17.   "President Trump's Trip Abroad," The White House, accessed August 8, 2017, https://www.whitehouse.gov/potus-abroad.

18.   Ibid.

19.   Sarah Pulliam Bailey, "Melania Trump Is Catholic, She Confirms After Vatican Visit," *Washington Post*, May 25, 2017, accessed August 8, 2017, https://www.washingtonpost.com/news/acts-of-faith/wp/2017/05/25/melania-trump-is-catholic-she-confirms-after-vatican-visit/?utm_term=.4cf08f4400f9.

20.   "President Trump's Trip Abroad," The White House.

CHAPTER 10—POLITICAL PRIORITIES

1.   Penny Starr, "FLASHBACK: Obama Says 'I Am Not a Supporter of Gay Marriage,'" CNSNews.com, June 29, 2015, accessed August 1, 2017, http://www.cnsnews.com/news/article/penny-starr/flashback-obama-says-i-am-not-supporter-gay-marriage.

2.   Zeke J. Miller, "Axelrod: Obama Misled Nation When He Opposed Gay Marriage in 2008," *Time*, February 10, 2015, accessed August 19, 2017, http://time.com/3702584/gay-marriage-axelrod-obama/.

3.   "Transcript: Robin Roberts ABC News Interview With President Obama," ABC News, May 9, 2012, accessed August 1, 2017, http://abcnews.go.com/Politics/transcript-robin-roberts-abc-news-interview-president-obama/story?id=16316043.

4.   Miller, "Axelrod: Obama Misled Nation When He Opposed Gay marriage in 2008."

5.   "FULL: Jon Voight at Voter Values Summit Washington, DC—Donald Trump," from the 2016 Voter Values Summit, televised by ABC, posted by "ABC15 Arizona," September 9, 2016, accessed August 1, 2017, https://www.youtube.com/watch?v=4G6lx_efQaU&list=PLgbKEZz9CBcggh34Sda71Y5TTmR6CJv04&index=9.

6.   Ibid.

7.   Ibid.

8.   "Presidential Candidate Donald Trump at Values Voter Summit," C-SPAN, September 9, 2016, accessed August 1, 2017, https://www.c-span .org/video/?415005-3/presidential-candidate-donald-trump-values-voter -summit.

9.   Ben Johnson, "Donald Trump's 4 Promises to the Values Voter Summit," LifeSiteNews.com, September 12, 2016, accessed August 19, 2017, https://www.lifesitenews.com/news/donald-trumps-4-promises-to-the -values-voters-summit.

10.   Ibid.

11.   Ibid.

12.   "George Washington Gives First Presidential Inaugural Address," History.com, accessed August 8, 2017, http://www.history.com/this-day-in -history/george-washington-gives-first-presidential-inaugural-address.

13.   Steven Waldman, "Inaugural Prayers Through History—The Ultimate Archive," Beliefnet, accessed August 8, 2017, http://www.beliefnet .com/columnists/stevenwaldman/2009/01/inaugural-invocations-and-pray .html.

14.   Emily McFarlan Miller, "Who's Praying at Trump's Inauguration? A Mix of Supporters, Critics and Firsts," Religion News Service, January 19, 2017, accessed August 8, 2017, http://religionnews.com/2017/01/19/whos -praying-at-trumps-inauguration-a-diverse-mix-of-supporters-critics-and -firsts/.

15.   Ibid.

16.   Miller, "Who's Praying at Trump's Inauguration? A Mix of Supporters, Critics and Firsts"; "Trump Presidential Inauguration 2017 (FULL EVENT)," ABC News YouTube channel, January 20, 2017, accessed August 8, 2017, https://www.youtube.com/watch?v=Nieiu8tmLIM.

17.   "Trump Presidential Inauguration 2017 (FULL EVENT)," ABC News YouTube channel.

18.   Donald Trump, "The Inaugural Address," The White House, January 20, 2017, accessed August 7, 2017, https://www.whitehouse.gov /inaugural-address.

19.   Ibid.

20.   Eugene Scott, "White Evangelicals' Support of Trump Holding Steady," CNN, April 28, 2017, accessed August 9, 2017, http://www.cnn .com/2017/04/28/politics/pew-analysis-white-evangelicals-trump/index.html.

21.   Gregory A. Smith, "Among White Evangelicals, Regular Church-goers Are the Most Supportive of Trump," Pew Research Center, April 26, 2017, accessed August 9, 2017, http://www.pewresearch.org/fact-tank /2017/04/26/among-white-evangelicals-regular-churchgoers-are-the-most -supportive-of-trump/.

22.   "Read President Trump's Liberty University Commencement Speech," *Time*, May 13, 2017, accessed August 8, 2017, http://time.com /4778240/donald-trump-liberty-university-speech-transcript/.

23.   "Presidential Executive Order Promoting Free Speech and Religious Liberty," The White House, May 4, 2017, accessed August 9, 2017, https://

www.whitehouse.gov/the-press-office/2017/05/04/presidential-executive
-order-promoting-free-speech-and-religious-liberty.

24.   Matt Hadro, "Pro-Life, Religious Freedom Leaders Cheer Confirmation of Neil Gorsuch," CNA, April 7, 2017, accessed August 9, 2017, http://
www.catholicnewsagency.com/news/pro-life-religious-freedom-leaders
-cheer-confirmation-of-neil-gorsuch-78077/.

25.   "Read President Trump's Liberty University Commencement
Speech," *Time*.

26.   "Trump Right to Make Cuba Pay for Its Intransigence." *Miami
Herald*, June 15, 2017, accessed August 19, 2017, http://www.miamiherald
.com/opinion/editorials/article156494959.html.

27.   Jennifer Rubin, "What Is Trump's Israel Policy?," *Washington Post*,
February 16, 2017, accessed August 19, 2017, https://www.washingtonpost
.com/blogs/right-turn/wp/2017/02/16/what-is-trumps-israel-policy/.

28.   Ibid.

29.   Pat Robertson, "Why Evangelical Christians Support Israel,"
PatRobertson.com, accessed August 1, 2017, http://www.patrobertson.com
/Speeches/IsraelLauder.asp.

30.   Virgil, "The Emerging Trump Doctrine: The Defense of the West
and Judeo-Christian Civilization," Breitbart, July 6, 2017, accessed August
19, 2017, http://www.breitbart.com/big-government/2017/07/06/virgil-the
-emerging-trump-doctrine-the-defense-of-the-west-and-judeo-christian
-civilization/.

31.   Ibid.; "Polish Crowd Chants 'Donald Trump,'" WND.com, July 6,
2017, accessed August 19, 2017, https://news.grabien.com/story-polish
-crowd-chants-donald-trumpusa-usa.

32.   "Remarks by President Trump to the People of Poland: July 6, 2017,"
The White House, July 6, 2017, accessed August 1, 2017, https://www
.whitehouse.gov/the-press-office/2017/07/06/remarks-president-trump-people
-poland-july-6-2017.

33.   Ibid.

34.   Ibid.

35.   Ibid.

36.   Ibid.

37.   Ibid.

38.   Abby Phillip, John Wagner, and Michael Birnbaum, "Western
Values Increasingly Endangered by Terrorism and Extremism, Trump
Warns Europe," *Washington Post*, July 6, 2017, accessed August 1, 2017,
https://www.washingtonpost.com/news/post-politics/wp/2017/07/06
/in-poland-trump-reaffirms-commitment-to-nato-chides-russia/?utm
_term=.7564396b7b11; Virgil, "The Emerging Trump Doctrine: The Defense
of the West and Judeo-Christian Civilization," Breitbart, July 7, 2017.

39.   "Remarks by President Trump to the People of Poland: July 6, 2017,"
The White House.

40.   "America First Foreign Policy," The White House, accessed August 1,
2017, https://www.whitehouse.gov/america-first-foreign-policy.

41.   "Bringing Back Jobs and Growth," The White House, accessed August 1, 2017, https://www.whitehouse.gov/bringing-back-jobs-and-growth.

42.   Ibid.

43.   Ibid.

44.   "An America First Energy Plan," The White House, accessed August 1, 2017, https://www.whitehouse.gov/america-first-energy.

45.   Ibid.

46.   Linda Doman, "United States Remains Largest Producer of Petroleum and Natural Gas Hydrocarbons," U.S. Energy Information Administration, May 23, 2016, accessed August 19, 2017, https://www.eia.gov/today inenergy/detail.php?id=26352.

47.   Anjli Raval, "US Oil Reserves Surpass Those of Saudi Arabia and Russia," CNBC, July 5, 2016, accessed August 19, 2017, http://www.cnbc.com/2016/07/05/us-oil-reserves-surpass-those-of-saudi-arabia-and-russia.html.

48.   "Statement by President Trump on the Paris Climate Accord," The White House, June 1, 2017, accessed August 29, 2017, https://www.white house.gov/the-press-office/2017/06/01/statement-president-trump-paris-climate-accord.

49.   Ibid.

50.   Ibid.

51.   Ibid.

52.   Ibid.

Chapter 11—Friends and Supporters

1.   Marlene Lenthang, "David Letterman on Donald Trump," *People*, October 8, 2016, accessed August 2, 2017, http://people.com/politics/david-letterman-donald-trump-new-yorker-festival/.

2.   Angela Mosconi, "Trump Patriarch Eulogized as Great Builder," *New York Post*, June 30, 1999, accessed August 19, 2017, http://nypost.com/1999/06/30/trump-patriarch-eulogized-as-great-builder/.

3.   Jonathan Mahler and Maggie Haberman, "For Rudy Giuliani, Embrace of Donald Trump Puts Legacy at Risk," *New York Times*, September 9, 2016, accessed August 19, 2017, https://www.nytimes.com/2016/09/10/us/politics/rudy-giuliani-donald-trump.html.

4.   Rush Limbaugh, *Rush Limbaugh Show*, podcast audio, June 21, 2017.

5.   Jennifer Calfas, "Twitter Founder Apologizes for Giving President Trump a Platform: 'It's a Very Bad Thing,'" *FORTUNE*, May 21, 2017, accessed August 2, 2017, http://fortune.com/2017/05/21/donald-trump-twitter-evan-williams/.

6.   Donald J. Trump's Facebook page, October 7, 2016, accessed August 2, 2017, https://www.facebook.com/DonaldTrump/videos/1015784464 2270725/.

7.   Lance Wallnau, "Why I Believe Trump Is the Prophesied President," Charisma News, October 5, 2016, accessed August 2, 2017, http://www

.charismanews.com/politics/opinion/60378-why-i-believe-trump-is-the
-prophesied-president.

8. Rachael Bade, "Trump's Early Backers Seize Power in Congress," POLITICO, November 28, 2016, accessed August 20, 2017, http://www .politico.com/story/2016/11/trump-endorsement-congress-231777.

9. Jennifer G. Hickey, "Donald Trump's Early Congressional Supporters Find Their Loyalty Rewarded," Fox News, December 2, 2016, accessed August 20, 2017, http://www.foxnews.com/politics/2016/12/02 /donald-trumps-early-congressional-supporters-find-their-loyalty-rewarded .html.

10. Eli Stokols, "Sen. Jeff Sessions Endorses Trump," POLITICO, February 28, 2016, accessed August 3, 2017, http://www.politico.com/story /2016/02/sen-jeff-sessions-endorses-trump-219939.

11. Hickey, "Donald Trump's Early Congressional Supporters Find Their Loyalty Rewarded."

12. Ibid.; Nick Gass, "Haley: I'll Support Trump if It Comes to That," POLITICO, February 26, 2016, accessed August 3, 2017, http://www .politico.com/blogs/2016-gop-primary-live-updates-and-results/2016/02 /nikki-haley-donald-trump-marco-rubio-219848.

13. Melissa Quinn, "All You Need to Know About U.N. Pick Nikki Haley," *Newsweek*, November 28, 2016, accessed August 3, 2017, http://www .newsweek.com/all-you-need-know-about-un-pick-nikki-haley-525955.

14. Donald J. Trump's personal Twitter account, January 26, 2016, accessed August 3, 2017, https://twitter.com/realdonaldtrump/status/692028 126189199360?lang=en.

15. Sarah Rodriguez, "Falwell Speaks," *Liberty Champion*, March 8, 2016, accessed August 20, 2017, https://www.liberty.edu/champion/2016/03 /falwell-speaks/.

16. Ibid.

17. Ibid.

18. Ibid.

19. Susan Berry, "Black Leader Endorses Donald Trump: Democrats 'Ask Us for Everything, Give Nothing Back,'" Breitbart, November 4, 2016, accessed August 3, 2017, http://www.breitbart.com/big-government /2016/11/04/black-leader-endorses-donald-trump-democrats-ask-us-for -everything-give-nothing-back/.

CHAPTER 12—FAITH, HOPE, AND CHARITY

1. "Remarks by President Trump at the National Prayer Breakfast," The White House, February 2, 2017, accessed August 8, 2017, https://www.white house.gov/the-press-office/2017/02/02/remarks-president-trump-national -prayer-breakfast.

2. Michael D. Shear, "Trump Discards Obama Legacy, One Rule at a Time," *New York Times*, May 1, 2017, accessed August 8, 2017, https://www .nytimes.com/2017/05/01/us/politics/trump-overturning-regulations.html.

3.   Joel B. Pollak, "Trump's Use of the Congressional Review Act Is a Legislative Milestone," Breitbart, April 15, 2017, accessed August 20, 2017, http://www.breitbart.com/big-government/2017/04/15/trump-congressional -review-act-legislative-milestone/.

4.   Donald J. Trump, *Great Again: How to Fix Our Crippled America* (New York: Simon & Schuster, 2015), 80.

5.   Jessica Chasmar, "Obama on Capitalism vs. Communism: 'Just Choose From What Works,'" *Washington Times*, March 25, 2016, accessed August 8, 2017, http://www.washingtontimes.com/news/2016/mar/25/obama -on-capitalist-versus-communist-theory-just-c/.

6.   YouTube video created by Victims of Communism Memorial Foundation, posted October 12, 2016, accessed August 22, 2017, https://www .youtube.com/watch?v=7yaPUL-oGjI&feature=youtu.be.

7.   Dan Alexander, "Where Did Trump's Foundation Donate Its Money? IRS Documents Reveal Surprising Answers," *Forbes*, February 9, 2017, accessed August 8, 2017, https://www.forbes.com/sites/danalexander /2017/02/09/where-did-trumps-foundation-donate-its-money-irs-documents -reveal-surprising-answers/#4b1aa8e47b52.

8.   Ibid.

9.   John Cassidy, "Trump and the Truth: His Charitable Giving," *New Yorker*, September 24, 2016, accessed August 8, 2017, http://www.newyorker .com/news/john-cassidy/trump-and-the-truth-his-charitable-giving.

10.   Alexander, "Where Did Trump's Foundation Donate Its Money? IRS Documents Reveal Surprising Answers."

11.   Ibid.

12.   Will Drabold, "Watch Rudy Giuliani's Energetic Speech at the Republican Convention," *Time*, July 18, 2016, accessed August 8, 2017, http://time .com/4412059/republican-convention-rudy-giuliani-transcript-video/.

13.   Sean Hannity, "Rep. Mike McCaul Rips Iran Prisoner Swap as 'Bad deal,'" Fox News, January 18, 2016, accessed August 8, 2017, http://www .foxnews.com/transcript/2016/01/18/rep-mike-mccaul-rips-iran-prisoner -swap-as-bad-deal.html.

14.   Ibid.

15.   "Donald Trump Writes $25K Check to Sgt. Tahmooressi #Marine-Freed," Fox News, November 10, 2014, accessed August 29, 2017, http:// nation.foxnews.com/2014/11/10/donald-trump-writes-25k-check-sgt -tahmooressi-marinefreed.

16.   Samuel Smith, "Pastor Confirms Donald Trump Gave $100K Donation for Louisiana Flood Relief," *Christian Post*, August 25, 2016, accessed August 8, 2017, http://www.christianpost.com/news/pastor-confirms-donald -trump-gave-100-thousand-dollar-donation-louisiana-flood-relief-168509/.

17.   Ibid.

18.   "Donald Trump, Mike Pence Visit With Franklin Graham and Samaritans Purse Flood Relief in Louisiana," Citizens for Trump, accessed August 20, 2017, http://citizensfortrump.com/2016/08/20/donald-trump -mike-pence-visit-franklin-graham-samaritans-purse-flood-relief-louisiana/.

19.   "Trumped Up," Snopes.com, accessed August 20, 2017, http://www
.snopes.com/luck/trump.asp. According to Digital Spy, Trump confirmed
the story on *The Celebrity Apprentice*, https://forums.digitalspy.com
/discussion/comment/84562632.

20.   "Intervention by Trump Helps Stave Off Foreclosure of Family
Farm," Associated Press, accessed August 9, 2017, http://www.apnews
archive.com/1986/Intervention-By-Trump-Helps-Stave-Off-Foreclosure-Of
-Family-Fawirerm/id-7b84fa6b5f9d67cd35f94363b48c03a4.

21.   Jim Galloway, "That Time When Donald Trump Saved a Georgia
Farm," Cox Media Group, December 12, 2016, accessed August 9, 2017,
http://politics.blog.ajc.com/2015/12/26/that-time-when-donald-trump-saved
-a-georgia-farm/.

22.   Trump with Schwartz, *The Art of the Deal*, 4–5, 236.

23.   Ibid.; Donald Trump, "Trump on Trump," *New Yorker*, November
16, 1987, 63.

24.   Justin Jouvenal, "In Donated Shoes and Suit, a Trump Supporter
Comes to Washington," *Washington Post*, January 18, 2017, accessed August
9, 2017, https://www.washingtonpost.com/local/dc-politics/in-donated-shoes
-and-suit-a-trump-supporter-comes-to-washington/2017/01/18/ccb691dc
-d839-11e6-b8b2-cb5164beba6b_story.html.

25.   Ibid.

26.   Justin Jouvenal, "'This Is the Greatest Guy': Trump Meets FedEx
Courier, Offers Him $10,000," *Washington Post*, January 19, 2017, accessed
August 9, 2017, https://www.washingtonpost.com/local/dc-politics/this-is
-the-greatest-guy-trump-meets-fedex-courier-offers-him-10000/2017/01/19
/e227a8fc-de98-11e6-acdf-14da832ae861_story.html.

27.   Hollie McKay, "She Guarded Trump's Star, but Still hasn't Saved
Herself From LA Streets," Fox News, January 6, 2017, accessed August 9,
2017, http://www.foxnews.com/us/2017/01/06/guarded-trumps-star-but-still
-hasnt-saved-herself-from-la-streets.html.

28.   Ibid.

29.   Kristinn Taylor, "BREAKING: Donald Trump Attorney Looking
for Homeless Woman Beaten by Hillary Clinton Supporters in Hollywood,"
GatewayPundit.com, October 28, 2016, accessed August 9, 2017, http://www
.thegatewaypundit.com/2016/10/breaking-donald-trump-attorney-looking
-homeless-woman-beaten-hillary-clinton-supporters-hollywood/.

30.   Jim Hoft, "Update: Homeless Woman Who Was Guarding Trump
Hollywood Star Is Found—Trump Camp Notified," GatewayPundit.com,
November 2, 2016, accessed August 9, 2017, http://www.thegatewaypundit
.com/2016/11/update-homeless-woman-guarding-trump-hollywood-star
-found-trump-camp-notified/.

31.   "Read Donald Trump's Full Inauguration Speech," *Time*, updated
January 24, 2017, accessed August 9, 2017, http://time.com/4640707/donald
-trump-inauguration-speech-transcript/.

32.   Abraham Lincoln, *The Portable Abraham Lincoln*, ed. Andrew
Delbanco (New York: Penguin Books, 2009).

33.   "Read Donald Trump's Full Inauguration Speech," *Time*.

34.   Lincoln, *The Portable Abraham Lincoln*.

CONCLUSION—FOR SUCH A TIME

1.   Egberto Willies, "Singing Make America Great Again, Evangelicals Say Trump Is 'God Giving Us Another Chance,'" Daily Kos, July 3, 2017, accessed August 9, 2017, https://www.dailykos.com/stories/2017/7/3/1677574 /-Singing-Make-America-Great-Again-Evangelicals-say-Trump-is-God -giving-us-another-chance.

2.   "President Trump Tribute to Veterans at Kennedy Center," C-SPAN, July 1, 2017, accessed August 20, 2017, https://www.c-span.org/video /?430774-2/president-trump-tribute-veterans-kennedy-center.

3.   Ibid.

4.   M. J. Lee, "God and the Don," CNN, June 2017, accessed August 14, 2017, http://www.cnn.com/interactive/2017/politics/state/donald-trump -religion/.

5.   Ibid.

6.   Ibid.

7.   Ibid.

8.   Meghan Murphy-Gill, "The Faith of Donald Trump," *U.S. Catholic*, January 19, 2017, accessed August 20, 2017, http://www.uscatholic.org /articles/201701/faith-donald-trump-30910.

9.   Ibid.

10.   Lee, "God and the Don."

11.   Lance Wallnau, "Why I Believe Trump Is the Prophesied President," *Charisma*, October 2016, 36–37; in communication with author.

12.   R. T. Kendall, "Donald Trump and Toby," rtkendallministries.com, November 28, 2016, accessed August 14, 2017, https://rtkendallministries .com/donald-trump-and-toby.

13.   Ibid.

14.   Ibid.

15.   Wallnau, "Why I Believe Trump Is the Prophesied President."

16.   Willies, Singing Make America Great Again."

17.   Todd Starnes, "Will the Real Church Please Stand Up?," *Charisma*, July 2017, 41–42.

18.   Todd Starnes, *The Deplorables' Guide to Making America Great Again* (Lake Mary, FL: FrontLine, 2017), xvi.

19.   In communication with author.

20.   Ibid.

21.   Ibid.

EPILOGUE—THE HERMIT OF LORETO

1.   Bret Thoman, "Tom Zimmer: The Hermit of Loreto and President Trump," *And Amazing Grace* (blog), March 8, 2017, accessed August 20,

2017, http://andamazinggrace.blogspot.com/2017/03/tom-zimmer-hermit-of
-loreto-and.html?m=1.

2.   Ibid.

3.   Ibid.; Giacomo Capoverdi, "Hermit of Loreto," YouTube.com,
posted February 19, 2017, accessed August 21, 2017, https://www.youtube
.com/watch?v=lyV7kwMRzdo.

4.   Capoverdi, "Hermit of Loreto."

5.   Thoman, "Tom Zimmer: The Hermit of Loreto and President
Trump."

6.   In communication with author.

7.   Thoman, "Tom Zimmer: The Hermit of Loreto and President
Trump."

8.   Ibid.

9.   Ibid.

10.   In communication with author.

11.   Ibid.

12.   Ibid.

INDEX

★★★★★

D

OTHER CHARISMA HOUSE
BOOKS WE RECOMMEND

The Paradigm by Jonathan Cahn. Is it possible that there exists an ancient master blueprint that lies behind current events, the rise and fall of leaders and governments, and reveals our future? *The Paradigm* will astonish you, answer your questions, and reveal things you never could have imagined. Be prepared to never see the world in the same way again.

The Harbinger by Jonathan Cahn. Before its end as a nation, there appeared in ancient Israel a series of specific omens and signs warning of destruction—these same nine Harbingers are now manifesting in America with profound ramifications for America's future and end-time prophecy.

The Book of Mysteries by Jonathan Cahn. Partake in the voyage and unlock the treasure chest to uncover the mysteries of the ages. With 365 mysteries, one for each day of the year, you will discover never before revealed keys to spiritual truth, the end times, and overcoming problems in your life.

Love Leads by Dr. Steve Greene. The one action verb most frequently missing from various manifestos on leadership is *love*. In *Love Leads* Steve Greene shares real-life examples, principles, and exhortations of the love of a leader. Greene dispels the myths and misconceptions many have come to accept about leadership.

The Bait of Satan by John Bevere. One of our perennial best sellers for the past two decades, this book exposes one of Satan's most deceptive snares to get believers out of the will of God—offense.

The Seven Pillars of Health by Don Colbert, MD. What if in just fifty days you could experience more energy, feel better, look better, decrease your stress, prevent disease, and be more efficient and effective in your work? In this book Dr. Colbert shares timeless biblical truths as he reintroduces you to the basics of good health.

23 Minutes in Hell by Bill Wiese. This *New York Times* best seller chronicles one man's journey to hell. Bill Wiese's trip to the devil's lair lasted only twenty-three minutes, but that was enough time to convince him that he would never want to return. Now he tells others about what he saw, heard, and felt so that they will steer clear of hell.

Jerusalem Countdown by John Hagee. In this warning Hagee anticipates Israel's strategies toward any Iranian threat and the resulting effect upon America. The author unveils the reasons radical Islam and Israel cannot dwell peaceably together as he paints a convincing picture explaining why Christians must support the State of Israel.

Fasting by Jentezen Franklin. When you fast, your spirit becomes uncluttered by the things of this world and amazingly sensitive to the things of God. Jentezen Franklin gives you the keys to experiencing this kind of transformation. Discover everything you need to know to unlock the power of biblical fasting.

Prayers That Rout Demons by John Eckhardt. Prayer and confession of Scripture are two of the most powerful weapons we have. They connect us to God and allow His power to flow to us in every situation. This book combines powerful prayers and decrees based on Scripture to help you overcome demonic influence and opposition in your life.

The Esther Anointing by Michelle McClain-Walters. Esther risked her life for the welfare of her people and the furthering of God's plan. Just as in biblical times, God is positioning women today and giving them divine opportunities to influence the culture for His kingdom. It doesn't matter where you came from or what skills and talents you have; if you let Him, God can use your life for His glory!

Dr. Colbert's Guide to Vitamins and Supplements by Don Colbert, MD. This balanced, natural health approach will inform you about vitamins, minerals, and other building blocks of nutrition. You can shop with confidence and know you are buying the right nutritional supplements to achieve your specific health goal, whether it's to lose weight, balance hormones, boost energy, or heal and prevent certain health conditions and diseases.

The Juice Lady's Guide to Fasting by Cherie Calbom. There is a new surge of interest in fasting, yet many are unaware how to navigate the numerous types. The Juice Lady offers her nutritional expertise on the how-tos of fasting. This comprehensive book provides menus, recipes, and strategic fasting guidelines. Discover the myriad of benefits derived from fasting the right way for a healthy life.

Total Forgiveness by R. T. Kendall. Best-selling author R. T. Kendall teaches how you can experience the incredible freedom forgiveness offers as he challenges you to root out the hidden and hardened places where resentments remain. Make the choice today, and step into a new dimension of freedom and peace.

These books are available wherever Christian books are sold in stores or online.

ALSO FROM CHARISMA MEDIA

The new Modern English Version (MEV) is the most modern translation produced in the King James Version tradition in more than thirty years. Our vision is to communicate God's Word anew with beauty and clarity for people everywhere. It comes in many styles such as thin line, large print, and giant print, plus many attractive colors. The MEV is also used in specialty topical Bibles such as the *SpiritLed Woman Bible*, *Spiritual Warfare Bible*, *Fire Bible* study Bible, and *The Promises of God Bible for Creative Journaling*. The MEV is available wherever Bibles are sold or visit www.mevbible.com.

Charisma magazine has been our flagship for forty-two years. Stay in touch with what the Holy Spirit is doing in the world with articles that will motivate you to radically change your world for Christ.

Charisma Media also publishes *Ministry Today*, *SpiritLed Woman*, and *Charisma's Best Christian Universities, Colleges and Schools*. For samples or to subscribe to any of our magazines, call 1-800-749-6500 during office hours EST or order online at Shop.CharismaMag.com.

The Charisma Podcast Network features many podcasts that will interest you—including the *Strang Report* by Steve Strang. Listen to his interesting interviews about spiritual topics, current events, and more. Check out what's available at CharismaPodcastNetwork.com.

Charisma Media has many free Christian newsletters and devotionals, including Stephen E. Strang's own *Strang Report* blog based on his four decades covering the Christian community and featuring his view of the world. Go to charismanewsletters.com to subscribe.

The CharismaNews mobile app offers up-to-the-minute Christian news on your smartphone. Available for Apple and Android devices

The Charisma Caucus mobile app provides breaking Christian news on the country's political landscape from a faith-based angle. Available for Apple and Android devices.

For our Spanish-speaking friends, we publish many of the most popular Christian authors through Casa Creación. To find out more, go to casacreacion.com.

Para todos nuestros amigos de habla hispana, nosotros publicamos muchos de los autores cristianos más populares a través de nuestro sello editorial Casa Creación. Para conocer más sobre estos títulos, visite casacreacion.com.

STAY IN TOUCH WITH STEPHEN E. STRANG

★★★★★

- Follow him on Twitter @sstrang.
- Like him on Facebook @stephenestrang.
- Subscribe to the *Strang Report* twice-weekly newsletter at charismanewsletters.com.
- Download the *Strang Report* podcasts at CharismaPodcastNetwork.com.
- Subscribe to *Charisma* magazine or other Charisma Media publications. Call 1-800-749-6500 during office hours EST or order online at Shop.CharismaMag.com.
- Watch for his next book from Charisma House!

If you enjoyed *God and Donald Trump,* tell your friends, including on social media. Also, leave a five-star rating for the book and your personal review at Amazon.com.

MORE EARLY PRAISE FOR
GOD AND DONALD TRUMP

★★★★★

For those seeking to understand the unlikely alliance forged between Donald Trump and evangelical Christians, *God and Donald Trump* is a must read. Steve Strang is one of the most effective and respected Christian leaders in the nation, and I highly recommend this book.

—RALPH REED
CHAIRMAN, FAITH & FREEDOM COALITION
ATLANTA, GEORGIA

US presidential elections are often divisive events politically as well as religiously. The 2016 election campaign and election of Donald J. Trump is no exception. In the midst of this continuing, and in some ways deepening, divide, Steve Strang offers an insightful perspective into the 2016 campaign, the life of Donald Trump, and the tensions and opportunities that evangelical Christians carry with this president. For those wishing to understand why and how conservative Christians voted for "The Donald," this book is a valuable resource.

—DR. DOUG BEACHAM
GENERAL SUPERINTENDENT,
INTERNATIONAL PENTECOSTAL HOLINESS CHURCH
BETHANY, OKLAHOMA

Evangelical and pro-life Catholic Christians turned out at the polls in record numbers on November 8, 2016. Eager to see the end of the lawless actions of the Obama administration, they helped elect Donald J. Trump president, the only president in American history to never have held public office or served in the military. Steve Strang has done Christendom a service in *God and Donald Trump* by documenting a miracle of God.

—DAVID LANE
AMERICAN RENEWAL PROJECT
WESTLAKE VILLAGE, CALIFORNIA

In *God and Donald Trump*, Steve Strang pens truth straight from the heart. This must-read book reaches far beyond politics into the redeeming frequencies that America surely needs. Let freedom ring!

—ALVEDA KING
EVANGELIST AND FOUNDER, ALVEDA KING MINISTRIES
ATLANTA, GEORGIA

Stephen Strang has written what is as close to an objective account of Donald Trump and his faith as you are likely to find. What is more, you won't be able to put this book down!

—Dr. R. T. Kendall
Bible Teacher and Author
Nashville, Tennessee

Few people have the courage to swim against the tide of popular opinion in the way that Steve Strang does. This makes him very qualified to write *God and Donald Trump*. This book will both encourage and confront you to see President Trump through the lens of history having been made through an awakened evangelical church.

—Dr. Cindy Jacobs
Generals International
Red Oak, Texas

In his book Stephen Strang has put together the story of the greatest shock in American political history. There is no doubt that the hand of God raised up President Trump against all odds—the world's financial elite, the pope, former presidents, and the media—and yet there he is, the forty-fifth president of the United States of America. This is exciting for every believer as this means God is not finished with America. God gave us a last-minute reprieve. Great job, Steve.

—Rodney Howard-Browne
Revival Ministries International
Tampa, Florida

As only he can do, in *God and Donald Trump*, Stephen Strang brilliantly takes us move by move through one of the most contentious and consequential elections in American history, all along the way revealing the largely untold stories of faith that undergirded it all.

—Rev. Samuel Rodriguez
President, National Hispanic
Christian Leadership Conference
Sacramento, California

This book represents an immensely important addition to the literature surrounding the controversy of Donald Trump's election. Written by my forty-year friend and award-winning journalist Steve Strang—*Time* magazine named him one of the twenty-five "most influential Evangelicals in America"—this tour de force champions a perspective that would have otherwise been lost from history. My heart raced as I turned the pages to find out what was "really" happening behind the scenes to propel Donald Trump to office. Whether or not you share Steve's point of view, you will be a better educated, wiser, and more well-rounded person if you read this book. I highly recommend this inevitable best seller. It has the ring of truth.

—PATRICK MORLEY, PhD
BEST-SELLING AUTHOR, *MAN IN THE MIRROR*
WINTER PARK, FLORIDA

Steve Strang's new book, *God and Donald Trump*, is a must read. Donald Trump wasn't my first choice as a candidate, nor my second or third, but when it became clear that he was God's choice, like many Evangelicals I was all in. Steve had unique access to the candidate, and as I read *God and Donald Trump*, I became more convinced that God has granted us a window of opportunity to save America from moral decay.

—RICK SCARBOROUGH
PRESIDENT, VISION AMERICA ACTION
KELLER, TEXAS

A can't-put-it-down story behind the story of Donald J. Trump and God's role in the election of the forty-fifth president of the United States of America. I encourage you to read this book with a humble and open heart. Your prayer life will be upgraded. Arise and shine, America, your light has come!

—LEIF HETLAND
PRESIDENT, GLOBAL MISSION AWARENESS
PEACHTREE CITY, GEORGIA

From the base facts to the extreme prophetic, my dear friend Steve Strang brings it all to light in this timely book, *God and Donald Trump*. Having been blessed to be a firsthand witness and participant in this amazing journey into destiny, I can attest that Steve got it right. He, above all journalists I know, is uniquely designed for this particular assignment. He has employed his gifts as a writer, editor, investigative reporter, man of God, and truth seeker, along with his time-tested passion, to publish the on-time miracles of our faith. Thank you, Lord, for giving us this chance, and thank you, Steve, for writing it down on tablets to make the vision clear and simple to understand!

—FRANK AMEDIA
FOUNDER AND PRESIDENT, POTUS SHIELD
CANFIELD, OHIO

Few people understand the culture of the charismatic church as well as Steve Strang. For four decades he has observed and reported on the intersection of the life of the church and public policy issues. From this unique background Strang has watched the Trump story unfold, and his book offers an analysis that is sure to generate debate and discussion. The lens through which Strang views President Trump is both political and religious, and readers from both sides of the partisan divide will agree that his perspective is an important one.

—PAUL CONN, PhD
PRESIDENT, LEE UNIVERSITY
CLEVELAND, TENNESSEE

Trump won the 2016 election by a wide margin in the electoral college. However, this victory happened only because a remnant showed up in five swing states—a mere .008 percent of the total national vote—and in the process determined the outcome of history. Who made up that little remnant? Evangelical voters who overwhelmingly voted for him. Now that evangelical base is under heavy attack to abandon him. The battle for America has just begun. That is why this book is so important. There is history yet to write, and Stephen Strang is part of that ongoing story. Read this and join the battle.

—LANCE WALLNAU
CEO, THE LANCE LEARNING GROUP
DALLAS, TEXAS

If you cringe when a political leader mentions God, this book is a must-read. *God and Donald Trump* is less about a president's faith and more about the welfare of a nation's faith.

—GARY MCCULLOUGH
DIRECTOR, CHRISTIAN NEWSWIRE
ST. AUGUSTINE, FLORIDA

God and Donald Trump gives a unique look into the most shocking presidential election of our lifetime. Steve Strang gives special insight into how President Trump was elected and how God can use this pivotal time to bring revival to America. As followers of Christ and Americans, no matter our political affiliation, we are called to pray for our leaders and for our nation. I believe this book is a reminder to the church body that we need God in our nation now more than ever.

—ALEX CLATTENBURG
LEAD PASTOR, CHURCH IN THE SON
ORLANDO, FLORIDA

In his book *God and Donald Trump*, Stephen Strang lays out historical, political, and prophetic evidence that solidifies the fact that Donald J. Trump is indeed "God's man" for this hour. Reminding us that Trump came into office with every card stacked against him, it shows us what can happen when the church unites in fervent prayer. As you read, hope will arise in your heart for what lies ahead for America. God isn't finished.

—Brad Smith
Lead Pastor, First Assembly of God
Monticello, Arkansas

Within twenty-four hours of receiving *God and Donald Trump*, I completed it! This behind-the-scenes, in-depth examination of one of our most unusual and extraordinary candidates in one of the most consequential and dramatic presidential elections in US history is simply outstanding! Steve Strang is one of America's most experienced, insightful journalists, and I wholeheartedly recommend you lay hold of this phenomenal book.

—Larry Tomczak
Cultural Commentator and Best-Selling Author
Nashville, Tennessee

In *God and Donald Trump*, Stephen Strang gives insight no other author has ever attempted—to describe the spiritual component of the life of one of the best-known public figures in the world. The book is balanced and carefully documented by other reliable sources. Although many say Donald Trump has bitten off far more than he can chew, he has a motto to admire: to restore hope, prosperity, and freedom for all, regardless of race, color, and religion. Only then will America be great again. If you read only one book this year, make it *God and Donald Trump*.

—Robin Steinberg
Singapore

In *God and Donald Trump* we see the white smoke rising from the White House as the forty-fifth president of the United States of America takes office. We see the unfurling of the flag in the hands of the evangelical Christians as they pray a path toward Pennsylvania Avenue. The book is truly captivating and records for posterity this historical event as we see God's hand at work throughout the raising of a president.

—Martin Clarke
London, England

There are significant times that are marked by history. *God and Donald Trump* reflects such a time. This book provides hope that the hand of God still plays a significant role in our daily lives. Donald Trump, the forty-fifth president of the United States, needs our support and prayers. This book is a mandate for the Christian community to unite, humble themselves, and focus on God's hand on this great nation.

—Col. Evan Trinkle
US Army (Retired)
Lexington, Kentucky

God and Donald Trump is about the really big picture. This book exposes how God moved through various people and circumstances to bring His choice for president to the White House. This is a must-read if you want to understand the agenda of God and the tool He uses in the form of Donald J. Trump. Steve Strang has done a magnificent job canonizing a move of the Spirit of God brooding over a man to make him a world leader.

—Douglas Weiss, PhD
Psychologist, Author
Colorado Springs, Colorado

They say there is always "a story behind the story," and Steve Strang has painstakingly documented this backstory in his book *God and Donald Trump*. In my opinion the liberal media has been hugely influential, if not responsible, for outcomes of several of the last presidential elections, especially those of Bill Clinton and Barack Obama. However, in this fascinating book Steve Strang shows that even with all its might the secular media couldn't stop the "God thing" of Donald Trump's being elected the forty-fifth president. Congratulations, Steve! Someone had to tell this story—glad it was you!

—Ben Ferrell
CEO, BMC Ferrell
Tulsa, Oklahoma

This is an amazing inside look at who President Donald Trump is and the spiritual forces that brought him to the presidency. Deuteronomy says that the secret to possessing the land is not your righteousness, but rather to be strong and courageous and not to be afraid or discouraged. Regardless of what you think of President Trump, he followed this biblical mandate to become president. The fascinating behind-the-scenes insights in the book have definitely got me praying for him more and for God's plan to unfold in and through his life. You will be gripped in this book by the many unexpected turns of events that brought Trump to the White House. I couldn't put the book down until I finished it, and neither will you.

—Peter Lowe
Founder, Get Motivated Seminars
West Palm Beach, Florida

Ultimate humility has been described as when the King of kings became a poor human, driven by a core motive of love. Until now the story has not been told of the sacrifice President Trump paid—walking away from ten billion dollars to run for president. Who better than one of *Time* magazine's "most influential Evangelicals in America" and the publisher of *The Faith of George W. Bush* to write it?

—GREGORY J. SWAN
CHRISTIANSINCHURCHES.COM
DETROIT, MICHIGAN

Christians know things could be better in our country, but few of us do anything about it—choosing to hide our faith rather than express it publicly. Steve Strang is a man who takes risks, expresses his faith openly, and has now written about Donald Trump, one of the world's most influential leaders who is not afraid to boldly support Christians and their freedom to live out their faith in public. This nation has a much better chance when our leaders aren't afraid to pray and bring God into politics and every area of life. Faith is an important part of our lives, and it's refreshing and exciting to see Steve describe a president who has surrounded himself with people of faith and wants to provide citizens greater freedom to express themselves in a godly fashion.

—LARRY IHLE
RETIRED BUSINESSMAN
BURNSVILLE, MINNESOTA

Steve Strang's new book, *God and Donald Trump*, is a unique look into the improbable rise to the presidency of Donald J. Trump. Strang gives the reader an "inside baseball view" of the struggle and intrigue of how Trump captured his most critical voting bloc, the Evangelicals. He also details the courageous support for Trump from many evangelical leaders who withstood tremendous internal opposition within their own ranks. The book is a must-read in the historical accounts of the battle for America.

—THOMAS ERTL
MEDIA DIRECTOR, CHRISTIANS FOR DONALD TRUMP
TALLAHASSEE, FLORIDA

God and Donald Trump by Steve Strang unveils the powerful spiritual element involved in the recent election of this desperately needed candidate to the office of the president of the United States. Every chapter is gripping, intensely interesting. Well-written and well-documented, this inspiring book makes it all-the-more clear that the Most High God was very involved in the whole process and much to the consternation of liberals, He succeeded in overturning previous advances made by corrupt men and women of political influence. Thank you, Steve Strang, for such an illuminating and timely work. May your influence and the impact of this book help to advance God's kingdom in our modern-day culture in ever-increasing ways.

—MIKE SHREVE
AUTHOR, TEACHER
CLEVELAND, TENNESSEE

It's amazing to read about the hand of God that orchestrated to bring change in the presidency in the present days. The destiny of America was at stake, hence God raised up President Trump and his family to build on the roots and foundations of the forefathers. Trump is an answer to the cry of millions that impacts the future of Israel and the world.

Stephen Strang clearly narrates the key role of the Evangelicals in the elections. Strang has his finger on the pulse of God's direction for America and the presidents of the United States of America.

—SAM KUMAR
PRESIDENT, UCM BIBLE UNIVERSITY
PANGIDI, INDIA

There are instances in Scripture where God used nonbelievers to accomplish His purposes. He even used a donkey. Only God knows Trump's heart but his fruit is arguably the most pro-Christian of any president in recent history. This well-referenced book can open our eyes to these truths and set the bar for how Christians vote in the future. *God and Donald Trump* is a must-read book for every believer regardless of party. Great job, Steve!

—K. C. CRAICHY
FOUNDER AND CEO, LIVING FUEL INC.
ORLANDO, FLORIDA

As a conservative who had quite a few reservations about Trump, I found this book to be fascinating. Steve Strang, in *God and Donald Trump*, presents a strong case to the reader regardless of where they sit on the political spectrum and provides insight from a unique perspective that can only be described as "prophetic." In addition, the book makes a strong case as to why God used what many considered a politically unpolished candidate to shake up the status quo for His purposes and plans.

—WOODLEY AUGUSTE
ADVERTISING CONSULTANT
APOPKA, FLORIDA

God and Donald Trump is a powerful and compelling extension of Steve Strang's reporting of Donald Trump's miraculous road to the White House. The book is a shining example of his dedication to reporting the truth in a time when many Americans have lost faith in the mainstream media.

—SHAWN A. AKERS
CONTENT DEVELOPMENT EDITOR
CASSELBERRY, FLORIDA

Many who voted for Donald Trump in November 2016 never thought they would be doing so. Most are unaware of the divine intervention that orchestrated Donald Trump's path to the presidency. My friend Steve Strang has written an important, insightful book that shares the untold story of the miraculous ways God influenced Trump's election. Pray with me that this could position our nation for a return to its godly heritage.

—JIM GARLOW, PhD
PASTOR, SKYLINE WESLEYAN CHURCH
SAN DIEGO, CALIFORNIA

No one is better qualified than Stephen Strang to explain the extraordinary rise of Donald Trump and the decisive role played in his election victory by American Evangelicals. A chronicler of events affecting Christians in the United States and around the world for more than four decades through his publication *Charisma*, Strang knows personally many of the people who propelled Trump to run and to win. Uniquely he is also better qualified than most other Trump chroniclers because of his deep understanding of the charismatic movement, some of whose prophets forecast the Trump victory long before it occurred.

—DAVID AIKMAN
FORMER SENIOR CORRESPONDENT FOR *TIME*
IRELAND

Donald J. Trump energized Evangelicals as no presidential candidate in American history. That they voted for Trump in the millions and continue to stand by their man has shocked the pundits. *God and Donald Trump* is excellently researched, fast-paced, provocative, and easy to read, and it documents the fascinating evangelical love affair with Trump. From his unique vantage point as a leading publisher in the Spirit-filled Christian community Stephen Strang proves that he never forgot his early days as a professional journalist. No matter how you voted in 2016, if you care about America and if you believe God still cares about America, read this book.

—DR. MARK RUTLAND
PRESIDENT, GLOBAL SERVANTS
BUFORD, GEORGIA

To say *God and Donald Trump* is an incredible book is an understatement! This clearly chronicled account is so moving that it will leave even the staunchest critic of Donald Trump inspired and saying, "God really does move in the affairs of nations!"

—RON JOHNSON
PASTOR, ONE CHURCH
ORLANDO, FLORIDA